# When Labels Fail

# When Labels Fail

POLITICS, VALUES,
AND IDEOLOGY ON THE
SUPREME COURT

C.B. Shotwell

| | | |
|---|---|---|
| Library of Congress Control Number: | | 2006903553 |
| ISBN 10: | Hardcover | 1-4257-1352-1 |
| | Softcover | 1-4257-1351-3 |
| ISBN 13: | Hardcover | 978-1-4257-1352-2 |
| | Softcover | 978-1-4257-1351-5 |



This book was printed in the United States of America.

To order additional copies of this book, contact:
Xlibris Corporation
1-888-795-4274
www.Xlibris.com
Orders@Xlibris.com

33216

# Contents

## Appendices

# Dedication

*To Jan, for encouragement and inspiration throughout this effort*

# Composition of the U.S. Supreme Court: Chronological Charts

1. The Marshall Court in 1803
2. The Taney Court in 1857
3. The Court of Field and Miller in 1865
4. The Court of Fuller in 1902
5. The Court of the New Deal Era in 1936
6. The Warren Court Era in 1954
7. The Burger and Rehnquist Court Eras (1969 to 2005)

# PREFACE

As this book is being concluded, a series of nominations to the U.S. Supreme Court have been subjected to political litmus tests by politicians, interest groups, and various judicial watchers. The successive nominations of District of Columbia Circuit Court of Appeals Judge John Roberts, Deputy White House Counsel Harriet Miers (later withdrawn), and Third Circuit Court of Appeals Judge Samuel Alito, following the announced retirement of Associate Justice Sandra Day O'Connor and the death of Chief Justice William Rehnquist, provided President George W. Bush with the opportunity to mold the Court in his "strict constructionist" vision.[1] But the debate on the merits of the nominations belies the reality that though a president may have the opportunity to shape the Supreme Court in some manner and to some degree through nominations, a president will not always be able to predict and control the behavior of nominees once they are confirmed and impaneled. More to the point and as has been seen throughout the history of the Supreme Court, politically inspired labels have provided poor criteria for predicting future performance of justices on the Court.[2]

This writing comes at a time when the public has been unusually focused on the Supreme Court. In the close presidential election of 2004, the composition of the Court as well as issues like abortion and medical malpractice stirred strong reactions in the electorate. Former U.S. House of Representatives majority leader Tom DeLay, talk show host Mark R. Levin, and others denounced the "tyranny" of the judiciary and the Supreme Court. The independence of the judiciary has been called into question with unprecedented vitriol.

In the midst of such criticism of the Supreme Court, labels such as "liberal," "conservative," "judicial activist," or "strict constructionist" are often used with politically laden, if not pejorative, connotations. But as columnist George Will pointed out, the Court's decisions are frequently fraught with ambiguities and political categorization is "not as easy as many suppose."[3] He was referring to the 2005 case of *Gonzales v. Raich* where a six-to-three majority on the Court held that federal regulatory authority over drugs, based upon Congress's interstate commerce power, preempted application of California's Compassionate Use Act. The latter act would have allowed marijuana use by individuals where their doctors had recommended it for relief of pain. At first glance, such a decision would seem to please social conservatives. Yet Associate Justice Sandra Day O'Connor dissented, joined by Chief Justice Rehnquist and Associate Justice Clarence Thomas, critical of the majority's expansive interpretation of the commerce clause. In this case, the marijuana was homegrown and never entered interstate commerce. The apparent conservative result in the case, upholding federal drug enforcement laws, was the result of reasoning akin to New Deal liberalism of seventy years prior.

This case underscores the point that contemporary meanings of political labels are often simplistic and at odds with their historical roots, as this book attempts to demonstrate. Fortunately, the framers of the Constitution, beset by political divisions in their own time, sought to devise a governmental system that would function despite partisanship and factionalism. George Washington and James Madison feared factionalism and divisiveness in the young republic. Madison, as one of the principal architects of the Constitution, intentionally devised a system of government that divided power among three branches to curb its destructive excesses to pit ambition against ambition.[4] Through frequently heated debates, hard bargaining, and ultimate compromise, fifty-five delegates to Philadelphia in 1787 agreed to a constitution that was relatively brief, with no mention of political parties, and was in many places deliberately vague. In commenting on the brevity and vagueness of the U.S. Constitution, Chief Justice John Marshall warned that an overly detailed constitution "would partake of the prolixity of a legal code and could scarcely be embraced by the human mind . . . Its nature, therefore, requires that only its great outlines should be marked, its important objects designated and the minor ingredients which compose those objects be deduced from the nature of the objects themselves."[5]

The foresighted Marshall adroitly described both the nature of a constitution and, by implication, the challenges for the courts charged with interpreting its meaning. The Constitution is neither cast in stone nor is it a shapeless conduit for the importation of values and principles deemed fitting by justices sitting on the Supreme Court at the time.

The Court distinguishes itself from the legislative and executive branches of government, the so-called political branches, by sets of rules, procedures, and principles unique to the judiciary. That does not mean that politics have no impact on the Court, its composition, and conduct; but rather that judicial politics are of a different nature because of the distinct role assigned to the judiciary in the Constitution and because of appointments for good behavior, which in practice has meant life. That difference is the result of an independent judiciary, the deliberate and intentional design of the framers of the Constitution. On this point, founding fathers as diverse as James Madison and Alexander Hamilton are in complete agreement. An historical survey of the Supreme Court, observing the politics surrounding selective significant cases and high-profile confirmations, demonstrates that the independence of the judiciary and, on occasion, countermajoritarianism has on the whole been a good thing for representative democracy and America.

The idea for this book coalesced after I taught classes entitled "The Politics of the Judiciary and the Supreme Court" and "Foreign Relations and National Security

Law," among others, while at the U.S. Air Force Academy. This effort benefited from the works of a politically diverse, articulate, and provocative group of writers. Among these was Professor Laurence Tribe, who in *God Save This Honorable Court* wrote of the "myth of the surprised presidency," which was a critical look at presidents who were surprised when their appointments to the Court failed to live up to political expectations. Coming from a different perspective, Judge Robert Bork in *The Tempting of America* was critical of both liberal and conservative activism on the Court, as he articulated the basis of the "original understanding" approach to the law. Comparing different approaches to interpretation of the Constitution, Professor Michael Glennon provides a useful basis to challenge widely held views about political stereotypes in the judicial context.[6] The works of Cass R. Sunstein, Antonin Scalia, Sandra Day O'Connor, Mark Tushnet, David O'Brien, Bernard Schwartz, and Lawrence Baum, among others, were also informative.

It is my goal in this survey of the Supreme Court to demonstrate that judicial "politics" are not the politics of the executive and legislative branches of government. My hope is that this writing will convince citizens across the political spectrum that, despite some decisions that we may disagree with, judicial independence is a good thing and that our representative government and constitutional liberties have been served well by the separation of powers of the three branches of government over the course of our nation's history.

# INTRODUCTION

Since the Constitution was ratified in 1788, there have been forty-three U.S. presidents, but only seventeen chief justices of the Supreme Court, as of this writing.[7] The terms of chief justices have ranged from as short as five months (John Rutledge) to as long as thirty-four years (John Marshall), with three successive chief justices (Earl Warren, Warren Burger, and William Rehnquist) each serving at least sixteen years in that capacity. Presidents have made 151 nominations to the Court (including the nominations of Judge John Roberts, Harriet Miers, and Judge Samuel Alito in 2005), but only 110 justices have actually been seated on the Court. Forty-one nominees failed to take a seat on the Court due to rejection by the Senate, withdrawal by the administration, or by their own declination. Thus, the confirmation process has provided ample opportunities to scrutinize nominees for their judicial qualifications and, as this writing will show, their political orientations.

The Supreme Court may be one of the three "pillars" of the federal government, but it differs fundamentally from the two others. Its primary output derives from the roughly seven thousand petitions for review it receives each year and approximately eighty rulings it produces in response. Methodologically it stands in marked contrast to Congress and the presidency, the so-called political branches of government. But is the Court truly nonpolitical? Is the Court capable of rising above partisanship and politics to provide detached and dispassionate judicial reasoning to disputes? Before one can adequately answer those questions, one must define politics.

*Politics* is about values, power, and about human behavior based upon sets of values and distribution of power. For Aristotle, *politikè* was about the distribution of political and economic power in society and about the behavior of individuals and groups in relation thereto.[8] Political scientist Harold D. Lasswell famously defined politics as simply "who gets what, when, and how." By long-standing tradition in Western pluralistic democracies, legal and judicial institutions, including the U.S. Supreme Court, play a practical role in handing down decisions on legal issues affecting tangible property rights. And by the same tradition, those institutions are bound to make these decisions based upon prescribed rights which are, in turn, based upon broader sets of values. In this vein, Aristotle's *politikè* concerned obligations of the state to pursue "justice," "equality," and "what is good for the whole community."[9] Recognizing that politics is about much more than power and mere economic or material rights, political scientist David Easton defined politics as the "authoritative allocation of values in a society."

When the Supreme Court is called upon to rule on questions about reasonable expectations of privacy, the rights of a fetus, or flag burning, among other things, it faces issues of fundamental values, not all of which enjoy broad societal consensus. The very divisiveness of the "hot" issues that brings them to the political branches of government frequently leads to contentious laws and executive mandates, inviting parties to seek judicial resolution.

But the politics of the judicial branch differs from the legislative and executive branches of government. The values of individual justices are subject to substantive principles and accepted rules of judicial procedure, including those governing jurisdiction and standing, affecting the very right of the Court to hear and decide specific issues. In this manner, political inputs are channeled to the Supreme Court in particular ways unique to this branch of government. The Court lacks the authority to take up as broad an array of issues as the legislative branch, though constitutional prohibitions against bills of attainder and ex post facto laws limit Congress's ability to render judgments against individuals. But jurisdiction aside, judicial methodology provides limitations on the Court's freedom of action based upon values of individual judges. Are defined values imbedded in the Constitution? Is the Constitution a "living" document that can expand to deal with new situations? Can the justices "discover" new rights "implicit" in the Constitution? These questions engender differing responses depending upon one's judicial methodology which may be a product of one's ideology.

*Ideology* has been defined by political scientist James Q. Wilson as "a coherent and consistent set of beliefs about who ought to rule, what principles rulers ought to obey, and what policies rulers ought to pursue."[10] In the context of the courts, ideology is more specifically a philosophy about how government should operate through law as well as its desired objectives and purposes. On the surface, one would expect that the traditional categories of strict constructionism and judicial activism describe ideology as applied to the judiciary. But as this historical survey of the Supreme Court will indicate, the traditional categories are neither consistent nor reliable gauges for performance on the Court nor necessarily indicative of political orientations. They reflect procedural *means* rather than political *ends* that can be used to serve purposes across the spectrum. In fact, either approach has been used in varying degree by conservatives and liberals on the Court alternately to reach desired end results. And some justices, such as Holmes and Black, have made conscious efforts to adhere to consistent methods of judicial interpretation regardless of the political result.

What remains clear is that politics on the Supreme Court is of a different nature than that of the other branches of government. The constitutional convention of 1787 provides insight into the intended role of the Supreme Court and why the judiciary is a different institution by design.

# CHAPTER 1

## THE CONSTITUTIONAL CONVENTION AND THE INDEPENDENT JUDICIARY

*After the American Revolution and the departure of the British loyalist Tories, there were no cognizable political parties in America. External threats to independence of the nation and internal squabbles between the states challenged the viability of the Articles of Confederation. Deficiencies of the confederation motivated the founders to devise a new charter or constitution for government. The new constitution was not based upon the existence of political parties but instead upon a division of power between the branches of government and between the states and federal government to prevent the aggregation of power to any one group or "faction." There was a decided distrust in governmental power and in the excesses of majoritarianism. The judiciary would become a major instrument in protecting against the concentration and, hence, abuses of power.*

**Problems with the Confederation.** In the early years of the American Republic, full independence had yet to be realized, despite a peace treaty with Britain. British soldiers occupied the Ohio Valley in defiance of the 1783 Treaty of Paris which ceded this territory to the United States. Britain demanded payment of prerevolutionary debts as agreed to in the treaty. On the extreme western frontier, Spanish ships increased patrols down the Mississippi River in 1785 in an attempt to tighten control over the transit of American freight. Spain controlled the Louisiana Territory since 1762 when King Louis XV of France ceded the lands to King Carlos III.

Additionally, cooperation between the states was less than exemplary or, in some cases, openly hostile. Virginia and Pennsylvania nearly went to war with each other over disputed territory in the western frontier. States charged customs and duties for goods traveling over state borders. Virginia charged tolls for ships entering the Chesapeake Bay. Under the Articles of Confederation adopted in 1781, there was no central court to arbitrate disputes between states (though there was provision for jurisdiction over admiralty cases), nor did the articles provide for the free transit of goods between the states. The articles placed most of governmental power in the thirteen states, leaving the Continental Congress with limited powers to collect revenue and pass laws affecting the states. There was no single currency. States issued their own currency. Foreign currency, such as Spanish reals, were commonly used in domestic trade.

George Washington, among others, inveighed against the confederal system that hindered interstate commerce and impeded his Potomac Company's efforts to build a canal system to carry goods to and from the western territories.[11] The canal system required the cooperation of Maryland since that state held rights to use of the Potomac River under a preexisting royal charter. Washington invited commissioners from Virginia and Maryland to meet in Mount Vernon in 1785 to discuss the problem. Subsequent to the meeting and with the encouragement of Washington, Virginia, commissioner James Madison urged the Virginia Assembly to support giving the power to Congress to regulate interstate commerce, as opposed to the thirteen states severally. The assembly, conscious of protecting its own sovereign prerogatives, cautiously approved a resolution calling for a convention of states to discuss commercial matters and to make recommendations to Congress.[12]

This led to a poorly attended meeting of state delegates in Annapolis in September1786. Only three states (Virginia, Delaware, and New Jersey) had quorums, and seven states had no representatives at all. Though few in number, the delegates were united in belief in the cause to rewrite the Articles of Confederation. They drafted a resolution calling for a convention the following year in Philadelphia "to devise such further provisions as shall appear to them necessary to render the Constitution of the federal government adequate to the exigencies of the Union."[13] Though by appearances the Annapolis meeting was a failure, it was influential in gaining support within the Virginia Assembly for a more ambitious convention. Naming George Washington to the state delegation enhanced the credibility of the convention and helped overcome the reluctance of other states to join in. That reluctance evaporated with the outbreak of Shays's Rebellion in Massachusetts in late 1786. Though the rebellion was contained by January 1787, the fear of citizen tax revolts, foreign intervention, and continuing Indian threats along the frontier stirred support for a stronger central government. All states but Rhode Island agreed to send delegations to the constitutional convention in Philadelphia.

**The Constitutional Convention of 1787.** Of the seventy-four delegates named by states for the constitutional convention in Philadelphia, only fifty-five attended. Those of the anti-Federalist persuasion correctly deduced that the organizers intended to use the Philadelphia meeting as a venue to *replace* rather than *amend* the Articles of Confederation. Patrick Henry, an ardent libertarian (famous for his revolutionary proclamation "Give me liberty or give me death"), "smelt a rat" and refused to attend the meeting in Philadelphia.

Among those favoring a new constitution, young lawyer James Madison accompanied Washington as a member of the Virginia delegation. Also attending the conference was New York delegate Alexander Hamilton. Hamilton was an accomplished lawyer and the former executive officer to General George Washington during the Revolutionary War. He was a hero at the battle of Yorktown, having commanded and led the final assault on the British redoubt. He became an important and essential ally of Madison's in the fight for the Constitution.

**Philosophical Foundations for the Court: Separation of Powers.** James Madison had prepared in advance with his own particular agenda for the convention. He put together the foundations for the Virginia Plan, which would have provided for proportional representation in the legislature based upon population (favoring large and populous states like Virginia). Contrary to the creed of the anti-Federalists who would leave governmental power primarily with the states, Madison believed that liberty could be secure in a new federal government, especially where powers were separated between three branches. Countering the anti-Federalist claims that a federal government would bring back the "tyranny" experienced during British rule, he proclaimed that "if men were angels, no government would be necessary."[14]

At the same time, Madison believed it would be unrealistic to rely on "mere parchment" to prevent concentration of power in the hands of a few. In answer to this concern, he later wrote in "Federalist No. 51":

> The great security against a gradual concentration of the several powers in the same department consists in giving to those who administer each department the necessary constitutional means, and personal motives, to resist encroachments of the others . . . Ambition must be made to counteract ambition.

Madison wrote this out of concern for the powers of the executive and legislative branches of government. Yet there was movement to create the judiciary as a coequal branch of government.

We owe much to the influence of French philosopher Montesquieu for championing the concept of separation of powers and particularly the notion of an independent judiciary. In his 1748 work, *The Spirit of the Laws,* he wrote,

> When the legislative and executive powers are united in the same person, or in the same body of magistracy, there can then be no liberty.[15]

He was an Anglophile who believed that the British Constitution embodied the principle of separation of powers, though the highest court, the King's Bench, was intrinsically part of the House of Lords, the upper house of Parliament, at a time when that body held relevant legislative powers. Nevertheless, Montesquieu's concept became the basis for the American departure from the British model to create a more independent judiciary.

Under the simple constitutional concept, the legislature passes laws under Article I, the executive executes laws under Article II, and the judiciary adjudges and applies laws under Article III. Nowhere in the Constitution can an explicit provision for judicial review be found, though the powers and responsibility for adjudication, particularly of constitutional questions, is clear. Much as ambiguities and omissions in appropriation of powers between the legislative and executive branches remained to be determined later, the full powers and role of the Court were to become evident over time. Yet the judiciary, not an entirely independent body under European tradition at the time, was somehow different than the "political branches" of government.

**The Debate on the Court's Role.** Most of the delegates to the constitutional convention were fairly united in a desire to create a single "supreme" court with jurisdiction over disputes between states. But many republicans opposed the concept of a court that could override state and federal legislatures since they believed that sovereignty should reside with the people, and as such there should be no higher authority than the people's legislative representatives. By this view, giving unelected judicial officials authority over legislatures undermined the emergent concept of democratic legitimacy.

**The Supremacy Clause.** Madison intended to make certain that federal law would take precedence over and preempt state law because of his concerns over state abuses of power. Fresh in the memory of many delegates were the cases of Rhode Island's law, forcing creditors to accept paper money (which depreciated well below its ascribed value) and Pennsylvania's disenfranchisement of Quakers. Madison placed in his delegations' proposal, known as the Virginia Plan, a clause authorizing the federal government "to negative all laws passed by the several states contravening in the opinion of the national legislature the articles of the Union."[16] Madison's proposed veto power over state legislation initially passed.

Although many delegates agreed with the necessity to overrule state legislation, they did not want to provide too large a power to a federal judiciary nor cede all power from the states. When South Carolina delegate Charles Pinckney proposed to strengthen this provision to give Congress authority "to negative all (state) laws which they should judge to be improper," other delegates from the South balked. They feared this authority would be used to strike down state slavery laws. Even Northern delegations thought this "universal veto" power went too far. The resolution was overwhelmingly defeated, despite the support of Madison. The mood had changed, and the initial support for Madison's legislative veto waned.

Delegate Luther Martin proposed a compromise to control errant state laws, a provision making federal laws and treaties "the supreme law of the respective states" similar to language contained in the New Jersey Plan.[17] The proposal passed without dissent. Though the antinationalist Martin did not intend for this language to give federal authority over state constitutions (as opposed to state legislation), the convention's Committee of Detail amended the language for broader coverage:

> The acts of the legislature of the United States made in pursuance of this Constitution, and all treaties made under the authority of the United States, shall be the supreme law of the several states, and of their citizens and inhabitants; and the judges in the several states shall be bound thereby in their decisions; anything in the constitutions or laws of the several states to the contrary notwithstanding.

The language would be amended additional times; but the final version of Article VI made the Constitution, laws of the United States, and treaties "the supreme law of the land."

**Jurisdiction of the Court.** The jurisdiction of the Court spurred a separate but equally spirited debate. The initial language for Article III modestly proposed that the Supreme Court would have jurisdiction over "cases arising under the laws passed by the legislature of the United States."[18] This wording assigned a role of enforcement of laws passed by Congress rather than questioning the constitutional consistency thereof. Connecticut delegate William Samuel Johnson proposed changing the language to the farther-reaching "The jurisdiction of the Supreme Court shall extend to all cases arising *under this Constitution* and the laws passed by the legislature of the United States." (emphasis added)

A lone Madison argued against the change, opining that the Court ought to be limited to "cases of a judiciary nature," impliedly resisting a role of constitutional or judicial review for the Court over congressional legislation. Johnson's language went forward with modifications, though Madison's notes condition approval on an understanding by the delegates of its limitation of the Court to considering only cases "of a judiciary nature." Since there were no official transcripts of the convention and since Madison took the most complete notes, we have little more than Madison's own words to rely upon. Nevertheless, the final language of Article III did not contain Madison's limitations:

> The judicial power shall extend to all cases, in law and equity, arising under this Constitution, the laws of the United States, and treaties made, or which shall be made under their authority.

There are indications that the delegates wanted the Court to have the power to overturn *state* legislation. Delegate Alexander Hamilton declared that the judiciary had a duty "to declare all acts contrary to the manifest tenor of the Constitution void."[19] Delegate Oliver Ellsworth, in his later capacity as a legislator and author of provisions of the Judiciary Act of 1789, would make explicit the power of the Supreme Court to declare state laws unconstitutional.[20] The power of the Court relative to federal laws remained ambiguous. It would not be until 1803, in the case of *Marbury v. Madison*, that John Marshall would interpret and apply Article III and Article VI authority to establish a precedent for the power of judicial review over federal laws.

**The Ratification Effort: Strengthening the Weakest Branch.** In the months ensuing after the drafting of the new constitution, Alexander Hamilton, along with then-Federalists James Madison and John Jay, authored several articles in New York newspapers making the case for the new constitution. The prolific Hamilton authored over fifty articles or two-thirds of the *Federalist Papers*. He wrote the most articles on the judiciary.[21] In "Federalist No. 78" (appendix 1), Hamilton laid out his vision of the proper role of the Court. He wrote of the importance of the life tenure of justices' "good behavior" to support "judicial magistracy." In his view, this was the "best expedient . . . steady, upright, and impartial administration of the laws." This tenure furthered the imperative of separation of powers:

> The judiciary, from the nature of its functions, will always be the least dangerous to the political rights of the Constitution; because it will be least in a capacity to annoy or injure them.[22]

Paraphrasing Montesquieu, Hamilton reasoned that "the judiciary is beyond comparison the weakest of the three departments of power."[23] As he explained, this is the case because "the judiciary has no influence over the sword or the purse."[24] The judiciary "may truly be said to have neither force nor will but merely judgment and must ultimately depend upon the aid of the executive arm even for the efficacy of its judgments."[25]

Hamilton drew heavily from Montesquieu who argued that "there is no liberty if the power of judgment be not separated from the legislative and executive powers."[26] Hamilton believed that "the complete independence of the courts of justice is peculiarly essential in a limited Constitution." The Constitution contained clear limitations on actions of the legislature that would appear to take upon a judicial role, prohibiting bills of attainder and ex post facto laws.

In a similar vein, Hamilton sought to prohibit legislative roles for the courts: "It can be of no weight to say that the courts, on the pretense of a repugnancy, may substitute their own pleasure to the constitutional intentions of the legislature."[27] Even in his anticipation of a power of judicial review, he saw a limited role for the courts. In judicial review, the courts preserve a "limited Constitution" via the duty to declare all acts contrary to the "manifest tenor of the Constitution" void.[28]

Hamilton sought to define the power of judicial review. He stated that "no legislative act, therefore, contrary to the Constitution, can be valid."[29] Only the courts would have the power to determine this.[30] He continued, "A constitution is, in fact, and must be regarded by the judges as, a fundamental law."[31] The proper role of the courts is

> To avoid an arbitrary discretion in the courts, it is indispensable that they should be bound down by strict rules and precedents which serve to define and point out their duty in every particular case that comes before them.[32]

Neither Hamilton nor many other framers of the Constitution subscribed to the optimistic Enlightenment Age view of human nature. Instead, their inherent distrust of human nature led them to divide and distribute power of government to prevent abuses. As John Marshall would later declare in *Marbury v. Madison,* our constitutional system is a "government of laws, not of men." And inevitably, as Tocqueville observed, political questions work into judicial questions, providing abundant opportunities to test how well the Constitution worked in this regard.

**The Anti-Federalists and the Bill of Rights.** Not everyone was enamored with the new Constitution. Delegates George Mason and Edmund Randolph of Virginia and Elbridge Gerry of Massachusetts refused to sign the Constitution.[33] Opponents of the Constitution, known collectively as the anti-Federalists, took issue with Hamilton and the potential for abuse of federal judicial power. A rebuttal to Hamilton appeared in a writing of early 1788 now known as "Anti-Federalist Paper No. 80" (appendix 2), believed to be authored by Robert Yates of New York. The paper was particularly critical of the Constitution's arrangement for one court "with supreme and uncontrollable power." The author feared that the Supreme Court would be "rendered completely independent, both of the people and the legislature."

But Hamilton, in "Federalist No. 81" (appendix 3), argued that the separation of judicial power from the legislative branch is a valid application of the principle of separation of powers already endorsed by the constitutions of nine states. He defended the tenure of justices based upon on good behavior as opposed to appointments for a "limited period" as further distinction and independence from the legislative branch. He pointed out that legislators are rarely selected for reasons of judicial knowledge or temperament. Instead, he feared the excess influence of legislators would pose threats of infringement of the Constitution:

> On account of the natural propensity of such bodies to party divisions, there will be no less reason to fear that the pestilential breath of faction may poison the fountains of justice.[34]

Thus, Hamilton made the case that the Constitution bolstered by an independent judiciary would strengthen rather than weaken liberty.

The agitations of anti-Federalists like Patrick Henry and George Mason generated demands by the states for a "bill of rights," borrowing from the English antecedent. Though eight state constitutions already had bills of rights, Elbridge Gerry's proposal at the convention, seconded by Mason, to include a bill of rights in the federal Constitution had been defeated with the majority of delegates believing it was not necessary.[35] But the absence of a bill of rights remained an issue after the convention, one that became critical for ratification in Virginia and Massachusetts.[36] Both states ratified in 1788, but with recommendations for amendments including a bill of rights. The authors of the *Federalist Papers* were also persuasive in the contentious states of New York and Pennsylvania. By 1788, the requisite nine states had ratified the Constitution. By 1790, the remaining four states had done so.

In June 1789, James Madison presented his draft of the bill of rights to the House of Representatives. He borrowed much from the Virginia Declaration of Rights, which had been drafted by George Mason and was part of the constitution of the Commonwealth of Virginia. The declaration included rights against excessive bail, freedom of the press, the right to trial by jury, the right to a speedy trial, the right to confront witnesses in criminal proceedings, the right against search and seizure without specific warrant, the right against self-incrimination, and the right to free exercise of religion, among others.

Madison's draft underwent revisions by both houses of Congress, but much of his original language remained intact. By 1791, the first ten amendments were ratified. The final version of the Fifth Amendment to the U.S. Constitution declared that "no person shall be . . . deprived of life, liberty, or property, without due process of law," incorporating Locke's natural rights. This due process clause closely resembled the language of Article VIII of the Virginia Declaration "that no man be deprived of his liberty except by the law of the land or the judgment of his peers." This, in turn, resembled chapter 39 of the original English Magna Carta, which ensured that "no free man shall be taken or imprisoned or disseized or outlawed or exiled . . . except by the lawful judgment of his peers or by the law of the land."[37] While the English barons who forced King John to sign this document at Runnymede in 1215 were no doubt motivated to seek guarantees of their own protection from the crown, these rights inured to the broad benefit of all citizens, becoming a hallowed part of English constitution law and tradition.

With the ratification of the Constitution, the Supreme Court was created, with institutional measures to maintain independence from the other branches of government. Madison and Hamilton anticipated the formation of factions and parties and divided power to prevent any one faction from abusing positions of authority within government. Their success in dividing authority would eventually invite spiteful attacks from factions frustrated in their quest for domination of all branches of government. Many of those participating in the constitutional convention would later play prominent roles in the judiciary. Delegates Oliver Ellsworth, John Rutledge, James Wilson, and John Blair served as justices of the Supreme Court.

# CHAPTER 2

## THE EARLY YEARS OF THE COURT AND THE EMERGENCE OF PARTIES: 1790-1835

*President George Washington's efforts to prevent division and factionalism in the early American Republic slowed but did not prevent the formation of political parties. His successor, John Adams, could not hold back zealots within the Federalist Party, who succeeded in dividing their party and the country. But since the Constitution effectively distributed power among the branches of government, attempts by the Republicans to dominate the government would be fettered. In the role of final arbiter of the Constitution, the Supreme Court would invoke the ire of frustrated majoritarian politicians, from Thomas Jefferson to Andrew Jackson.*

**The Washington Administration and the Court's Beginning.** As the first president under the new Constitution, George Washington selected justices for the Supreme Court who strongly supported the Constitution and were inclined to broad interpretations of constitutional provisions regarding federal power.[38] Since Washington presided over the 1787 constitutional convention in Philadelphia, he was keenly aware of the implications of the new federal system of government and residual resistance by the anti-Federalists. There were no political parties in existence in America at the time, and Washington loathed even the notion of "factionalism" as dangerous to the unity of the new republic. But the seeds of factionalism had already been planted. By 1791, Hamilton and his followers had founded the Federalist Party, consisting of supporters of a strong central government. The following year, anti-Federalists and states' rights advocates formed the Republican Party.

Drafters of the Constitution contemplated a limited role for the judiciary. In its structure, the enumerated judicial powers of Article III are much shorter than the legislative powers of Article I or the executive powers of Article II. The Constitution laid out limited "original jurisdiction" and gave Congress the power to regulate appellate jurisdiction. It also specified the mode for selection and tenure for justices. But Article

III was silent as to the Court's power to overrule actions of other branches and its role, if any, in policy-making. Furthermore, the Court would be dependent upon the enabling legislation before it could even convene. Congress passed the Judiciary Act of 1789, establishing a federal court system, setting the size of the Court at six justices, and giving the Supreme Court broad appellate jurisdiction. The chief drafter of the legislation was Oliver Ellsworth, who would later join the Court. Congress would change the number of associate justices many times over the next decades until the Judiciary Act of 1869 set the number at nine justices, where it remains today.

In keeping with his intent to establish a strong federal government, Washington nominated only those supporting the federal system as embodied in the Constitution. John Jay was his choice to serve as the first chief justice. Jay had drafted a constitution for New York State, had been elected as a delegate to the Continental Congress, served as American minister to Spain during the Revolutionary War, was appointed secretary for foreign affairs under the Articles of Confederation, became New York State's first chief justice, and was author of several of the *Federalist Papers*. Jay would serve as chief justice of the U.S. Supreme Court until 1795. Of the five initial associate justices on the Court, John Rutledge of South Carolina, James Wilson of Pennsylvania, and John Blair of Virginia had been delegates to the constitutional convention in Philadelphia in 1787 and had signed the Constitution. Washington would also nominate William Cushing from Massachusetts to sit on the original Court. Over his two terms as president, Washington also appointed James Iredell (1790), Thomas Johnson (1791), William Paterson (1793), Samuel Chase (1796), and Oliver Ellsworth (1796). Both Paterson and Ellsworth had been delegates to the constitutional convention.

The Court's beginning was slow. It heard only fifty cases between 1790 and 1799. The Court did not convene until February 1, 1790, nine months after Washington took office, and then began work with only three justices in attendance.[39] Their courtroom and offices were located in the Merchant's Exchange Building in New York City, then the nation's capital. In a political deal between Hamilton and Southern members of Congress, it was agreed to move the capital to a new federal "District of Columbia" with an interim location in Philadelphia. In the fall of 1790, the Court would move to the former city hall in Philadelphia when that city became the capital. The Court's first opinion would not be delivered until 1792. In addition to duties on the Supreme Court, the justices were required to perform circuit court duty twice a year, which involved arduous travel to remote regions.

One of the earliest significant cases was *Chisholm v. Georgia* (1793).[40] The Court was called upon to decide a dispute between citizens of South Carolina and the state of Georgia relating to property seized from Tories during the Revolutionary War. The Court decided against Georgia, whose lawyers failed to appear before the Court. Shocked members of Congress responded by initiating a constitutional amendment which would deny the jurisdiction of the Court to review cases brought by citizens of one state against another state. The measure was ratified by the requisite number of states by February 1795, resulting in the Eleventh Amendment to the Constitution. This would be the first of several times that Congress would initiate amendments to the Constitution in order to, in effect, reverse decisions of the Supreme Court.

**The Court and American Neutrality.** Larger political issues would work their way to the Court. The Court was not immune from the continuing enmity (now a war) between the French and British which dominated Washington's foreign policy concerns during his presidency. In 1793, the ruling French Girondists sent Edmond Charles Genet to the United States as their ambassador. His involvement in plans to attack British and Spanish territories from American soil, compounded by disparaging remarks about President Washington, resulted in his being declared persona non grata by the administration. During this time, Washington sought a legal basis to establish American neutrality. In furtherance of this objective, he sent the Court twenty-nine questions on international law and treaties. However, the Court refused to provide advisory opinions, believing that such would constitute an exercise of executive powers in violation of the Constitution. Washington ultimately promulgated a Neutrality Proclamation in an attempt to keep the United States out of the growing conflict between Britain and France. The precedent against providing advisory opinions stands today, though courts in other countries, including the International Court of Justice, do otherwise.

Nevertheless, the Supreme Court would later support Washington's policy of U.S. neutrality in practical legal terms. In *Glass v. Sloop Betsey* (1794), the Court denied French jurisdiction over a Swedish ship, the *Betsey,* carrying cargo owned by an American citizen, Alexander Glass, which was seized by a French raider, the *Citizen Genet,* on the high seas and taken to Baltimore.[41] It had up to that point been the French practice to bring such ships into U.S. ports for French consuls to decide the disposition of contents as spoils of war. The Court's decision struck a strong note in defense of American sovereignty and independence.

Other issues involving foreign powers, such as the British occupation of the Ohio territories, also had an impact on the Court. To secure British withdrawal from rightful American territories, Washington decided to pursue a settlement with England. He sent Chief Justice Jay to England in 1794 to negotiate a new peace treaty. He had been one of three commissioners, along with John Adams and Benjamin Franklin, who negotiated the Treaty of Paris in 1785, which provided for peace with England and recognition of America's sovereignty. By the terms of the Jay Treaty of 1794, the British agreed to, among other things, end occupation of the Ohio Valley in exchange for settling outstanding claims by Tories. This treaty was immensely unpopular with the American public because of the monetary obligation it saddled onto states to pay off debts to Tories and provisions requiring the extradition and return of British sailors who had deserted. The Jay Treaty also alarmed the French, who considered it a new alliance with their old enemy, England. It would herald the beginning of difficult relations and an undeclared war with France, fueling republican and anti-Federalist sentiment out of sympathy for the French Revolution. Ironically, in the only case he argued before the Supreme Court, attorney John Marshall lost his case on behalf of a Virginia law which challenged the Jay

Treaty's mandate to pay British creditors.[42] By virtue of the supremacy clause, the Court held that such treaties are supreme over state laws. As indicated by the events leading up to and including the drafting of the Constitution, that clause was intended to cure the deficiencies of the Articles of Confederation which had hindered the effectuation of peace with England. Ironically, the supremacy clause would form the foundation for later significant decisions by Marshall and the Supreme Court.

**The Senate's First Rejection of a Nomination.** In 1795, John Jay resigned his seat on the Court, having been elected governor of the state of New York, a post he considered more prestigious. The resignation of Chief Justice Jay left a hard-to-fill vacancy on the Court. During a congressional recess, George Washington named former associate justice John Rutledge from South Carolina, who had left the Supreme Court in 1791 to preside over South Carolina's highest court, to replace Jay as chief justice. Rutledge served as chief justice from August to December of 1795 by virtue of a temporary commission from Washington issued with the hope of being confirmed by the Senate to permanently hold that position. But a speech he made denouncing the Jay Treaty during a visit to his hometown of Charleston, South Carolina, would defeat those plans. Rutledge's remark that he would "rather the president die than sign the treaty" deeply offended Washington's supporters. When the Senate reconvened in December 1795, it rejected his nomination by a vote of 14-10, the first rejection by the Senate of a presidential nomination for the Supreme Court. The ten supporters of Rutledge were, not surprisingly, opponents of the Jay Treaty. The Philadelphia-based Republican newspaper *Aurora* criticized the vote as politically motivated.

Washington considered nominating Patrick Henry, but Henry declined. Washington then offered the chief justice nomination to Associate Justice William Cushing, but Cushing declined in 1796. Thereafter, the nomination went to Oliver Ellsworth who served as chief justice until 1801. Ellsworth had been one of the fourteen senators voting against Rutledge. By the time Washington left the presidency in 1797, he had made fourteen nominations and ten appointments to the Supreme Court,[43] a number matched by no other president.

**The Adams Administration.** President John Adams, serving only one term, would make three appointments to the Supreme Court; but two justices, John Marshall and Bushrod Washington, would each stay on the Court for over three decades. John Marshall from Virginia would change the direction of the Court and substantially enhance the influence of the Court on the other branches of government. At a precarious position with a rising Republican chorus from Southern states, the New England-born and raised Adams would consistently appoint justices from Southern states. In 1798, his first nominee to a seat as an associate justice, Bushrod Washington, was a Virginian and nephew of President George Washington. He would serve for thirty-one years on the Court. Alfred Moore from North Carolina, the most junior justice on Court, was appointed in 1799 and served only five years on the Court.

Though Adams opposed factionalism and the development of political parties as much as Washington did, his administration was wracked by a growing division between the Federalists and the Republicans, who favored the limitation of federal power. Vice President Jefferson, though a longtime friend and confidant of Adams (dating back to their days together as fellow commissioners to France), worked behind the scenes to support Republican causes and undermine the Federalists. Even under Washington's administration, he had covertly stirred forces against Hamilton and other ardent Federalists through financial support to the opposition press, in particular journalist James Callender and the dissident Philadelphia newspaper *Aurora*.

Growing concerns about French political intrigue preoccupied the Federalists, who did not hide their pro-English sentiments. They feared French attempts to pull America into its fight with England, as Citizen Genet had tried. Their fear was fueled further by the "XYZ" Affair. In 1797, President Adams dispatched a commission consisting of Elbridge Gerry, John Marshall, and Charles Pinckney (code-named X, Y, and Z) to meet with the infamous ruling French Directory (now dominated by the radical Jacobins) to negotiate a peace treaty with France, similar to the Jay Treaty with England. The demand by French Foreign Minister Charles Maurice de Talleyrand-Périgord for fifty thousand pounds sterling in addition to a considerable loan to the republic of France caused the U.S. agents to depart in disgust (with the exception of Gerry, who remained behind to take care of other business). News of the incident generated popular outrage in America.

Anti-French sentiment was so high that the Federalists endeavored to tarnish the Republicans by referring to them as Democratic-Republicans, a moniker associating them with the French and the excesses of the French Revolution. The Republicans for their part were not altogether offended by the label since they officially adopted the "Democratic-Republican" name for their party in 1798.

**The Alien and Sedition Acts.** In response to fears of foreign intervention and the publication of the XYZ letters publicizing the incident in France, the so-called High Federalists in Congress sponsored the Alien and Sedition Acts of 1798.[44] This group of Federalists was firmly aligned with Britain and vitriolic in their enmity toward the French. Hamilton was most visible of the High Federalists in the executive branch. The Sedition Act made it a federal crime to publish "false, scandalous, and malicious" statements against the Congress or the president. Jefferson's ally James Callender was among twenty-five people arrested and ten convicted under this act. He was charged with accusing President Adams of agitating for war with France. The judiciary, especially one dominated by Federalists, had no desire to challenge the constitutionality of abridgements of freedom of speech, especially against legislation sponsored by leading members of their own party. Though the Supreme Court would later stake out a claim as defender of individual civil liberties under the Constitution, at this time such an assertive challenge to congressional authority was not contemplated. The Alien Act gave the president the right to expel any foreigner he deemed "dangerous."[45] But President Adams never invoked the Alien Act before it expired in 1800 despite the urging of anti-French, pro-war Secretary of State Timothy Pickering. Though Vice President Jefferson also signed the Alien Act and though the laws were largely the product of the High Federalists in Congress rather than the president, Adams's name would forever be associated with these laws, if for no other reason than he did not actively oppose them.[46] Notably, not all Federalists supported the Sedition Act. John Marshall, among others, opposed the act and would likely have voted against it were he in Congress at the time.[47] The Sedition Act expired in March 1801. The popular reaction to the Sedition Act would affect the Supreme Court's views about the importance and meaning of the First Amendment and freedom of speech long into the future.[48]

The unpopular Alien and Sedition Acts became fodder for Republican rallies against the Federalists, viewed as attempts to stifle dissent and political voice for the Republicans, especially timed to impact the election of 1800. The growing unpopularity of the Federalists helped ensure that Adams, the senior member of the party, would not be elected to a second term as president.

In spite of his own role in passage of the legislation, Vice President Jefferson distanced himself from the administration. He and James Madison secretly drafted the Kentucky and Virginia Resolutions of 1798, which declared that each state had a "natural right" to nullify federal actions it deemed unconstitutional.[49] This "nullification doctrine" would later have repercussions far beyond the scope of the Alien and Sedition Acts. Opposition to the acts became a cause celebré for Jefferson and his followers, who would be swept into office in the election of 1800. Upon taking office in 1801, President Jefferson exercised his constitutional authority to pardon all publishers convicted under the Sedition Act. The Republicans had planted a seed on behalf of civil liberties that would germinate later on the Court.

Other legislation would be used to curtail contacts with foreign governments. The Logan Act, which was designed to prevent Republicans from aiding and assisting France, prevents private citizens from negotiating with foreign governments on behalf of the United States without prior authorization. It was named after Dr. George Logan, a Republican Quaker from Philadelphia who attempted to negotiate peace with French officials, including Talleyrand, in 1798. Though no one has ever been convicted under the Logan Act, the threat of charges has been invoked during the Vietnam War against self-appointed peace delegations and even against Associate Justice William O. Douglas.[50]

**The Division of the Federalists.** Adams paid a political price for his careful balancing act between the "High Federalists" like Hamilton, who wanted war with France, and the Republicans, who wanted peace. While building a sizeable American Navy, he quietly pursued peace with the French, securing an agreement in the form of the Convention of Mortefontaine, which ended the so-called Quasi-War in October 1800.[51] The treaty was the result of negotiations of commissioners Chief Justice Oliver Ellsworth, Patrick Henry, and William Vans Murray, facilitated by the breakup of the infamous French Directory and Napoleon's appointment as first consul of France. Adams had fired Hamilton's ally Timothy Pickering as secretary of state because of Pickering's opposition to the peace mission to France and replaced him with Congressman John Marshall, who favored peace with the French. But the news of the peace treaty did not reach the United States until after the presidential election, denying Adams any political benefit from his efforts. In the meantime, Hamilton, who had lobbied George Washington behind Adams's back for an appointment as inspector general of the army, and other High Federalists actively worked to undermine Adams's reelection, publishing accusations of his alleged mishandling of relations with France, among other things. But the Republicans became the actual beneficiaries of Federalist divisions, with Jefferson taking the presidency and Aaron Burr, a former Federalist and senator from New York, taking the vice presidency.[52] The Twelfth Amendment of 1804 eliminated the Constitution's original requirement that the candidate with the second largest majority become vice president.

**John Marshall and the Federalist Legacy.** When the ailing Oliver Ellsworth announced his retirement as chief justice, Adams offered the post to his old colleague and former chief justice John Jay.[53] After Jay declined, Adams nominated his secretary of state, John Marshall, on January 31, 1801.[54] This appointment was made in the last months of the Adams administration, knowing that Jefferson's Republicans would be remaking the government according to their own designs. But Adams correctly predicted that Marshall, who was in good health and vigor at the age of forty-five, would likely serve for many years on the Court.[55] In fact, Marshall presided over the Court for thirty-four years, until 1835, when he was eighty years old. He had been a company commander during the revolutionary war, serving under Washington at Valley Forge through the frigid winter of 1777-1778. A sense of duty to country remained with him after his military service. Marshall became active in Virginia politics, an ardent Federalist with a view toward strengthening the power of the federal government vis-a-vis the states. Prior to his appointment to the Court, he was known more for his skills in politics and diplomacy than adeptness as a litigator. Adams had high regard for Marshall's loyalty, good sense, and for his belief in Federalism.[56] Only under John Marshall would judicial review emerge as a tool to challenge the powers of the other branches of the federal government. Marshall would abandon the British practice of all justices providing their opinions separately *ad seriatim* in favor of a single opinion of the Court. President Adams's appointment of Marshall would later come to be regarded as one of Adams's greatest contributions to his country.[57]

**Jefferson and the Republicans Face the Court.** In Jefferson's inaugural address of March 1801, he called for national unity, declaring that "we are all Republicans, we are all Federalists." But his actions as president proved less conciliatory. Jefferson proceeded to systematically appoint members of the Republican Party to senior posts in government. However, the Constitution's mandated life tenure for justices limited his influence on the Supreme Court. Jefferson correctly viewed the judiciary as a stronghold for Federalists, where life tenures made it almost impervious to his influence. He recognized the Federalist agenda on the Court and fought it where he could. One of his appointees to the Court, William Johnson, would establish a precedent by writing the first dissenting opinion on the Marshall Court not long after his appointment to the Court in 1804.

**The Court Asserts Constitutional Authority: Marbury v. Madison.** It would not be long after his appointment for the opportunity to come for Marshall to establish a more substantial constitutional role for the Court. The opportunity was provided by William Marbury, one of the forty-two so-called midnight judges nominated and confirmed, with commissions signed by Adams during the waning hours of the administration. Marbury was commissioned to be justice of the peace for the District of Columbia. But his commission was never delivered during the final hours of the John Adams administration nor during the succeeding administration of Thomas Jefferson. When James Madison, the secretary of state under Jefferson, refused to deliver the judicial commission, Marbury filed a writ of mandamus to compel him to do so.

When the case of *Marbury v. Madison* came to the Supreme Court in 1803, Marshall struck down a portion of the Judiciary Act of 1789 where Congress had attempted to redefine the original jurisdiction of the Supreme Court in violation of Article III of the Constitution.[58] Applying the supremacy clause of Article XI, Marshall asserted that "it is emphatically the province and duty of the judicial department to say what the law is. Those who apply the rule to particular cases must of necessity expound and interpret that rule." The result denied the Court's jurisdiction over Marbury's writ of mandamus for his judicial appointment. Although the immediate result supported the Jefferson administration's position (opposing the preceding Adams administration's attempts to dominate the judiciary at a time when Federalists were losing electoral support in the legislative and executive branches of government), the methodology struck a chord against legislative power and, by implication, executive power, where acts of either branch exceeded their constitutional authority. A few years later, the ruling would be applied to overturn state statutes.

The case came before the Court as part of a larger fight between Federalists and Republicans over who would control the future direction of government. In an effort to thwart Republican opportunities to appoint Supreme Court justices, the Federalists in Congress had reduced the number to five, with the occurrence of the next vacancy, in the Judiciary Act of 1801.[59] A Republican-dominated Congress repealed this portion of the act in 1802. A judicial challenge to congressional authority was somewhat risky since the authority of the Supreme Court to declare a law passed by Congress unconstitutional and void was not explicitly mentioned in the Constitution. Furthermore, the Court had the misfortune of being a "tenant" in the Capitol building which was controlled by the legislative branch (as it would until 1935).

The animosity between the outgoing Federalist administration and the new Republican administration of Jefferson could be seen in other aspects of the Judiciary Act of 1801. The Federalists used the act to create several new judgeships to which the outgoing president could make lifetime appointments. The act added three new circuits, for a total of six, and ten additional district courts. To President Jefferson's chagrin, the act made the judiciary a political stronghold for Federalists for years to come. But the circuit court system was abolished in 1802 when the Republicans took over a majority of seats in Congress. Though Congress could do little else about the Federalist appointments, it succeeded in effectively shutting down the Supreme Court for over a year (from December 1801 to February 1803) by resetting the Court's term dates.[60] But ultimately Congress could not prevent the Court from reconvening, and Marshall boldly issued the *Marbury* decision in the ensuing term.

**The First Impeachment.** Jefferson's fight against the Federalist agenda led to a more direct challenge to the Court. His supporters in the House of Representatives impeached Associate Justice Samuel Chase in 1805 on charges of promoting Federalist philosophy while riding circuit and presiding over the sedition trial of James Callender.[61] Old Bacon Face, as Chase was known, was the first justice of the Court to be impeached. He has been described as an able lawyer, "a man of violent opinions, overbearing manners, fierce temper, and center of controversy."[62] He had led the Sons of Liberty in subversive activities against the British in 1765 and was later chief judge of the highest court of Maryland. Of more concern to the Republicans, he ran Adams's unsuccessful reelection campaign in 1800, engendering their enmity. The Senate trial included the testimony of fifty-one witnesses, of which Marshall was a witness for the defense of Chase. But to Jefferson's disappointment, the Senate failed to convict (and remove) Chase. He would remain on the Court until 1811. No attempt to impeach a Supreme Court justice would be successful again until almost one hundred fifty years later. The latter impeachment (Associate Justice William O. Douglas) also ended in failure to convict.

**Republican Changes to Composition of the Court.** In addition to William Johnson, Jefferson appointed two other justices to the Court: H. Brockholst Livingston in 1806 and Thomas Todd in 1807. Despite three appointments to the Court, Jefferson was not able to influence nor shape the Court to the extent he desired. He would suffer the indignity of having to comply with Marshall's subpoena for documents during the treason trial of Aaron Burr, Jefferson's former vice president, in 1807.

Nor did the two judicial appointments of President Madison and the one appointment of Monroe successfully challenge Marshall's domination of the Court. Even a prominent Democratic-Republican Party appointee, Joseph Story, nominated by President James Madison in 1811, found himself under the considerable influence of Marshall. Story's nomination came on the heels of the Senate's rejection of a previous nominee, Alexander Wolcott, and the declination of two others, Levi Lincoln and John Quincy Adams. As a former speaker of the Massachusetts statehouse, U.S. congressman, speechwriter for Daniel Webster, one-time leader of the Jeffersonian Republicans, and one of the most learned and prolific lawyers of his time, Story was seemingly an easy choice for Madison. Thus, there was ample evidence that Story would be the Republican "intellectual counterweight" to Marshall on the Court.[63] But Jefferson ominously warned Madison that Story was a "Tory" who would disappoint the Democratic-Republicans.[64] Story, who was thirty-two years old at the time of his nomination, would remain on the Court until 1845.

Marshall's stature and his congenial but persuasive nature would continue to carry great weight with his associate justices throughout his tenure on the Court. Marshall remained on the Court well beyond the demise of the Federalist Party and the passing of Jefferson's two terms as president, supporting strong national powers over state power in *McCulloch v. Maryland* in 1819[65] (upholding the constitutionality of the Bank of the United States) and *Gibbons v. Ogden* in 1824.[66]

In *McCulloch*, the Court held that the Bank of the United States could not be taxed by the state of Maryland. Marshall relied upon the supremacy clause contained in Article VII of the Constitution, which states that the constitution, treaties, and laws of the United States shall be the "supreme law of the land." Under this provision, federal law would be superior to state law where in conflict. But Madison and fellow Democratic-Republican opponents of the bank believed that the federal government lacked authority to create such a bank in the first place since such a power was never explicitly mentioned in the Constitution. In response, Marshall relied upon powers implicit in the Constitution. Taking into account the explicit powers in the Constitution to create currency, tax, and borrow funds, Marshall pointed to Article I, Section 7 which gave to Congress the power "to make all laws which shall be *necessary and proper* for carrying into execution the foregoing powers and all other powers vested by this Constitution." (emphasis added) Marshall continued,

> Let the end be legitimate, let it be within the scope of the Constitution, and all means which are appropriate, which are plainly adapted to that end, which are not prohibited, but consistent with the letter and spirit of the Constitution are constitutional.

The fight over the Bank of the United States would not end with this decision. Enmity over the bank would dominate later Democratic-Republican Party agendas in the other branches of government.

In another case decided in 1819, the Marshall Court used the Constitution to invalidate an act of the New Hampshire state legislature. Marshall supported the application of the contract clause of the Constitution to corporations in *Dartmouth College v. Woodward*.[67] Article I, Section 10 prohibits states from "passing any law impairing the Obligation of Contracts." The Court held that corporate charters were in the nature of a contract and thus protected from government impairment. Some credit this case with promoting American economic expansion by protecting property rights of corporations and providing them with legal "personality."[68]

In 1824, the Marshall Court again ruled in favor of federal supremacy over state law in *Gibbons v. Ogden*. Thomas Gibbons challenged New York's grant of an "exclusive right of navigation" to Robert Livingston's and Robert Fulton's steamboats on the Hudson River between Elizabethtown, New Jersey, and the city of New York. Steam ferry transit between New York and New Jersey was a highly lucrative enterprise. Congress gave Gibbons a license for coastal trade in 1793. The Supreme Court ruled that under the interstate commerce clause of the Constitution, congressional power was explicit and superior to any purported state power. Therefore, New York's exclusive license was invalid in the face of Gibbons's license from Congress.

**The Andrew Jackson Era.** The Democratic-Republican Party dominated American politics after the demise of the Federalist Party in 1816. But by the 1820s, the party divided into two factions. Particularly divisive was the selection of a party nomination to succeed James Monroe as president in 1824, the first presidential election in which nonlandowning white men could vote. The faction consisting of many former Federalists became the National Republican Party. The followers of Populist Andrew Jackson, who backed the expanded franchise, emerged as the Democratic Party. In the sharply contested race between John Quincy Adams and Andrew Jackson, neither had the requisite majority of electoral votes cast. By virtue of the Twelfth Amendment, the election was to be decided by the House of Representatives. With the support of Henry Clay and former Federalists, the House awarded the presidency to Adams by a one-vote margin.

But four years later, Andrew Jackson defeated Adams and the National Republican Party by a clear majority. His accession to the presidency in 1828 marked a turning point for Justice Marshall and the Supreme Court, who faced an openly hostile administration. President Jackson had earlier in his life practiced law in North Carolina's western territories (an area later becoming the state of Tennessee) and had served for a time as a judge. He later was elected to Congress and the Senate, representing Tennessee. His exploits as a major general during the War of 1812, including devising the successful strategy for the Battle of New Orleans in 1815, made him a national hero. He became the first president from a state west of the Appalachian Mountains.[69]

An ardent states' rights advocate, Jackson loathed the Bank of the United States and its supporters, especially John Marshall. When Marshall ruled in *Worcester v. Georgia* (1832)[70] that the United States must honor its treaty obligations with the Cherokee Indians, he met with Jackson's resistance. Jackson was a veteran Indian fighter, having led campaigns against the Creek and Seminole Indians which ended with the eviction of both tribes from their native lands. In open defiance of the

Supreme Court's decision, Jackson declared, "Marshall has made his decision, now let him enforce it."[71]

Recognizing that the Court had no "power of the sword," President Jackson refused to implement the judicial order protecting the Cherokee nation. The Cherokees were subsequently forced to leave their native lands, following the infamous "trail of tears" to the west. But Jackson's cynical rejection of judicial power hardly foretold the demise of the third branch of government's influence, nor did it detract from Marshall's lasting legacy to the judiciary and the nation.

**The Marshall Legacy.** Only the death of Marshall in 1835 brought an end to Jackson's enmity with the Court. He appointed Roger Taney, a solid states' rights advocate (who was a Federalist earlier in his political career), as chief justice. Marshall's lasting legacy was elevating the Court to a coequal branch of government. His influence extended thirty-four years beyond Adams and the Federalists' loss of political power. He saw the potential power of the Court more than his predecessors Jay and Ellsworth. His great ability was to articulate principles of enduring value and relevance, which would be called upon by future generations of jurists for causes across the political spectrum.

The early Supreme Court established its independence from the legislative and executive branches of government, frustrating attempts by the parties to control its direction. After the departure of the Adams administration, the Court earned the opprobrium of President Jefferson as a stronghold of Federalists. It took the administrations of five presidents to reshape the Court.

## THE COURT OF JOHN MARSHALL IN 1803

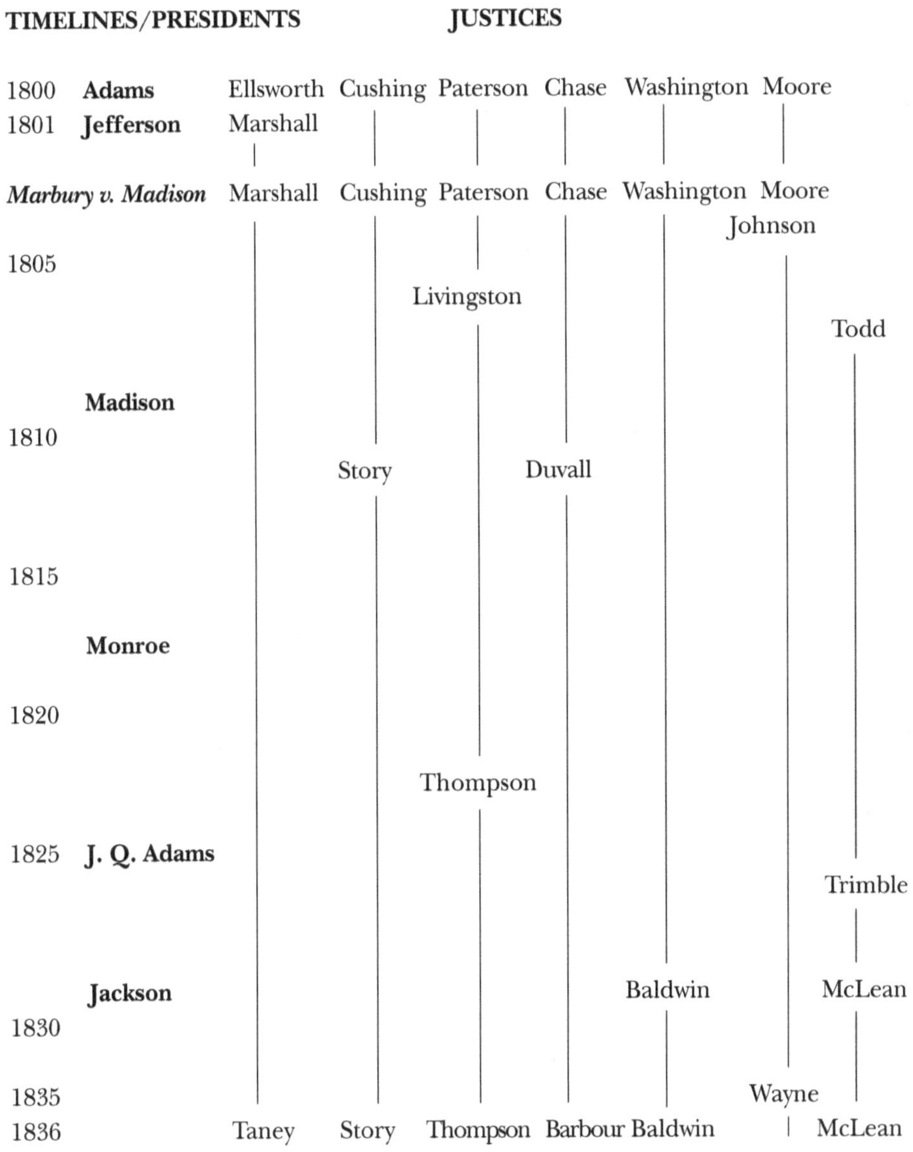
TIMELINES/PRESIDENTS
JUSTICES
1800 Adams
Ellsworth Cushing Paterson Chase Washington Moore
1801 Jefferson
Marshall
*Marbury v. Madison*
Marshall Cushing Paterson Chase Washington Moore
Johnson
1805
Livingston
Todd
Madison
1810
Story
Duvall
1815
Monroe
1820
Thompson
1825 J. Q. Adams
Trimble
Jackson
Baldwin
McLean
1830
1835
Wayne
1836
Taney Story Thompson Barbour Baldwin McLean

# CHAPTER 3

## STATES' RIGHTS AND CIVIL WAR: 1836-1865

*The independence of the Supreme Court would continue to frustrate leaders of the political branches of government. Changes in composition of the Court did little to end the institutional friction with the executive and legislative branches. Regional differences in the nation would eventually result in a civil war, but the Constitution and the separation of powers between the branches of government would survive and outlast the challenges of the war.*

**The Taney Court.** The Supreme Court was a bastion of stability in terms of composition in contrast to the executive branch of government. During the sixty-three-year period from 1801 to 1864, there were fifteen presidents but only two chief justices. The Democratic Party held the presidency for twenty of twenty-eight years (from 1832 to 1860). Roger Brooke Taney's succession to the post of chief justice after Marshall opened a new era for the Court, lasting from 1836 to 1864. Taney came from an aristocratic Southern Maryland tobacco family.[72] He began the practice of law in Frederick, Maryland, at the age of twenty-two. A Roman Catholic, he was married to the sister of Francis Scott Key. He was elected to the Maryland House of Delegates in 1799 as a Federalist. After a break with the party leaders during the War of 1812 (Taney supported the war), Taney returned to the Federalist fold, being elected to a five-year term in the Maryland Senate in 1816. In 1824, he abandoned the Federalists to support Democrat Andrew Jackson's unsuccessful (and hotly contested) run for the presidency against John Quincy Adams. He supported Jackson in his second campaign against Adams in 1828. President Jackson later appointed Taney attorney general in 1831, where he served until 1833. Taney successfully advocated that President Jackson veto the congressional rechartering for the Bank of the United States and wrote Jackson's 1832 veto message. After his appointment as secretary of the treasury in 1933 (by President Jackson during a congressional recess), he implemented the withdrawal of federal funds from the bank, ensuring the dismantlement of one of the most visible symbols of federal power.[73] But Taney's highly visible role generated opposition in the

Senate, where Adams's National Republican Party still held sway. Jackson's nomination of Taney to be secretary of the treasury was rejected by a 28-18 vote when the Senate reconvened in 1834.[74] The Senate also failed to confirm Jackson's 1835 nomination for Taney to be an associate justice on the Supreme Court. But upon the death of John Marshall in 1835, Taney was nominated for the position of chief justice of the Supreme Court. Assisted by a changed membership in the Senate the following year, Taney's nomination was confirmed. He was fifty-nine years old and would serve for twenty-eight years on the Court, witnessing changes in the country at least as significant as in Marshall's tenure.

Yet the Court of Taney's tenure left most of Marshall's opinions intact, merely giving states more room for regulation. For this reason, many commentators, including Chief Justice Rehnquist, have been quick to point out the fallacy in referring to the institution as the "Taney Court."[75] Even accepting the varying leadership and intellectual abilities of persons appointed to that post, chief justices do not have the institutional powers to control associate justices the way that presidents can influence their cabinets or executive departments. The latter's powers of appointment and removal of officials serve to promote a measure of unity of purpose and effort in the executive branch; but such powers are denied to the chief justice, making the judiciary an institution more dependent upon the powers of persuasion of the members therein.

Thus, the Court could offer more toleration for independent-minded associate justices like Joseph Story. Story, who had been nominated by President James Madison, would continue his intellectual development while on the Court, teaching at Harvard beginning in 1829 and publishing extensively. His leading treatises on law included *A Familiar Exposition on the Constitution of the United States,* published in 1840. Like Jefferson, he was an adherent to natural law theory.

As previously mentioned, Story did not emerge as a precast Republican of the Jeffersonian mold. The impact of having served on the Marshall Court for twenty-four years seems to have outweighed the influence of Taney, on whose Court he served for only ten years. In the latter years, Story remained a significant philosophical link to the Marshall Court. In *A Familiar Exposition,* he was very critical of the deficiencies of the Articles of Confederation in respect to federal power. In his opinions, he often supported federal power at the expense of state power, as in the case of *Martin v. Hunter's Lessee,* where writing for the majority he upheld the Supreme Court's authority to review state court decisions on federal constitutional questions. This stance often put him at odds with the Jacksonians on the Court. Needless to say, his strident opposition to slavery as seen in the *Amistad* decision, where slaves who mutinied on a Spanish ship were freed, did not sit well with the Southern states.

**Shift to States' Rights.** A new orientation of the Court could be seen from the beginning of Taney's term. In the *Charles River Bridge* case (1837), owners of a bridge across the Charles River had sued to prevent the state of Massachusetts from chartering the construction of a second bridge across the Charles River because it would impair their "exclusive" right under a charter with the state to collect tolls. The plaintiff, Charles River Bridge Company, pointed to the "contract clause" of the Constitution (Article I, Section 10) which stated that "no state shall . . . pass any law impairing the Obligation of Contracts."

Attorneys Daniel Webster and Simon Greenleaf argued the case for five days. The Court ruled against the plaintiff declaring that there was no contractual obligation (implied or otherwise) that prevented the state from chartering another bridge. The result clearly favored sovereign state power vis-a-vis individuals or companies. Justice Story dissented, joined by Justice Thompson, based on the precedent of the *Dartmouth College* case of Marshall Court. He accepted the argument that the state had granted a monopoly to Charles Bridge Company.

The trend was continued in the case of *Cooley v. Board of Wardens of Port of Philadelphia* where the Court declared that public ports (and by analogy, states) are not prohibited from regulating all areas of interstate and foreign commerce. The case upheld the port's requirement to use harbor pilots or alternatively pay a set fee. It limited the effect of *Gibbons v. Ogden*, where the Court had ruled against state power in favor of federal interstate commerce power.

Not all cases supported state power or restricted federal power. The *Propeller Genesee Chief* case upheld a congressional statute providing for admiralty jurisdiction over accidents on the Great Lakes. The Act of 1845 used the new term "navigable waterways" and lakes. It was contrary to English law which limited admiralty jurisdiction to areas within the "ebb and flow" of the ocean. In the process, the Court reversed an 1825 ruling of the Court adopting English law on the subject.

**Dred Scott and Its Aftermath.** In the years leading to the Civil War, President James Buchanan labored hard to prevent the division of the United States through the implementation of political compromises between North and South, an effort which became increasingly futile. The Court itself was not insulated from the growing divisions between the states. The Court became a venue for the litigation of states' rights. Although the states' rights agenda was imbedded in the minds of Taney and Jackson, they did little to reverse powers of national government beyond terminating the Bank of the United States. The doctrine of judicial review was well accepted by the time of the infamous *Dred Scott* decision (*Scott v. Sandford*, 1857), which effectively struck down federal law prohibiting slavery in some states and negated U.S. citizenship for blacks.[76]

A divided Court denied the standing of Scott, a sixty-two-year-old slave, as a citizen to claim freedom as a result of his extended sojourn with his master in the state of Illinois and Fort Snelling in the Louisiana Territory (now Minnesota and Wisconsin). Slavery had been banned in both places, the former by state legislation and the latter as a result of regional demarcation of the territory included in the Missouri Compromise of 1820. Instead, the Court affirmed the ruling of Missouri's highest court that Scott's return to Missouri, a slave state, made Scott a slave. Taney wrote an opinion stating that "the right of property in a slave is distinctly and expressly affirmed in the Constitution." The majority consisted of five justices from border and Southern slaveholding states: Roger Taney of Maryland, John Catron of Tennessee, James Wayne of Georgia, John Campbell of Alabama, and Peter Daniel of Virginia, joined by two Northern Democratic justices, Robert Grier from Pennsylvania and Samuel Nelson from New York. Justices John McLean of Ohio and Benjamin Curtis of Massachusetts dissented. Of those, Taney, McLean, Wayne, and Catron were appointed to the Court by Andrew Jackson. Daniel was appointed by President Martin van Buren in 1841. Nelson was President John Tyler's sole appointee to the Court in 1845. Grier was appointed by President James Polk in 1846, and Campbell had been appointed by President Franklin Pierce in 1853.

In 1820, Congress had tried to resolve the issue of the future of slavery in the Louisiana Territory by allowing slavery south of the latitude of 36° 30', as well as in one state north of that demarcation, Missouri. This "Missouri Compromise" outlawed the holding of slaves in free states. But as part of the Compromise of 1850, Congress passed the Fugitive Slave Act, which repealed the Missouri Compromise. Scott argued that he was free because of his residence with his master on "free soil" prior to 1850. In the opinion written by Taney, the Missouri Compromise had exceeded Congress's constitutional powers by declaring the prohibition of slavery in certain areas in contravention of the original intent of the framers of the Constitution that African Americans "were not intended to be included under the word 'citizens' in the constitution and can therefore claim none of the rights and privileges which that document provides for."

Taney cited other provisions of the Constitution, treating African Americans as property, such as the provision ensuring that "property" taken to other states would be protected as property in other states as in the state of origin. Specifically, Article IV, Section 2 obligated states to return slaves to their state of origin. This provision was part of a political compromise to Southern states at the constitutional convention in 1787, which abolitionist William Lloyd Garrison referred to as the covenant with hell. This provision remained in the Constitution until the Thirteenth Amendment was ratified in 1865.

But internal dynamics divided the "majority." Only Justices Wayne and Daniel agreed with Taney that Negroes could not be citizens. On the more specific issue that Scott was still a slave, Justices Curtis and McLean dissented. Justice Nelson opined that Missouri state law governed, therefore Scott remained a slave. Justice Campbell joined most of Taney's opinion.

The internal dynamics had external dimensions. Justice Catron was a partisan whose involvement in politics did not end after Jackson appointed him to the Court. He was a close advisor to Presidents James K. Polk and James Buchanan.[77] During the deliberations on *Scott*, he wrote to President Buchanan successfully urging him to get Grier to join the majority. Justice Grier was from Pennsylvania, the same state as new president Buchanan.

The public and press reactions were loud and unprecedented to the decision. In addition to a reaffirmation of slavery, the *Dred Scott* decision allowed the spread of slavery throughout the western territories. The decision inflamed the antislavery sentiment in the North and is considered one of the seminal events leading to the Civil War, along with John Brown's ill-fated slave rebellion at Harpers Ferry.[78] Horace Greeley, editor of the *New York Tribune*, argued that the opinion carried no "moral weight." William Cullen Bryant called the decision a "disgrace," not a "free man's constitution." The issue became a subject of the famous Lincoln-Douglas debates in their quest for a U.S. Senate seat in 1858, a key step in Lincoln's ultimate election to the presidency. For his part, President Buchanan pledged to "cheerfully submit" to the decision of the Court.

Later justices have been sharply critical of the *Dred Scott* decision. Chief Justice Charles Evans Hughes would later call the decision "a self-inflicted wound." In the view of Chief Justice Rehnquist, the Court violated canons of constitutional interpretation by deciding a question of constitutional law not absolutely essential to disposition of the case and by declaring an act of Congress void based upon the sense that the law was unfair.[79]

But was the constitutional question in *Dred Scott* truly avoidable? Would that have been a wiser course of action? Would avoiding a ruling through application of the political question doctrine have been a judicially honorable course, especially when the political branches of government were incapable of resolving the issue and where the Constitution did indeed cover the issue? The ultimate solution came in 1865, with the ratification of the Thirteenth Amendment, which removed the offending portions of the Constitution. The *Dred Scott* decision was merely a way stop on the road to fighting over larger political questions, such as Northern versus Southern political power in Congress and the future of slavery.

The facade of a unified Democratic Party of President Buchanan did not survive beyond his presidency. The remnants of the Whig Party formed the Constitutional Union Party.[80] They selected wealthy slaveholder John Bell from Tennessee as their presidential candidate. The Democratic Party was seriously divided between regional factions. Southern Democrats walked out of the party convention in Baltimore in 1860 and formed their own party. They named Buchanan's vice president, John Breckinridge of Kentucky, as their presidential candidate. Lincoln rival Stephen Douglas of Illinois received the Northern Democratic nomination for president. In competition against Senator Salmon Chase and former Whig William Seward, Lincoln prevailed in securing the Republican Party's nomination for president. This new party was not a re-creation of the earlier party of the same name but rather the result of an emerging coalition of groups including Free-Soilers, Anti-Nebraska Democrats, and various antislavery advocates.[81] These events resulted in a four-way presidential race, between Douglas, Breckinridge, Bell, and Lincoln. This unprecedented division of the electorate enabled the Republican Party to prevail against the other parties in the electoral college and thus delivered the presidency to Lincoln.

**The Civil War's Challenge to the Court**. Following Lincoln's election, the Supreme Court changed substantially in both composition and environment. Construction of new chambers for the U.S. Senate and House of Representatives allowed the Supreme

Court to move from its inauspicious quarters on the first floor (sometimes referred to as the basement) of the Capitol to the old Senate chamber in 1860. Reflecting the national schism, the Supreme Court itself was a "house divided," with consequences impacting the composition of the Court. The most immediate impact of secession was the resignation of Justice John Campbell who reluctantly left the Court when his home state of Alabama joined the Confederacy, though he personally disagreed with secession. But other proslavery justices, such as John Catron of Tennessee and James Wayne of Georgia, remained on the Court because of strong Unionist feelings. In fact, Wayne consistently sided in favor of federal wartime powers during the war. In addition to the departure of Campbell, other vacancies resulted from the deaths of Justice Peter Daniel in 1860 and Justice John McLean in 1861.

Lincoln nominated Noah Swayne, Samuel Miller, and David Davis to fill these three vacancies. Congress added a tenth seat to the Court in 1863, to which Lincoln appointed Stephen Field. This partial change of composition would not result in a Court that was compliant and submissive to Lincoln's interpretation of the Constitution. Chief Justice Roger Taney's continued presence on the Court would emerge as an obstacle to Lincoln's ability to prosecute the war. Though Taney's home state of Maryland never seceded, it was the home of much actively prosecessionist sentiment. Union troops passing through Baltimore on their way to reinforce Washington were stoned by angry crowds in early 1861. In fact, Lincoln was so concerned about an anticipated vote for secession that he used questionable executive powers to shut down the Maryland General Assembly. The Civil War was the ultimate consequence of the fight over states' rights, a hallmark of the Taney Court. Taney would remain on the Court until he retired in 1864, fully three and one-half years after Lincoln's inauguration. He died the following year at the age of eighty-eight. In all, he had served twenty-eight years as chief justice.

**Secession and War Powers.** The Civil War raised fundamental legal questions: Could states lawfully secede under the Constitution? Was state sovereignty superior to federal sovereignty? Lincoln's interpretation of the Civil War is significant in understanding his approach to this great challenge to the Constitution. Similar to views held by the departing president Buchanan, he believed that there was no legal right to secede from the Union; and therefore, the states themselves remained officially part of the Union, notwithstanding the existence of a "rebellion" and "rebel" forces.[82] Under this interpretation, congressmen, senators, and Supreme Court justices from secessionist states could continue to sit and carry out their respective federal functions. Throughout the conflict, Lincoln refused to acknowledge the legitimacy of the Confederacy as a separate sovereign entity. In his view, "The Union is older than the states; and in fact, it created them as states." State withdrawal from the Union was "against law, and by revolution."[83] In this view, it was more in the nature of an insurrection than a war.[84]

Over the course of the Civil War, the Court supported many of Lincoln's war powers. In 1861, he added twenty-two thousand men to the army and eighteen thousand to the navy, mobilized seventy-five thousand state militia, and imposed a naval blockade on the South without a congressional declaration of war.[85] But the Court would ensure that presidential powers in wartime were not without limitation. In 1861, in *Ex Parte Merryman*, a federal circuit court ordered the release of John Merryman, a Maryland secessionist.[86] He had been arrested for burning bridges and tearing down telegraph wires.[87] The presiding circuit court judge was Taney, who was acting in his dual capacity as a circuit judge, a common responsibility for judges on the Supreme Court at the time. Lincoln had suspended the writ of habeas corpus on April 27, 1861, after the attack on Union troops in Baltimore. He did this without the approval of Congress, which remained out of session. Judge Taney, in circuit, issued a show cause order to General George Cadwalader, commander of Fort McHenry, where Merryman was held prisoner. Taney held that habeas corpus cannot be suspended without congressional authorization in accordance with Article I, Section 9 of the Constitution, in effect declaring Lincoln's action unconstitutional.

Lincoln defended his suspension of the writ before Congress as necessary recourse against rebellion, "Are all the laws, but one [the right of habeas corpus], to go unexecuted, and the government itself to go to pieces, lest one be violated?"[88] Merryman was released after seven weeks at Fort McHenry and indicted in federal court, but the case never went to trial because of the fear that a Maryland jury would never convict him. The Northern press supported Lincoln and criticized Taney. In 1863, Congress authorized the president to suspend the writ during time of rebellion.

In a remarkable assertion of war powers on September 22, 1862, Lincoln declared that all slaves in secessionist states would be emancipated under his executive authority as commander in chief effective January 1, 1863. The net effect at the time was the symbolic liberation of approximately four million persons in Southern states. Long before Lincoln's declaration, Major General John C. Frémont, commander of the Western Department of the Union army, had in August 1861 confiscated property and freed slaves of Confederates in Missouri as "contraband" or "war booty" without presidential authority.[89] Though the characterization of slaves as "property" harked back to the infamous *Dred Scott* decision, the result was an effective legal theory for the liberation of slaves. The colorful Frémont was a Southerner by birth and had been an explorer of the West, a Mexican War veteran, a senator from California, and the Republican candidate for the presidency in 1856, the first-ever candidate for that newly formed party. But fearing the reaction of slave states remaining in the Union, Lincoln felt that Frémont had exceeded his authority and revoked the order in 1861. However, a year later Lincoln's Emancipation Proclamation went farther than Frémont's declaration by its application to all slaves owned by Confederates and by declaring their freedom effective immediately and not conditioned upon physical liberation as "prizes of war." The proclamation left slavery intact in states remaining part of the Union (e.g., West Virginia, Maryland, and Kentucky). But those states relinquished slavery with the ratification of the Thirteenth Amendment to the Constitution in 1865, forever ending the debate on the legality of slavery in the U.S.

In 1863, the Court once again took up the question of executive war powers, considering the constitutionality of Lincoln's blockade of Confederate ports in the *Prize Cases*, where four merchant ships were seized.[90] By this time, however, the Court's composition had changed significantly. The states' rights faction suffered from the resignation of Justice Campbell and the deaths of Justices Daniel and McLean. Lincoln's three appointees, Swayne, Miller, and Davis, were making an impact on decisions of the Court. In the *Prize Cases*, the Court upheld Lincoln's commitments to prosecute a war without a formal declaration by Congress. The Court noted that Congress was in recess during the president's proclamations of April 19 and 27, 1861. The majority held that the existence of an insurrection provided the president with the same authority as if there had been a congressional declaration of war. In fact, Congress meeting in extraordinary session on July 13, 1861, ratified the president's actions after the fact. Lincoln justified his action to Congress as a "public necessity."[91] As expected, Chief Justice Taney dissented.

The following year posed an unusual test for a democracy. In 1864, despite the Civil War, presidential elections were held. Former Union army general McClellan ran on the Democratic Party ticket against Abraham Lincoln. The end of the Civil War settled long-pending disputes about whether either the states or the federal government would prevail. The adoption of the Thirteenth Amendment (ending slavery) in 1865, the Fourteenth Amendment (granting citizenship and providing protection of all persons born or naturalized in the U.S.) in 1868, and the Fifteenth Amendment (guaranteeing the right to vote to all citizens) in 1870 were strong demonstrations of newly asserted federal power. Disputes between the states and the federal government would reemerge but in the form of issues decidedly different than before the war.

When Taney died in 1864, Lincoln sought to replace him with a chief justice "who will sustain what has been done in regard to emancipation and the legal tenders."[92] He chose former presidential contender and secretary of the treasury Salmon P. Chase. He had been a two-term governor of Ohio and a one-term senator, a leader of the Republican radicals in the latter capacity. Chase's legal qualifications were modest, having spent most of the fifteen years prior to his appointment in politics. He still held an ambition for the presidency, and his political drive was noted to have colored his judicial temperament.[93] In one such case, Chase wrote the majority opinion-finding legislation to finance the war to be unconstitutional, defeating one of Lincoln's key objectives in his appointment to the Court.[94]

**Civil Liberties and Civil Rights in Wartime.** Even after Taney's departure, the Court would continue to deal with the issue of war powers. Lincoln's suspension of the writ of habeas corpus, censorship of the press in selective instances, arrests of thousands of suspected disloyal citizens, and trials of civilians before military commissions provided ample fodder for litigants. The latter issue formed the basis of a cause of action in the 1866 case of *Ex Parte Milligan*, where the Court struck down the application of martial law for Indiana. Lambdin P. Milligan was a member of a group of Peace Democrats known as the Sons of Liberty, who supported peace even if it meant accepting the Confederacy's independence from the Union. He was charged with conspiracy to forcibly release Confederate prisoners in the Midwest (and join them up with rebel forces in Missouri and Kentucky) and seize government stores in Louisville, Kentucky, in violation of Order No. 38 issued by General Ambrose Burnside, commander of the military district of the Ohio (which covered Indiana, Illinois, Ohio, Kentucky, and Michigan). Burnside's order was, in turn, based upon President Lincoln's proclamation of September 1862 subjecting those "discouraging volunteer enlistments, resisting militia drafts, or guilty of any disloyal practice affording aid and comfort to rebels" to martial law and trial by court-martial.[95] He was tried by a military commission in 1864 and sentenced to death by hanging. A lawyer himself, he protested his trial by the military as opposed to civil authorities. He petitioned for a writ of habeas corpus. A five-man majority on the Court held it unconstitutional to try Milligan by court-martial. They held that the state of Indiana was sufficiently removed from the battlefield, negating the "necessity" to apply martial law. The U.S. attorney general argued that the president is "sole judge of the exigencies, necessities, and duties of the occasion." Among the three counsel arguing on behalf of Milligan, attorney James A. Garfield asserted that

> A republic can wield the vast enginery of war without breaking down the safeguards of liberty; can suppress insurrection, and put down rebellion, however formidable, without destroying the bulwarks of law; can, by the might of its armed millions, preserve and defend both nationality and liberty.[96]

In a case of historic irony, Garfield would later be elected to the highest executive office, the presidency, whose powers he sought to limit. Garfield's arguments carried the day. Writing for the majority on the Court, Associate Justice David Davis declared that

> The Constitution is a law for rulers and people, equally in war and in peace, and covers with the shield of its protection all classes of men at all times.

The Court found that the activities occurred in districts remote from the war and insufficient cause to justify the use of military tribunals against citizens.[97]

In the majority view, martial law must be "confined to the locality of actual war." Notably, Lincoln appointee Justice Field joined the majority. In his dissent, Chief Justice Chase, joined by Swayne and Miller, stated that no one contended that Congress authorized a trial of Milligan. In 1869, in an angry response to the Court's action, a radical Reconstruction era Congress redefined the Court's statutory jurisdiction to exclude the right to hear habeas corpus actions.

**Lincoln's Legacy for the Court.** Lincoln left a lasting legacy on the Supreme Court. By the time of his assassination in 1865, he had made five appointments to the Court, including an abolitionist as chief justice. One of Lincoln's appointees, Justice Stephen J. Field, would remain on the Court until 1897. When Lincoln began his presidency, the Court was a redoubt for states' rights and Jacksonianism. When he died, the Court had accepted expanded federal powers. As the late Chief Justice William Rehnquist noted, the challenge of the suspension of civil liberties during the Civil War, the addition of three new amendments to the Constitution, and the war-driven industrial expansion of the North left the Court in a very different legal environment by the war's end.[98]

# THE COURT OF ROGER BROOKE TANEY IN 1857

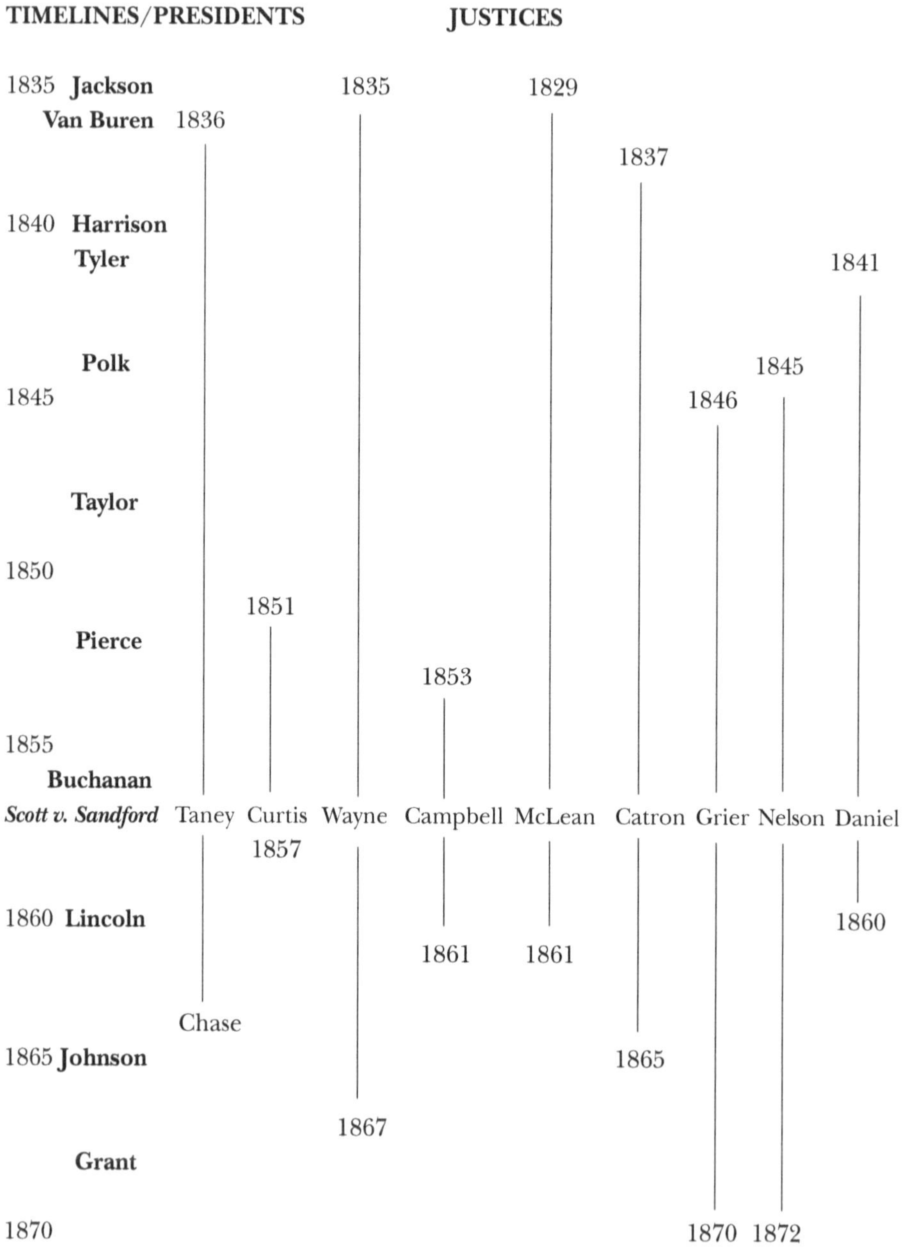

# CHAPTER 4

## RECONSTRUCTION AND INDUSTRIAL REVOLUTION: 1865-1910

*The changes to the nation as a result of Civil War and industrialization brought new challenges to the Supreme Court and its role in interpreting the Constitution. The changes witnessed the emergence of political and ideological causes related to new societal trends, such as economic liberties as applied to trusts and corporations and attempts to counter the excesses of unregulated business practices. The institutional division of power under the Constitution would ensure that the judiciary would clash with the executive and legislative branches over those issues finding their way to the courts.*

**The Court of Chase, Miller, and Field.** The Civil War had forever changed the political dynamics on and off the Court. The retirement of Chief Justice Taney in 1864 signified not only the end of the Jacksonian states' rights agenda, but the end of a sixty-three-year period in which two chief justices, Marshall and Taney, had dominated the Court. No chief justice achieved the same level of dominance on the Court for another fifty years.[99] Lincoln appointed former senator and treasury secretary Salmon P. Chase to replace Taney. Chase, along with William Seward, had run for the Republican presidential nomination in 1860. A Radical Republican, Chase could be relied upon to support emancipation and the political agenda of the Republicans. Yet in the view of some, he lacked the intellectual and leadership qualities needed to dominate the Court.[100] Instead, associate justices like Stephen Field or Samuel Miller assumed leadership roles. They were both Lincoln appointees as well.

The legislative branch also exercised its influence over the Court. The Radical Republicans who dominated the Congress after the Civil War sought to rid themselves of the vestiges of the Taney Court. In 1867, Congress abolished the seats held by Wayne who died in 1867 and Catron who died in 1865, reducing the number on the Court to nine. Members of Congress, unhappy with the failure of the Senate to convict on the impeachment of President Andrew Johnson, wanted to deny him the right to fill those seats on the Court. The number of justices on the Court remains fixed at nine since that time. Changing the number of justices on the Court was not the only way that Congress influenced composition of the Court. To encourage the retirement of aging judges on the Court, Congress passed the Judiciary Act of 1869 which offered a continuing salary to justices who retired. Justices Grier suffered paralysis in 1867 but did not retire until 1870. Nelson retired in 1872. Altogether, the departure of Justices Wayne, Catron, Grier, and Nelson represented the demise of pre-Republican administration influence on the Court. The 1869 act, also known as the Circuit Judges Act of 1869, created judgeships for each of nine circuit courts. The act did not abolish circuit-riding duties for Supreme Court justices but reduced the frequency of duties to once every two years.

The Radical Republican Congress set out to assert its agenda on the South, which remained occupied by Union troops. In contrast to Lincoln, who insisted that the Southern states never legally left the Union, these Republicans insisted that the Southern states reratify the Constitution (as amended by the Thirteenth, Fourteenth, and Fifteenth Amendments) before being allowed full rights and privileges as states. Not until after the election of Rutherford B. Hayes as president in 1876 did Union troops end the occupation of the South. The much-contested election, with proper blame of corruption on the part of both parties, led to a compromise allowing the Republican candidate Hayes to take the presidency on the condition that, among other things, the program of radical Reconstruction and occupation of the South would end.

Samuel Freeman Miller was born in Kentucky in 1816. He received a medical degree in 1838. By 1845 he was bored with medicine and turned to the study of law. By 1847, at the age of thirty-one, he was admitted to practice of law. In 1850, he moved to Iowa because of his opposition to Kentucky's support of slavery. He joined the Republican Party in 1854, supporting Lincoln's election campaign. Lincoln appointed him as an associate justice to the Court in 1862. He was the first justice on the Court born west of the Appalachian Mountains. He served on the Court until he died in 1890. As Chief Justice Rehnquist described him, he had a limited legal education, but a virtue of common sense. His dissent in the *Gelpcke* case, against federal jurisdiction over matters of state law, was vindicated years later. Miller's view of the Fourteenth Amendment, which would apply due process rights to persons and situations within the original postslavery intent of its framers, ultimately lost to Field's view.

Stephen J. Field was born in Connecticut in 1816. He practiced law in New York until 1845 when he moved to California. He promptly secured an appointment as a magistrate. In 1850, he became a member of the state legislature. In 1857, he was elected to the Supreme Court of California. In 1863, Lincoln appointed Field as justice for the newly created Tenth Circuit. Field was known as a War Democrat who supported Lincoln. He acted like a part-time legislator, sponsoring bills in the California legislature. However, he grew senile in his later years and resigned in 1897. The late Chief Justice William Rehnquist described him as lacking in proper judicial temperament. He was combative and dogmatic, though a lucid writer. Yet over time, Field's view of the Fourteenth Amendment prevailed.

**The Post-Civil War and Reconstruction Period.** An ambitious Congress had secured approval of the Thirteenth, Fourteenth, and Fifteenth Amendments to the Constitution, as well as the Civil Rights Act of 1866, which was intended to outlaw public and private discrimination against the newly freed slaves. Union troops remained in the South to protect them for over ten years. The Reconstruction era laws would be the cause of litigation for over the next 130 years.

Many of the cases in the immediate postwar period dealt with resolution of issues pending from the Civil War and its aftermath, such as loyalty oaths for former Confederates and the meaning of due process and equal protection under the Fourteenth Amendment. In the case of *Ex Parte Garland*, a lawyer sought readmission to the Supreme Court bar without the requirement to take a loyalty oath. He had served in the Confederate Senate, representing Arkansas.[101] The particular oath required affiants to declare they had never taken up arms against the United States or given aid or encouragement to enemy. The Court by 5-4 vote found the oaths in question to constitute a bill of attainder and an ex post facto law, both prohibited by the Constitution (Article I, Section 9). Field wrote the majority opinion, stating that these oaths had the same effect as a bill of attainder and an ex post facto law. He was joined by Wayne, Catron, Grier, and Nelson. The dissenting justices were Miller, Chase, Swayne, and Davis, who opined that the bills were not really bills of attainder or ex post facto laws.

In another case, *Cummings v. Missouri*,[102] a Catholic priest from Missouri refused to take an oath of loyalty. Missouri was a fiercely divided state during the war. It was the locus of Confederate guerilla fighter William Clarke Quantrill's atrocities against civilians, pro-Union towns, and farms.[103] At one point in the war, the Union forced evacuation through Order No. 11. After the war, Missouri enacted the most sweeping test-oath requirements. These oaths were applied not just to attorneys and officeholders but also to clergymen and voters. The measures promoted by Radical Republicans effectively deprived former secessionists of any political power. The actual oath required the affiant to declare that he had never engaged in armed hostility against the U.S. government or that he never by act or word manifested adherence to enemies of the United States, aided any person, or ever indicated "disaffection for the government of the United States in its contest with the rebellion." At the time, the First Amendment only applied to Congress, not to the states. That was done later, using the Fourteenth Amendment due process clause. Similar to the result in *Garland*, the Court struck done the oath.

The *Milligan, Garland, and Cummings* cases were among the earliest significant civil liberties cases heard by the Court. Civil liberties in this context usually involved claims of an individual against the government. The claims asserted rights, usually involving individual freedom. But civil liberties cases were soon to be overtaken by a plethora of economic cases. The *Slaughterhouse* cases of 1873 were the first notable efforts to apply the Fourteenth Amendment to purposes beyond freed slaves. Louisiana law gave a commercial monopoly for certain slaughterhouses with the purported purpose to protect the health of citizens. State courts and the Supreme Court (by a narrow margin) upheld the law. Justice Miller wrote for the majority that post-Civil War amendments showed a unity of the intent and purpose, supporting nothing more than the freedom and protection for newly freed slaves.

For the dissent, Justice Field, supported by three others, criticized the majority's interpretation as making the Fourteenth Amendment's equal protection clause a "vain and idle enactment." Some considered this case the beginning of the end for this early era of civil rights because of the Court's narrow approach.[104] Although the intent of the framers of this amendment in 1868 was clear as concerns ending the vestiges of slavery for African Americans, the language of the amendment itself was general and not limited in application to African Americans. Indeed, the general language of the amendment invited application to issues like those in the *Slaughter-House* cases, which had nothing to do with racial discrimination. But continued adherence to the original intent of the framers of the Fourteenth Amendment in subsequent cases would most likely have benefited civil rights for the ex-slaves and their progeny rather than detracted from it. It is plausible that applying the *intentionalist* approach rather than solely the *textualist* approach would have led to a different result twenty-three years later in *Plessy v. Ferguson*, where segregation of schools was upheld and African Americans were denied equal protection of the law.[105] Indeed, Associate Justice John Marshall Harlan wrote in his dissent in *Plessy* that the majority's decision would, in effect, "defeat the beneficent purposes which the people of the United States had in view when they adopted the recent amendments of the Constitution." But Harlan also relied on the plain meaning of the words "equal protection," warning that the "thin disguise of equal accommodations . . . will not mislead anyone, nor atone for the wrong this day done." Harlan was perhaps ahead of his time in advocating a precursor for the "original understanding" approach.

**The Grant Administration.** President Grant had bad fortune with his first two nominations for the Court. Former secretary of war Edwin Stanton was confirmed by the Senate to be an associate justice in 1869 but died four days later.[106] In 1870, Attorney General Ebenezer Hoar was rejected by the Senate, where many members of that body were offended by Hoar's disinclination to support the senators' recommendations for judicial appointments.[107] Hoar also disappointed the Radical Republicans by his failure to support the impeachment of President Andrew Johnson. Nevertheless, Grant was more successful in three subsequent nominations for associate justices to the Court: William Strong and Joseph Bradley in 1870 and Ward Hunt in 1873. When Chief Justice Chase died in 1873, finding a replacement was not easy. During a carriage ride to the chief justice's funeral, President Grant offered the nomination of a replacement to Senator Roscoe Conkling from New York, but Conkling declined.[108] Grant would offer the nomination to six others before Morrison Waite accepted.[109] Waite, who like his predecessor was from Ohio, was confirmed in 1874 and would serve as chief justice for fourteen years.

**Legal Tender Act.** Presidents have been surprised when individuals change their views on issues as they move from the executive branch to the judiciary. In 1862, Lincoln's attorney general, Salmon Chase, drafted the law (albeit with personal reservations about its constitutionality) that allowed the Union to use paper money to pay debts during the Civil War. But when the law was challenged before the Court in the case of *Hepburn v. Griswold* in 1870, Chief Justice Chase and a 4-3 majority on the Court struck them down.[110] The three dissenters were Lincoln appointees. Those dissenters were joined later that year by two justices appointed by President Grant: William Strong and Joseph Bradley. When the issue was revisited the next year in the *Legal Tender* cases, Chase was in the minority and dissented when the Court overturned the decision.[111]

**Presidential Politics: The Court and the Election of 1876.** Grant left the presidency after completing two full terms. Though his personal integrity was beyond reproach (aside from recurring bouts of drinking), his administration was tainted by corruption and scandal. The scandals tainted the election of his successor as well. The election of 1876 was rife with fraud on the part of both parties. The worst allegations of voting fraud involved the states of Louisiana, North Carolina, South Carolina, Oregon, and Florida. The Constitution assigns responsibility to the House of Representatives to decide the winner when no presidential candidate has a majority of votes from the electoral college. Such was the case for the Republican Rutherford B. Hayes and Democrat Samuel J. Tilden, as a result of contested ballots. The Senate had a Republican majority and the House a Democratic majority, leading to stalemate.

The leaders of both parties agreed to set up a fifteen-member commission, composed of five members of the House, five senators, and five justices of the Supreme Court. Originally, the composition would have been seven Democrats, seven Republicans, and one independent, to be appointed from the Court. The prime nominee for the latter position, Justice David Davis, unexpectedly resigned from the Court when he was elected to the Illinois Senate.[112] Consequently, the nomination fell to Justice Joseph P. Bradley, noted for his supposed judicial impartiality. The only other choices on the Court were Republicans.[113] In the end, Bradley, thought to be the least partisan of the Republicans, cast the deciding vote for Hayes.[114] The result was an electoral college vote of 185-184 in favor of Hayes, though Tilden admittedly had more of the popular vote.[115] There were after-the-fact accusations that Justice Bradley had changed his vote as a result of pressure from Republicans and railroad executives.[116] The capable justice would remain haunted by these accusations and challenges to his integrity. Other justices regretted their service on this commission and how it sullied the members of the Court with charges of partisanship.[117] Similar charges would be repeated in the electoral dispute of 2000.

Dissatisfied with the results of the commission, Tilden, with the support of House Speaker Samuel J. Randall (D-Pa.), urged a filibuster. Within days before the end of the Grant administration, a secret political arrangement that later became known as the Compromise of 1877, was reached. By the terms of the arrangement, the Democrats in Congress agreed to accept the Hayes presidency in exchange for an agreement by the Republicans to withdraw federal troops from Louisiana, South Carolina, and Florida. Unlike other Southern states, which had already regained control of their legislatures, these three states still had carpetbagger governments. Federal troops remained there since the end of the Civil War for the purpose of enforcing federal reconstruction laws and protecting the Fourteenth and Fifteenth Amendment rights of newly freed slaves. Union occupation came to a head when in 1874, during the Battle of Liberty Place in New Orleans, black federal troops were used to subdue a white supremacist mob push to take over the state's carpetbagger government.[118] The political reaction against this resulted in the Democrats gaining control of the House of Representatives. The *Posse Comitatus* law was later passed prohibiting the use of federal troops for civil law enforcement functions.

Many considered the Republican move a betrayal of African Americans in the South in order for the party to gain the White House.[119] The move left the ex-slaves with even less protection for constitutional rights than they had before and spelled the end of the Reconstruction governments of the Southern states, where African Americans had exercised the right to vote and even held elective offices in state legislatures. The end of Reconstruction also spelled problems for the future of the Fourteenth and Fifteenth Amendments' equal protection and voting rights.

**Hayes's Appointments.** As president, Hayes nominated John Marshall Harlan to replace David Davis on the Court in 1877. Though Harlan came from a slave-owning family in Kentucky, he would dissent from the majority in *Plessy v. Ferguson,* foreshadowing desegregation cases over fifty years later. Hayes also nominated William B. Woods and Stanley Matthews in 1880. Woods was confirmed but Congress took no action on Matthews until 1881, after President Garfield took office and resubmitted the nomination.

**The Gilded Age of Industry, the Railroads, and the Grange.** The Civil War had transformed the country in more ways than civil rights for freed slaves and federal-state relations. The wartime economy had furthered the industrial development of the North. Technological developments, coupled by revolutions in the areas of communication (telegraph) and transportation (railroads), had begun to shift the nature of the U.S. economy from its predominantly rural, agricultural focus. Industrial and financial barons, such as Jay Gould and Cornelius Vanderbilt, amassed great fortunes. Industry depended upon a large pool of labor. This, in turn, brought about changes in society and new social challenges to the existing regime of legal rights and obligations.

The transcontinental railroad which began in 1864 under Lincoln's stewardship was completed in 1869 when the Union Pacific track was joined with the Central Pacific track at Promontory, Utah. The building of the railroads created national markets for farmers. Cities and counties agreed to give one-third of local land (the usual formula) to the railroads in exchange for laying tracks to their locality.

These arrangements did not always please local citizens. When individuals could not succeed in challenging state and local governments through political means, they resorted to taking their cases to the courts. *Gelpcke v. Dubuque* (1864) was one of the earliest cases. Gelpcke and others who paid money for railroad bonds sued to recover interest on the bonds after the city of Dubuque defaulted on the bonds.[120] The Supreme Court of Iowa held the issuance of the bonds was invalid, even though the issuance of bonds was approved by the state legislature, since the state constitution limited debt and forbade the state from owning stock in private corporations. Gelpcke took his claims to federal district court in 1857 (using "diversity" jurisdiction since Gelpcke was not from Iowa). The Supreme Court supported the bondholders by rejecting the state court's invalidation of contractual obligations of the bond. The opinion read that "we shall never immolate truth, justice, and the law, because a state tribunal has erected the altar and decreed the sacrifice." Miller dissented, objecting to the Court deciding issues of state law. The Court would continue to provide special protection and consideration to contracts, even where it invalidated state laws.

In *Munn v. Illinois* (1876), the state of Illinois tried to establish maximum rates for the storage of grain but was challenged on the basis of the due process clause of the Fourteenth Amendment.[121] The Court upheld the Illinois law as a legitimate exercise of state "police power" to regulate private property when in the public interest. In a view foretelling the later expanded use of the "political question doctrine," Chief Justice Waite stated that if the state abuses its power, "people must resort to the polls, not to the courts." His view did not prevail for long.

The Court in the *Railroad Commission* cases of 1886 changed its approach to the Fourteenth Amendment due process clause. The Court held that states could not require the railroad companies to carry people or freight without a return, considering the act a "taking" of property. In *Chicago, Milwaukee, and St. Paul Railway v. Minnesota* (1890), a Minnesota statute making a final rate determination without opportunity for judicial review was deemed unconstitutional.[122] In *Wabash, St. Louis, and Pacific Railway v. Illinois* (1886), states were limited to regulating only intrastate railroad matters.[123] The result left most railroads without state or federal regulation. Consequently, Congress created the Interstate Commerce Commission in 1887.

The Court also did much to limit powers of the federal government through the Constitution. It limited federal powers to tax and regulate commerce contained in the Interstate Commerce Act and interpreted the Tenth Amendment broadly to give states power and to prohibit federal action. It even upheld the Fourteenth Amendment protection of corporations, treating them as legal persons for purposes of standing in 1886. During this time, strong support emerged for use of the due process clause to protect liberty of contract and to protect property rights of business owners. The Court's increasingly antigovernment trend continued until the 1930s, running headlong into the New Deal.

In the latter third of the nineteenth century, farmers blamed the railroads for the Depression. The large profits of railroads were the visible targets as well as monopolistic grain elevator owners and other middlemen that skimmed the earnings of farmers. Up to this time, most people, especially farmers, favored laissez-faire economic liberalism. They had been Jeffersonian Republicans and Jacksonian Democrats. But in the minds of farmers of the day, the railroad companies had too much power in state legislatures and elsewhere. As a counterbalance to the railroads, the farmers flocked to the National Grange, an agrarian advocacy and support organization founded in 1867. The Grange and groups like the Farmers' Alliance, the Free Silver Movement, and the Greenback-Labor Party pooled their political capital to form the Populist Party in 1891. In 1896, the Populist Party fused with the Democratic Party in 1896 when William Jennings Bryan was selected as its presidential candidate.[124] Though Bryan lost to William McKinley, the Populist movement demonstrated considerable strength; and its legacy would be carried on in future years in the courts.

The railroads reacted with a plan of their own. When they lost political power in the legislatures, they turned to the courts and the Fourteenth Amendment. The states started creating railroad commissions in 1869. States in the Midwest started regulating railroad rates. The Interstate Commerce Commission created by Congress in 1887 and the Sherman Antitrust Act in 1890 moved further to erode the power of the railroads. The use of the Fourteenth Amendment due process clause for protection of railroads and others asserting economic rights was to have a significant impact, diverting attention from the original purpose of the constitutional amendment for over seventy years.

**Economic Growth and Regulation.** By 1900, the United States had emerged as a growing world economic and political power. The latter nineteenth century meant growth of economic regulation corresponding to the great growth in industry and commerce. At the same time, the concept of economic due process under the Fourteenth Amendment emerged. In the period from 1890 until 1935, while economic liberties enjoyed expanding interpretation by courts, there was a corresponding decline of attention and focus on civil rights under the Fourteenth Amendment.

As the protection of economic due process grew, the originally intended recipients of the Fourteenth Amendment equal protection clause were neglected. In the 1896 case of *Plessy v. Ferguson,* the Court took a narrow interpretation of equal protection under the law. The ruling supporting a system of "separate but equal" treatment for minorities. Justice John Marshall Harlan, a former slave owner, wrote a spirited dissent:

> But in the view of the Constitution, in the eye of the law, there is no superior, dominant, ruling class of citizens. There is no caste here. Our constitution is color-blind, and neither knows nor tolerates classes among its citizens.[125]

Harlan's dissent laid the groundwork for its eventual reversal by the Warren Court in *Brown vs. the Board of Education of Topeka* (1954).

The era heralded significant changes in American society. The population grew from approximately thirty-one million in 1860, to seventy-six million in 1900, and ninety-two million in 1910. Much of the increase was the result of immigration. Between 1860 and 1900, fourteen million immigrants arrived in America. By 1915, there were an additional fourteen and a half million. Many of them were from Southern and Eastern Europe: Italians, Slavs, and Jews. Many had left for political reasons or had been associated with budding labor movements in newly industrialized regions. This added impetus to the already-growing labor movements in the United States.

The United States had changed by virtue of geographic components. The nation had grown from thirty-three states in 1860 (most located between the Atlantic Ocean and the Mississippi River) to forty-five states in 1900 (reaching from the Atlantic to the Pacific Ocean). Historian Frederick Jackson Turner, in his famous essay on "The Significance of the Frontier in American History," noted the declaration of the 1890 U.S. Census that a true frontier no longer existed in the United States.[126] There began a trend in migration from rural to urban areas that was to continue throughout much of the twentieth century.

Between 1900 and 1914, national income grew from $16 billion to $31 billion. As industry grew, megasized "trusts" emerged. Later incorporation became the method of choice for industrial organizations. Revisions in state laws allowed corporations to "hold" stock in other companies. These holding companies included the railroads and industrial giants like U.S. Steel and Standard Oil. Acquisitions and consolidation within industry and finance resulted in two individuals, John D. Rockefeller and James Pierpont Morgan, dominating major trade and industrial sectors of the economy. Popular resentment against the megatrusts grew; and "trust-busting" became a popular rallying cry, leading to the Sherman Antitrust Act of 1890 outlawing "every contract, combination in the form of trust or otherwise, or conspiracy, in restraint of trade or commerce among the several states, or with foreign nations." This was followed by the Clayton Antitrust Act of 1914, which went further by outlawing exclusive sales agreements and interlocking directorates in large corporations in the same field of business, among other things. It also restricted the use of injunctions against labor unions.

For its part, labor had led a grand effort to consolidate disparate groups. The Knights of Labor was formed in 1869, followed by the Federation of Organized Trades in 1881 and the American Federation of Labor in 1886. With the growth of unionization, labor activism grew. Unions became more successful in their tactics, being able to shut down factories and even industries. Transportation was so greatly affected by the Pullman Strike of 1894 that President Cleveland authorized the use of force against strikers. Nor was labor's power restricted to the picket line. Over time, organized labor became enough of a power in the electorate to influence state legislatures. The Populist movement emerged as a key advocate for labor's causes.

Legislation, such as the Adamson Act of 1916 which established a maximum eight-hour day for all interstate railroad workers, was championed by this new and emerging voice in national politics.

The Pullman Strike in particular foreshadowed new legal questions regarding presidential authority and labor politics. President Grover Cleveland intervened with federal troops in Chicago for the claimed purpose of protecting federal property and removing obstructions to U.S. mail. This was done without consulting John P. Altgeld, the Democratic governor of Illinois, an unprecedented application of federal power during peacetime without explicit statutory authority.[127] When the legal issues reached the judiciary, the Supreme Court supported this expansive use of executive powers to arrest Eugene V. Debs and other strike leaders for conspiracy to obstruct the mails. In the case of *In re Debs,* the Court relied upon general Article II executive powers to protect the peace of the United States.[128] Though Cleveland won in the Supreme Court, the outrage of labor and allied interests contributed to the defeat of the Democratic Party candidate William Jennings Bryan in 1896. Instead, the Republican candidate, William McKinley, became president.

**A New Generation of Justices Join the Court.** As the Civil War era justices passed from the scene, new justices moved onto the Court with different views. Lincoln's chief justice Salmon Chase left the Court in 1873. President Grant appointed Morrison R. Waite to replace him. By 1890, Miller and Field were the only justices left appointed by Lincoln. President Grant had made five appointments to the Court, with his successors each making fewer nominations: Hayes 3, Garfield 1, Arthur 2, Cleveland 4, Harrison 4, and McKinley 1. Among the new crop of justices was Rufus Peckham, appointed in 1896 by President Grover Cleveland. He had been active in Democratic Party politics. Coming from the upstate New York wing of the party, he fought the corrupt Tammany Hall politicians in New York City as much as he fought the Republicans. He was a personal friend of President Cleveland. He served on the Court until he died in 1909.

**The Creation of the Federal Circuit Court of Appeals System.** During its first century of existence, the Supreme Court acted as an appellate court for federal trial courts. By the end of the late nineteenth century, it had become evident that the appellate load was too much for the Court. In 1891, the burden was finally relieved when Congress created the Federal Circuit Court of Appeals system. It put an end to circuit-riding duties of Supreme Court justices, allowing them to concentrate on their own caseload.[129] This would facilitate a growing caseload and a more prominent role for the Court in decisions of national political interest. It also ended the informal practice of appointing a justice from each of the circuits. Thereafter, it was not as rare to find justices on the Court from the same state.

# THE COURTS OF MILLER AND FIELD AS OF 1865 AND THEREAFTER

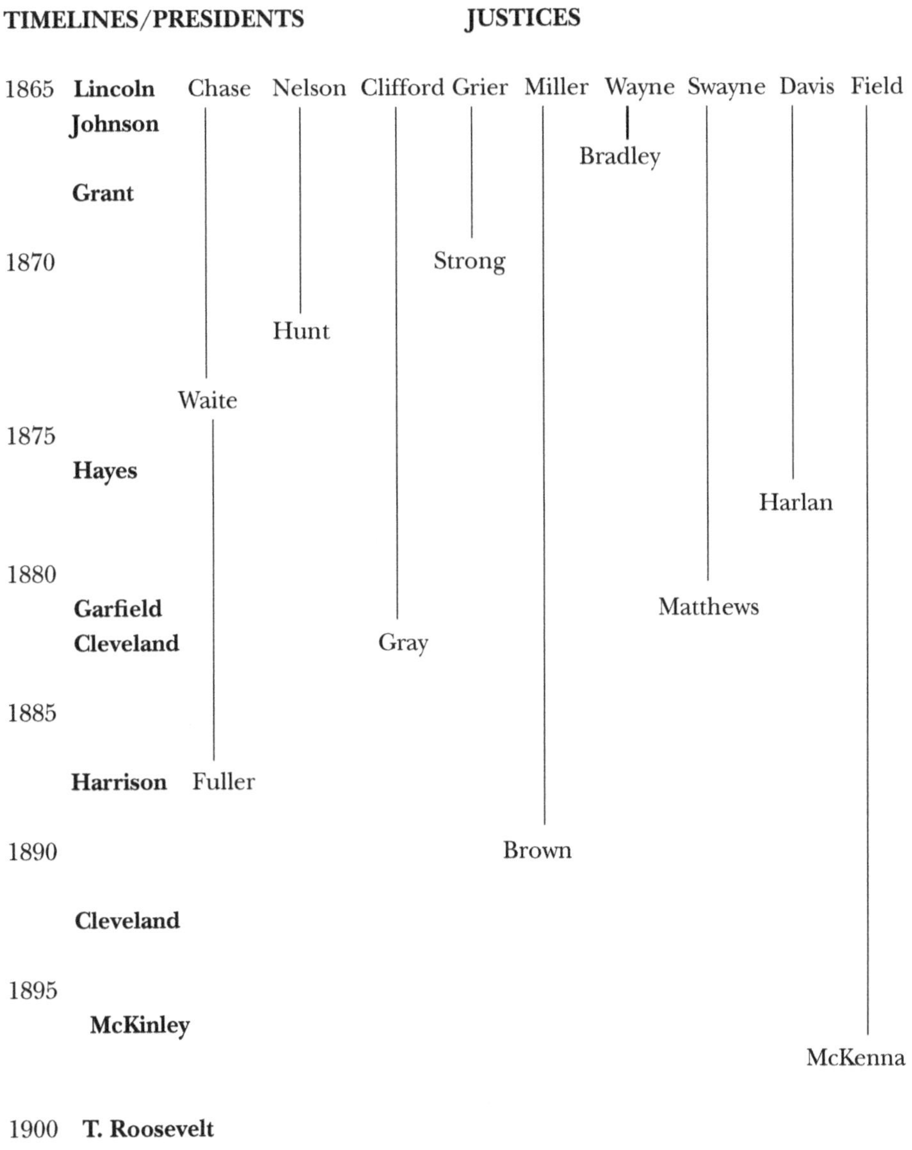

**The Era of Theodore Roosevelt.** Theodore Roosevelt succeeded William McKinley to the presidency after the latter was assassinated in 1901. He was feared by many in the Republican Party as a maverick with unorthodox, erratic tendencies. Roosevelt's opponents thought the vice presidency would anchor this energetic reformer in a position of insignificance. Instead, they unwittingly positioned Roosevelt to have a lasting mark on the presidency, the nation, and the judiciary. Roosevelt made three nominations to the Supreme Court, one of whom would serve on the Court for thirty years.

That nominee was Oliver Wendell Holmes, Jr., replacing Associate Justice Horace Gray who retired in 1902 after suffering a stroke. Holmes had been a respected judge on the Massachusetts Supreme Court, a progressive professor of law at Harvard, and a veteran of the Civil War. Holmes was born to a wealthy family in Boston in 1841. His father was a medical doctor and a well-known author. The junior Holmes entered Harvard but left before completing his studies, enlisting in the Union army after the fall of Fort Sumter, South Carolina, in 1861. He was commissioned a lieutenant in the Twentieth Massachusetts Regiment that same year.[130] In the course of his service in the war, he would be wounded several times. At the battle of Ball's Bluff, Virginia, in 1861, he was shot through the chest. In Antietam in 1862, he was shot through the neck. At Chancellorsville in 1863, Captain Holmes was wounded in the foot. It was the least serious of his wounds but required seven months recovery away from the front. Though offered the opportunity to return to his regiment as a major, he opted for a discharge in July of 1864 and entered Harvard Law School shortly thereafter. In 1881, he published *The Common Law* based on his series of lectures at Harvard Law School. He later was appointed to the Massachusetts Supreme Court, where he served for twenty years, rising to the position of chief justice. His progressive approach to legal interpretation, later to be known as legal realism, caught the attention of young president Roosevelt who, on the advice of Massachusetts senator Henry Cabot Lodge, appointed him to the Court. He would remain on the Court until he retired in 1932, at age ninety-two. He was forever shaped by his wartime experience which left him with lingering memories of comrades who had made the ultimate sacrifice in service to their country. Despite his legal realism and his disdain for "natural rights conferred by God," he would write decisions fundamental to the Court's protection of free speech and other constitutional rights.

In 1903, Roosevelt appointed William R. Day to the Court. He had served as McKinley's secretary of state and was considered reliable with "mild liberal tendencies," a counterbalance to conservatives on the Court like David J. Brewer, Rufus Peckham, Edward D. White, and Chief Justice Melville Fuller.[131] Day would join the aging libertarian John Marshall Harlan as well as Holmes to form the progressive wing of the Court. Day served until 1922.

In 1906, Roosevelt appointed William H. Moody to the Court. Early in his administration, Roosevelt appointed Moody to be secretary of the navy. When it came to filling a vacancy created by the departure of Associate Justice Henry Brown, Roosevelt consulted Secretary of War William Taft and former secretary of war Elihu

Root along with three sitting justices and four senators.[132] Among the justices supporting the nomination was Oliver Wendell Holmes, who had been favorably impressed by Moody's performance as a lawyer in the courts of Massachusetts.[133] Moody would serve on the Court until 1910. He went on to pursue a political career, being elected to the U.S. House of Representatives.

**Challenges within the Republican Party.** The Roosevelt presidency coincided with a struggle not just between the major political parties but within the parties themselves. The Democrats faced an insurgency from growing labor constituents. The Republicans faced an emerging fight between the Progressives, who fought against government corruption and for regulation of harmful business practices and corporate excesses, and the probusiness wing, who opposed broad regulation of businesses. The term "progressive" was associated with a broader political movement (and separate political party). Progressives championed social justice, using state power to protect the poor from the excesses of the marketplace. They pushed legislation to restrict child labor hours and conditions, to set minimum wages, to limit maximum hours, and to provide for workers' compensation. In 1911, ten states had instituted workers' compensation systems (twenty more by 1916). Almost all states had child labor laws by 1916. Thirty-seven states had maximum hours for women by 1917.

The national division over labor laws and economic regulation carried over into the Court. On the one side, Justice Peckham favored limited governmental regulation of business, preferring Herbert Spencer's theory of "social Darwinism." On the other side, Justices Holmes and William G. Sumner were more amenable to governmental regulation of excesses of business and industry. In *Holden v. Hardy,* where the Court upheld a Utah statute with maximum hours for coal mining in 1898, Peckham dissented, based on the decision of the Court during the previous term in *Allgeyer v. Louisiana.* The majority declared the statute to be a valid exercise of police power even though it interfered with the right of contract. Thus, the right to contract could not be an absolute bar to economic regulation but was subject to limitations.

**The Antitrust Cases.** Presidents have sometimes been disappointed by appointments to the Court not because of political disagreements but because a particular judicial methodology steers a justice in a different result. President Roosevelt had such an experience in pursuing antitrust actions. Early efforts to corral corporate excesses occurred under administrations prior to Roosevelt. The first major prosecution under the Sherman Antitrust Act was reviewed by the Court in 1895, *United States v. E. C. Knight Company* (otherwise known as the *Sugar Trust* case). The Court held that the defendant's acquisition of stock of competing sugar-refining companies did not fall within the scope of the commerce clause power of Congress to regulate. Manufacturing was viewed as a purely local activity.[134] That decision did not dampen the hopes of President Roosevelt and Attorney General Philander Chase Knox to squelch further monopolistic practices.

Roosevelt's and Knox's chance came when the Great Northern and Northern Pacific railways were joined through a holding company headquartered in New Jersey. Knox zealously launched an enforcement action under the Sherman Act against the railroads, naming as defendants some of the most powerful men in the country: J. P. Morgan (for the Northern Pacific), E. H. Harriman (Union Pacific), and James J. Hill (Great Northern). The case of *United States v. Northern Securities* reached the Supreme Court in 1904.[135] Justice Harlan wrote for the majority, "No scheme or device could more certainly come within the words of the (Sherman) Act . . . or could more effectively and certainly suppress free competition."[136] He was joined by Justices Day, Brown, and McKenna. Justice Brewer concurred, providing a majority in the result but denying a majority on the rationale for the decision.

To the surprise and chagrin of President Roosevelt, Holmes joined Chief Justice Melville Fuller and Associates Justices Peckham and White in the dissent. In announcing his opinion before an open session of the Court, Holmes stated that

> Great cases, like hard cases, make bad law. For great cases are called great, not by reason of their real importance in shaping the law of the future, but because of some accident of immediate overwhelming interest which appeals to the feelings and distorts the judgment.[137]

Roosevelt, who had been an admirer of Holmes and had him over for lunch in the White House frequently, was outspoken in his bitterness toward his appointee. He declared that "I could carve out of a banana a judge with more backbone than that."[138] Though he was personally hurt by Roosevelt's criticism, Holmes rested on principle, finding nothing in the evidence to support the finding that the Northern Securities Company had attempted to monopolize trade or commerce. The *Northern Securities* case was an anomaly since Holmes otherwise consistently supported legislation sponsored by Roosevelt.

Despite Holmes's admirable adherence to principle, the weight of public opinion in favor of trust-busting prevailed upon official policy makers in government. Muckrakers like Ida Tarbell continued to inveigh against trusts, with considerable influence on lawmakers and the judiciary. Only three years after the *Northern Securities* decision, the government succeeded in breaking up a larger enterprise, John D. Rockefeller's Standard Oil, a victory over the greatest symbol of corporate monopolization at the time.

**The Court, the Regulation of Labor, and Lochner.** In 1906, the Court struck down a municipal ordinance setting a maximum sixty-hour workweek for bakeries in New York City in the case of *Lochner v. New York.*[139] The case was a notable reversal of a trend begun with *Holden.* Justice Rufus Peckham, writing for the majority, held that the right to contract could be applied to the states via the Fourteenth Amendment due process clause. Though not in the Bill of Rights, the Court presumed that "liberty of contract" was superior to the state's power to regulate the industry absent a sufficient justification.

Four justices dissented, including Holmes, who sharply criticized the majority's use of the due process clause: "The Fourteenth Amendment does not enact Mr. Herbert Spencer's *Social Statics*" (appendix 4). He decried what he viewed as incorporation of external social and economic theories into the Constitution: "A constitution is not intended to embody a particular economic theory." The *Lochner* decision would be overturned thirty-two years later.

President Roosevelt himself had proudly championed labor rights in federal legislation he sponsored known as the Employers' Liability Act of 1906. The act was intended to protect workers by providing for liability of employers for certain acts or omissions endangering the safety and well-being of laborers. But in 1907, the Court, in an opinion written by Justice White, struck down the law because it reached beyond interstate commerce and applied even to intrastate corporations. To the dismay of Roosevelt, his appointee Justice Day concurred with the majority.

The Supreme Court scrutinized other federal labor laws as in the case of *Adair v. United States* (1908).[140] This case involved a law banning employers from exacting a promise not to join union as condition of employment. The Court held that these "yellow-dog" contracts violated right to contract. Holmes again dissented, joined by Justice McKenna. The Court would later strike down a similar Kansas law banning yellow-dog contracts, holding that the law was unconstitutional as it had no relevance to "health, safety, or morals or public welfare" in *Coppage v. Kansas* (1915).[141] Writing for the majority, Justice Mahlon Pitney held that the railroads could not be forced to bargain collectively.

Yet the course of the Court was inconsistent. In *Muller v. Oregon* (1909), the Court upheld the Oregon maximum hours work law for women in laundries and factories (ten hours per day).[142] The attorney arguing on behalf of the state of Oregon was Louis Brandeis, who used statistical evidence and commission reports to demonstrate a valid state interest in regulating these industries. In a seeming retreat from *Lochner*, Associate Justice Brewer, who wrote for the majority, said the right to contract is not absolute. The Court would continue to struggle over labor law for three more decades.

# THE COURT OF FULLER AS OF 1902

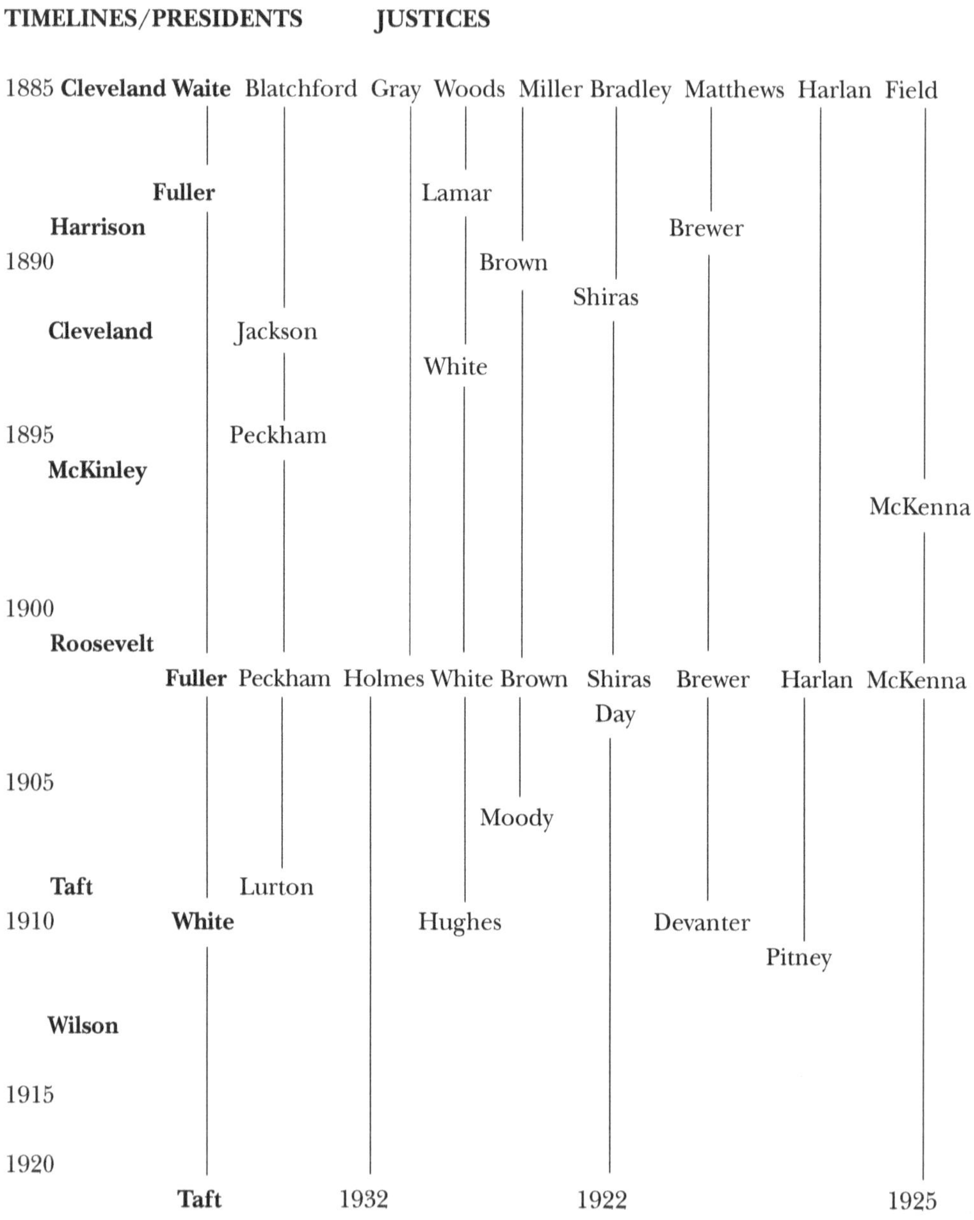
TIMELINES/PRESIDENTS
JUSTICES
1885 Cleveland Waite
Blatchford
Gray
Woods
Miller
Bradley
Matthews
Harlan
Field
Fuller
Lamar
Harrison
Brewer
1890
Brown
Shiras
Cleveland
Jackson
White
1895
Peckham
McKinley
McKenna
1900
Roosevelt
Fuller
Peckham
Holmes
White
Brown
Shiras
Brewer
Harlan
McKenna
Day
1905
Moody
Taft
Lurton
1910
White
Hughes
Devanter
Pitney
Wilson
1915
1920
Taft
1932
1922
1925

# CHAPTER 5

## THE COURTS OF WHITE, TAFT, AND HUGHES: 1910-1941

*Issues relating to industrialization and other changes in society would continue to challenge the Supreme Court in new ways. Settled law could not always be counted upon to provide cogent guidance, especially where new technology or novel social issues were involved. Again, the division of constitutional powers would ensure that the judiciary would come into conflict with the executive and legislative branches of government.*

**The Taft Administration.** In March 1909, William Howard Taft succeeded Theodore Roosevelt to the presidency. An able administrator, he had served as governor of the U.S. territory of the Philippines, Panama Canal supervisor, emissary to Japan, and secretary of war. As a lawyer, he had served as solicitor general and as a circuit judge. Though Taft only served one term as president, he nominated five justices to the Court and elevated Associate Justice Edward D. White to the position of chief justice. White remained on the Court until his death in 1921. Taft also filled an associate justice opening with Charles Evans Hughes, the "coldly brilliant Republican lawyer"[143] and former governor of New York. In addition to White and Hughes, Taft appointed Horace H. Lurton, Charles Evans Hughes, Willis van Devanter, Joseph R. Lamar, and Mahlon Pitney. Taft's nominees were decidedly conservative and would have a lasting influence on the Court. Justice Van Devanter would remain on the Court until 1937, emerging as a notable opponent of Franklin Roosevelt's New Deal legislation. Hughes resigned from the Court to run unsuccessfully for president against Wilson. Taft would later be appointed chief justice by President Warren G. Harding. In 1930, Hughes returned to the Court to replace Taft as chief justice. Hughes remained on the Court until his retirement in 1941.

**The Wilson Era.** When Theodore Roosevelt ran on a third-party ticket and split the Republican vote to the detriment of incumbent president William Howard Taft in 1912, Woodrow Wilson won the presidency. In answer to his lifelong ambition, Wilson would make three appointments to the Court: James C. McReynolds, Louis D. Brandeis, and John H. Clarke.

President Wilson nominated James McReynolds to replace Justice Horace Lurton who died in 1914. Wilson regarded his first appointment as a miscalculation when McReynolds failed to emerge as progressive as Wilson had hoped. But Wilson disliked McReynolds, and his motivations to remove him from his cabinet outweighed considerations of the best qualified candidates.[144] The conservative McReynolds frequently voted against Wilson's interests and remained on the Court for twenty-six years, long enough to vote against Franklin Roosevelt's New Deal program. McReynolds would lose influence among his colleagues on the Court as time went on. He became a target of Franklin Roosevelt's later efforts to purge conservatives from the Court. When Charles Evans Hughes left the Court in 1916 to run for president on the Republican ticket, Wilson nominated John Clarke to replace him. But Clarke did not remain on the Court for long, resigning in 1922.

When Associate Justice Joseph Lamar died in 1916, Wilson nominated Louis Brandeis to replace him. Brandeis was a Kentucky-born, Harvard-educated lawyer. He achieved prominence by taking many important pro bono cases, causing him to be known as the people's attorney. He supported and campaigned for Wilson in his successful run for the presidency in 1912. The Senate Judiciary Committee's confirmation hearings were contentious because, in Brandeis's view, he is considered "a radical and is a Jew."[145] Ex-President Taft and the American Bar Association opposed the nomination while the *Wall Street Journal* and *New York Times* ran articles against him.[146] Despite a narrow two-vote margin of approval in the committee, the Senate easily confirmed Brandeis by a vote of 47-22. Justice Brandeis would find common ground with established justices such as Holmes, who believed that the Constitution did not forbid economic regulation. Brandeis and Holmes also agreed on the preservation of freedom of speech and the press. Brandeis would remain on the Court long enough to hear the controversial *Schechter* case at the time of the New Deal controversy, at the age of seventy-nine.

**The Growth of Regulation.** Many domestic and international challenges pressured President Woodrow Wilson to exercise wide-sweeping federal executive powers. An influx of immigrants from Central and Eastern Europe over the preceding decades had swelled the market with cheap labor as well as fueled an increasingly politically active workers' movement. Labor unions had grown in strength, but the right of workers to organize and collectively bargain was not universally accepted and faced serious resistance from industry. Bolder and more confrontational tactics were used by both labor and management, with the government intervening on occasion. During Wilson's second term, he led America into the war in Europe, despite his 1916 campaign pledge, when Germany resumed its campaign of unrestricted submarine warfare. The war effort furthered industrial demands, continuing the trends that gave rise to new social challenges and demands for regulation. It also reinforced federal wartime powers, leading to an inevitable conflict with civil liberties.

**The Continuing Debate: Labor Laws and the Constitution.** The Court continued on an inconsistent path with regard to labor law, reflecting the lack of clear consensus among the justices. In *Bunting v. Oregon* (1917), the majority upheld a state law setting a ten-hour day for workers generally and requiring payment of "time and one-half" for hours worked over that limit, up to a maximum of thirteen hours.[147] Justice McKenna, writing for the majority, based his holding on statistical evidence on average work hours around the world. In another victory for labor, the Court struck down an Arizona law forbidding injunctions against workers picketing as a violation of the equal protection clause of the Fourteenth Amendment in *Truax v. Corrigan* (1921).[148]

Yet the right of contract was invoked again in *Hammer v. Dagenhart* (1918) to strike down a federal child labor law.[149] In addition to contract rights, the Court also denied authority to Congress to regulate in this area based upon their understanding of the limited reach of the interstate commerce clause. In the view of the Court, this was a matter for *state* regulation, not *federal*. Justices Holmes, McKenna, Brandeis, and Clark dissented. This foreshadowed the later New Deal era conflict between the Court and the other two branches over the scope of the commerce clause.

In *Adkins v. Children's Hospital* (1923), where it struck down minimum wages for women, a majority on the Court attempted to distinguish the *Bunting* case, reasoning that regulating minimum wages was different from regulating maximum hours.[150] Justices Taft, Sanford, and Holmes dissented. A divided Court would continue to chart an erratic course on labor rights for the next fourteen years.

**Criminal Law and Civil Rights.** In 1914, the Court established the exclusionary rule. Though it initially applied only to criminal trials in federal courts, the Court's decision in *Weeks v. United States*[151] was to have extensive consequences for years to come. The Court held that a seizure of private papers and items (lottery tickets) by police officers, acting under the sanction of the U.S. Marshall, when they entered the defendant's home without a search warrant violated the Fourth Amendment. Writing for the Court, Justice William Day declared that

> If letters and private documents can thus be seized and held and used in evidence against a citizen accused of an offense, the protection of the Fourth Amendment, declaring his right to be secure against such searches and seizures, is of no value, and so far as those thus placed are concerned might as well be stricken from the Constitution.

The rule to exclude evidence gathered in violation of the Fourth Amendment would not be applied to the states until forty-seven years later, but it set the course for further

Court ventures into criminal procedure and civil rights. Whatever progress was made in the name of civil rights at this time would be called into question during World War I.

**Civil Rights and Civil Liberties in Wartime.** Entry of the United States into the First World War brought tensions between advocates of wartime security measures and civil liberties. In June 1917, Congress passed the Espionage Act which outlawed the advocacy of "treason, insurrection, or forcible resistance to any law of the United States" including the use of U.S. mail for sending materials urging resistance to recruitment. This was amended by the Sedition Act of 1918, which prohibited oral or written attacks on the U.S. government, Constitution, or flag. Before the war was over, thousands of Americans had been arrested under the Espionage Act and related laws.

In one of the more well-known cases of that era, Eugene V. Debs's conviction for advocating resistance to the draft was upheld by the Court. Debs was prominent as the Socialist Party's presidential candidate in 1912 and carried 10 percent of the vote, a remarkable feat for a third party in American politics. In *Debs v. United States,* Holmes wrote for a unanimous Court that Debs's intent was to incite resistance to the draft.[152] Though President Wilson declined the opportunity to pardon Debs, he was ultimately pardoned by President Warren G. Harding in 1921.

In another well-publicized case, Charles T. Schenck was accused of distributing leaflets urging resistance to the draft. In the *Schenck* case, Holmes wrote for a unanimous Court that the First Amendment did not protect utterances that pose a "clear and present danger" of causing conduct that Congress had a right to prevent.[153] Though Schenck's conviction was upheld by the decision, Holmes had attempted to move the Court beyond the old standard which only prohibited prior restraints on speech as opposed to subsequent punishment for content of the speech.[154] On the basis of his new standard, which protected the right to express unpopular views, Holmes dissented when the Court voted to uphold the conviction in *Abrams v. United States* for publishing articles critical of the war.[155]

The challenge to civil rights did not end with the war, as the Sedition Act was not repealed until 1921. During the Red Scare of 1919-1920, Attorney General A. Mitchell Palmer arrested thousands of alleged communists and held them without trial before deporting them.[156] It would fall upon the Court in later years to place limitations on such practices in the name of civil rights. Holmes's view would prevail only after the Second World War.

**The Harding and Coolidge Administrations.** Wilson was succeeded by the Republican presidential administrations of Warren G. Harding and Calvin Coolidge. Though Harding died in office, serving less than two and a half years as president, he made four appointments to the Court. The most significant of those appointments was that of William Howard Taft, whom he appointed to be chief justice in 1921. Taft had long aspired to this position. Before taking his place on the Court, he was notorious for his meddling on behalf of nominees to the Court. The practice did not stop after he was seated on the Court, as he lobbied on behalf of Butler in 1922. Taft's judicial philosophy remained conservative, referring to those preferring more liberal approaches to the law, such as Learned Hand, Louis Brandeis, and Benjamin Cardozo, as destroyers of the Constitution.[157] On the Court, Taft was a believer in unanimity, opining that "most dissents don't do any good and only weaken the prestige of the Court." But Holmes, Brandeis, and Stone were undeterred in their dissents.

Though Taft's substantive performance on the Court may have been unremarkable, he left a lasting legacy on the judiciary, strengthening the Court's image and role as a coequal branch of government. He brought the prestige of a former president to the Court and won support for the construction of the Court's own building. The other legacy of Chief Justice Taft was more discretion for the Court on cases it would hear. Facing a five-year backlog of mandatory appeals from federal circuit courts and state courts of last resort, he pushed Congress to pass the Certiorari Act of 1925.[158] The act gave the Court the discretion to choose which appellate cases it would hear.

Harding would also appoint George Sutherland and Pierce Butler in 1922 and Edward T. Sanford in 1923. Sutherland and Butler would later play roles as antagonists of Franklin Roosevelt's New Deal programs. Harding's term as president was cut short by his death in August 1923. Vice President Coolidge succeeded him and was elected in his own right in 1924. President Coolidge's lone appointment to the Court was Attorney General Harlan Fiske Stone, who took his seat in 1925. Stone was a progressive Republican who had been dean of Columbia Law School and had headed litigation for the New York firm of Sullivan and Cromwell. This appointment would take on added significance, as Stone later earned the support of Roosevelt for his elevation to the post of chief justice. He remained on the Court until 1946. Though appointed by the conservative Republican Coolidge, Stone would frequently align himself with Holmes and Brandeis.

**Civil Liberties and Civil Rights.** Though this era is not noted for great advances in the recognition of civil rights and civil liberties, the opinions and dissents often formed the basis for later decisions that developed law in these areas. The advent of new technology, such as wiretapping, challenged traditional interpretations of constitutional rights. In *Olmstead v. United States* (1928), the Court held that a wiretap on private telephone conversations did not constitute a search and seizure within the meaning of the Fourth Amendment.[159] The case involved electronic eavesdropping leading to the conviction of the leader of a major bootlegging ring. Chief Justice Taft wrote for the majority, noting that the conversations were intercepted by the use of telephone lines but "without trespass upon any property of the defendants." Continuing, he stated that the Fourth Amendment applies to searches of "material things—the person, the house, his papers, or his effects." The wiretap was not a "physical entry." He noted that Congress may choose to enact laws to protect the secrecy of telephone conversations.

Associate Justice Brandeis, joined by Justices Holmes, Butler, and Stone, dissented, arguing that the framers of the Fourth Amendment to the Constitution intended to confer "the right to be let alone—the most comprehensive of rights and the right most valued by civilized men. To protect that right, every unjustifiable intrusion by the government upon the privacy of the individual, whatever the means employed, must be deemed a violation of the Fourth Amendment."

He also prophetically noted that "the progress of science and invention will make it possible for the government, by means more effective than the rack, to obtain disclosure in court of what is whispered in the closet." The *Olmstead* decision was later overturned, with Brandeis's dissent becoming the majority view.[160] Brandeis's dissent would also form the part of the basis for the *Griswold v. Connecticut* decision recognizing a right to privacy and the *Roe v. Wade* decision recognizing the right to an abortion.

**Forced Sterilization.** There were limits even to the progressivism of justices like Holmes when faced with the rising popularity of the pseudoscience of eugenics. Proponents of eugenics in the late nineteenth century maintained that "germ plasm" which predetermined characteristics was passed on from parents to children. Stopping reproduction, therefore, stopped the transmission of undesirable characteristics. In *Buck v. Bell* (1927), the Court was called upon to decide whether the state of Virginia had the authority to order the forced sterilization of a "mentally retarded adult."[161] The attorney representing Carrie Buck argued that the statute authorizing the act was void under the Fourteenth Amendment as it denied the plaintiff due process of law and equal protection of the laws. Carrie Buck was the daughter of an institutionalized woman and had herself already given birth to a "feebleminded" child. Writing for the Court, Justice Holmes upheld the Virginia statute, stating that "three generations of imbeciles are enough":

> It is better for all the world if instead of waiting to execute degenerate offspring for crime, or to let them starve for their imbecility, society can prevent those who are manifestly unfit from continuing their kind. The principle that sustains compulsory vaccination is broad enough to cover cutting the Fallopian tubes.[162]

By 1939, twenty-eight states had adopted similar laws, forcibly sterilizing two to four thousand people a year.[163] The practice would continue in Virginia until 1972, when the state abolished the procedure. By that time, 7,500 people in the state had been sterilized. Eugenics was later discredited, and the specific allegation such traits are genetically transmitted was disproved. Carrie Buck was located in 1979 and was reportedly found to be of normal intelligence.[164] Had Holmes treated eugenics as skeptically as he had regarded Spencer's statics, this specious "science" would not have tainted his record of otherwise thoughtful and insightful decisions.

**Executive Powers.** In 1926, the Court demonstrated once again that individual politics may take on different hues after appointment to the judiciary, as when the Court upheld an expansive interpretation of executive powers in removing officials from office. Writing for the majority in *Myers v. United States,* Chief Justice Taft held that an 1876 statute requiring the president to obtain the advice and consent of the Senate prior to removal of a postmaster was unconstitutional.[165] Frank Myers had been appointed postmaster for Portland, Oregon, by President Woodrow Wilson with the advice and consent of the Senate in 1917. But Wilson decided to dismiss him in 1920. Myers sued to challenge his removal. As Taft wrote for the Court, the power of removal of government officials was an inherently executive power. Taft, who as a Republican president took a decidedly narrow interpretation of executive powers, in this decision supported a Democratic president's ability to dismiss the postmaster without the approval of the Senate. Though Wilson had died two years before this holding, Taft's decision indicates that no enmity over the man who defeated him in his reelection bid for the presidency stood in the way of this ruling. There would be further Court decisions restricting the precedent of this ruling, but the course was set for an increasing expansion of executive power.[166]

**The Hoover Administration.** President Herbert Hoover took office in 1929. When Chief Justice Taft died in 1930, Hoover nominated Charles Evans Hughes to replace him. He had served as an associate justice of the Supreme Court from 1910 to 1916, when he resigned to accept the Republican nomination for president. He was narrowly defeated by incumbent president Woodrow Wilson. He went on to serve as the "reform Republican" governor of New York. President Warren Harding appointed Hughes secretary of state from 1921 to 1925, one of only two secretaries of state to later become chief justice.[167] He engaged in private law practice in between government appointments. Hughes would remain chief justice until 1941. He was seventy-seven at the time of Franklin Roosevelt's Court-Packing Plan.

When Edward T. Sanford died in 1930, Hoover nominated conservative North Carolina Circuit Court of Appeals Judge John J. Parker. A coordinated campaign against him led by labor groups and the NAACP resulted in a Senate rejection of Parker by a narrow margin of only two votes. A badly embarrassed Hoover then nominated Republican attorney Owen J. Roberts, from Pennsylvania, who was confirmed by the Senate.[168]

When Hoover looked for a replacement for Holmes in 1932, he initially sought to nominate someone from the West, to cover the lack of representation from that region. But Senator William Borah of Idaho, a key supporter of Hoover, recommended the president-nominate Benjamin Cardozo, the liberal chief judge on the New York Court of Appeals. Justice Stone, who had previously recommended Cardozo as a replacement for Sanford, strongly supported the nomination of Cardozo and actively campaigned on his behalf. Hoover's concerns about appointing a Democrat were assuaged by Cardozo's moderation in his approach to the law and his strong belief in traditional common law. Cardozo became the second justice of Jewish heritage on the Supreme Court.

**Taft's Legacy: A Permanent Home for the Court.** In 1929, Chief Justice William Howard Taft, who had served as president from 1909 to1913, used his considerable political influence to persuade Congress to fund the construction of the Supreme Court's first permanent home at One First Street Northeast, across the street from the Capitol at a cost of $9,740,000. It was Taft's desire to construct "a building of dignity and importance suitable for its use as the permanent home of the Supreme Court."[169]

Since first convening in the Merchant's Exchange in New York City in 1790, the Court had resided in six different rooms in the Capitol building in Washington, D.C. Taft never lived to see the realization of his dream as he died in 1930, two years prior to the start of construction. It was an ambitious project undertaken in the midst of a national Depression. The neoclassical Corinthian structure was completed in 1935, at $94,000 under budget. The white marble courtroom included friezes of eighteen lawgivers of historic note, including Hammurabi, Moses, Solomon, Octavian, Napoleon Bonaparte, John Marshall, William Blackstone, Hugo Grotius, Charlemagne, and Justinian.[170]

In the Court's new home, the justices emerged from under Congress's shadow both in the literal and symbolic sense, reinforcing its more-than-symbolic status as a coequal branch of government. From this point onward, a growing assertiveness of the Court would appear, significantly at a time when the Court experienced one of its greatest challenges to its independence and standing.

**The Roosevelt Years.** In an act symbolic of the old and the new, Franklin Delano Roosevelt met with Oliver Wendell Holmes on his inauguration day in 1933.[171] Holmes had retired from the Court the year before at the age of ninety-two. He had seen the nation's transformation from regional division during the Civil War to emergence as a global power. The Court had faced new challenges in that time. For over a quarter of a century, the Court wrote inconsistently on the subject of powers of the states and federal government to regulate labor and industry. The election of Roosevelt to the presidency would result in fundamental challenges to the orientation of the Court on those powers.

In his heralded first "hundred days" in the office of the president, Roosevelt used his constitutional authority to convene Congress in special session and to send more significant pieces of legislation for approval than any administration had before. Aided by Democratic majorities in both houses in the spring of 1933, Congress passed the Banking Act, the Beer Act, and the Economy Act with intent to prevent further bank failures, weaken Prohibition restrictions, and stabilize federal salaries and pensions. These measures foreshadowed more federal involvement in the affairs of states and businesses and challenges to the conventional understandings of limitations on the role of the federal government. The Court would be called upon to determine what the Constitution permitted.

**The New Deal and the Court-Packing Plan.** The 1930s also represented a significant shift in the direction and power of the Court. President Roosevelt pushed the National Industrial Recovery Act (NIRA) through Congress in 1933. With the backdrop of the stock market crash of 1929 and an ensuing Depression, Roosevelt's New Deal plan would increase governmental economic regulation substantially. It attempted to end cutthroat competition, protect labor, limit agricultural and industrial overproduction, and regulate the stock market. It set up new government institutions for these purposes: the National Recovery Administration (NRA) and the Securities and Exchange Commission (SEC). The 1935 Wagner Act guaranteed labor's right to organize.

During the approach to Roosevelt's run for a second term as president, Senator Huey Long from Louisiana challenged the president's leadership on economic recovery by offering a plan for old-age pensions and national unemployment compensation. Though European governments had introduced such social welfare plans beginning in the late nineteenth century (such as Germany's program which was sponsored by Chancellor Otto von Bismarck in 1881), the United States had yet to enact a similar plan on a federal level.[172] Roosevelt responded to Long with a plan of his own. But his plan for a "Social Security" system, as well as other new "extraordinary" economic measures for Depression relief, was viewed as beyond the powers of the federal government traditionally accepted by the Court. The Supreme Court in 1935 was dominated by justices who reflected the traditional, narrow approach to federal powers. With the cooperation of Congress, Roosevelt attempted to expand federal powers, under the would-be authority of the interstate commerce clause. His view failed to prevail in the Court, with the federal cases losing in 1935 and 1936 (both decisions lost narrowly by 5/4 votes). Among the twelve acts struck down by the Court in Roosevelt's first term were the Railroad Retirement Act, Bituminous Coal Conservation Act, and the Agricultural Adjustment Act.

Three decisions in particular angered FDR: *Louisville Joint Stock Land Bank v. Radford*, *Humphrey's Executor v. United States*, and *Schechter Poultry Corp. v. United States*.[173] In the *Louisville* case, the Court struck down foreclosure-delay provisions of the Frazier-Lemke Act, designed to protect farmers. The Court ruled that Congress could not do this without compensation. In *Humphrey's Executor v. United States*, the Court denied the president's authority to remove a member of the Federal Trade Commission, an independent regulatory body. Perhaps the attitude of the Court was best reflected by Justice Robert's majority opinion in *Nebbia v. New York*: The "state is free to adopt whatever economic policy may reasonably be deemed to promote public welfare . . . With the wisdom of the policy adopted . . . the courts are both incompetent and unauthorized to deal."[174]

The most significant case, however, was *Schechter Poultry*, sometimes referred to as the sick chicken case. The NIRA of 1933 authorized the president to establish and enforce "codes of fair competition" for businesses.[175] Pursuant to the NIRA, a code of competition was set for poultry dealers in the greater New York City area, setting minimum wages and maximum hours. Chief Justice Hughes wrote for the majority, stating that the Schechter business was local in nature and beyond the scope of interstate commerce clause power since it had no direct effect upon interstate commerce. A majority of the justices believed in the viability of the Tenth Amendment that "those powers not delegated to the United States by the Constitution nor prohibited by it to the States are reserved to the States respectively or to the people." This ruling undermined the foundation for the NIRA. Part of the problem was that the NIRA was so vague it gave unlimited power to the president and the NIRA.

In *United States v. Butler* in 1936, the Court held the Agricultural Adjustment Act of 1933 unconstitutional by a 6-3 vote.[176] The act authorized the Secretary of Agriculture to pay farmers to reduce their cultivated acres and production in order to stabilize produce prices. The Solicitor General tried to defend the legislation based upon Congress's power to tax and spend "for the general welfare." The Court found that regulating agricultural production was a power reserved to the states via the Tenth Amendment.

During his second inaugural address in February 1937, President Roosevelt responded to the judicial "assault" on his New Deal agenda by proposing to add six new justices to the Court (one for every justice over the age of seventy for a total of fifteen). The plan would change the formula for nine justices that had existed since 1869. This was not the first attempt to add seats to the Court with the purpose of influencing its balance and composition. President Jefferson succeeded with the assistance of Congress in adding one seat in 1807, as did President Jackson in 1837 (adding two seats), President Lincoln in 1863 (one seat), and President Grant in 1869 (one seat).

At the time, the Court included only two justices, Brandeis and McReynolds, appointed by the last Democrat to hold the presidency, Woodrow Wilson. Chief Justice Hughes was a Hoover appointee in 1930. Roosevelt was most adamant about the anti-New Deal "four horsemen"(of apocalyptic allegory): Justices Devanter, McReynolds, Sutherland, and Butler. Justice Willis van Devanter was appointed by Taft in 1911. James C. McReynolds was appointed by Wilson in 1914. George C. Sutherland was appointed by Harding in 1922. Pierce Butler was appointed by Harding in 1923.

The age of the justices and political party of the appointing president were not valid discriminators when it came to votes on the Supreme Court. Owen Roberts, appointed by Hoover in 1930, was a swing vote. The "liberal" Harlan F. Stone was a 1924 Coolidge appointee, and the "liberal" Benjamin Cardozo was a 1932 Hoover appointee. The pro-New Deal justice Brandeis was seventy-nine years old at the time of the Court-Packing Plan.

Unlike Presidents Jefferson, Jackson, Lincoln, and Grant before him, Roosevelt failed to muster sufficient votes in Congress to add judges to the Supreme Court, despite growing criticism of the Court's protection of business interests and its attack on congressional power. But many congressional Democrats were shocked by the radical change proposed for the Court. Even liberal pro-New Deal Democrats, such as Senator Wheeler, opposed Roosevelt's Court-Packing Plan.

The media was also critical of Roosevelt. Chief Justice Hughes sent a letter to Wheeler, with the approval of Associate Justices Brandeis and Van Devanter, stating that the Court was not behind in its docket and that an increase in the number of justices would not increase the Court's efficiency. Wheeler produced the letter in the midst of the Senate Judiciary Committee's hearing on the matter, an act that became instrumental in defeating

Roosevelt's plan.[177] The Court-Packing Plan subsequently died in the committee by a vote of 10-8. In rejecting the bill, the committee condemned the proposal as a "needless, futile, and utterly dangerous abandonment of constitutional principle."[178]

Nevertheless, popular discontent appears to have brought pressure to bear on the Court. Justices Hughes and Roberts changed their position on the constitutionality of New Deal legislation. Devanter announced his retirement the morning on the day of the Judiciary Committee's vote, encouraged by Congress's providing of retirement benefits for Supreme Court justices via the Judiciary Act of 1937.[179] Others retired not long thereafter, such as Sutherland in 1938, Butler in 1939, Cardozo in 1938, and Brandeis in 1939. In a variation of the old proverb, it was said that the "switch in time saved nine."

**Reshaping the Court.** The reversal of the course of the Court could be seen within two weeks after the vote to defeat Roosevelt's plan in *West Coast Hotel v. Parrish* (1937), upholding Washington State's child labor laws and minimum wage laws for women (overruling the 1923 *Adkins* decision) and defeating arguments on behalf of employers for "freedom of contract" as a constitutional economic right.[180] In effect, the Supreme Court reversed a forty-year trend and allowed an expansive reading of the interstate commerce clause power to benefit expanded federal power. The Court reached deep into its history to invoke the name of John Marshall as a would-be supporter of such an expansive interpretation of federal powers.

Shortly thereafter, the Court upheld the Wagner Act in *National Labor Relations Board v. Jones & Laughlin Steel Corp.*[181] The Wagner Act, otherwise known as the National Labor Relations Act of 1935, had established a comprehensive labor relations regime, which guaranteed labor the right to organize and bargain collectively. In a 5-4 vote, the Court accepted the scope of congressional authority over interstate commerce in this legislation because by its own terms, "it purports to reach only what may be deemed to burden or obstruct (interstate or foreign) commerce."

**Roosevelt's Legacy on the Court.** Within a span of four years, Roosevelt appointed Justices Black, Reed, Frankfurter, Douglas, Murphy, Byrnes, and Jackson. Roosevelt's 1937 nominee, Hugo Black, had spent ten years in the Senate, representing the state of Alabama, at the time of his nomination. He was one of the Senate's most reliable supporters of the New Deal and was the Senate's leading proponent for Roosevelt's Court-Packing Plan. He was considered by some to be a Roosevelt "crony."[182] When news of Black's previous membership in the Ku Klux Klan surfaced, Roosevelt claimed to have been unaware. Though Black had resigned his membership prior to the nomination, newspapers fanned the flames of opposition, nearly costing Black confirmation by his fellow senators. Paradoxically, Black became a hard-line enforcer of constitutional rights on the Court and a supporter of desegregation in the *Brown* decision in 1954. He would have a lasting impact on the Court, serving for thirty-four years.

Solicitor General Stanley Reed was appointed in 1938 to replace George Sutherland who had retired. Though conservative in many respects, Reed could be counted on to support New Deal programs and federal power.[183] He served on the Court until 1957. A native of Kentucky, he would grudgingly concur with the desegregation decision in *Brown v. Board of Education*.

The 1939 nominee, Justice Felix Frankfurter, was a Vienna-born lawyer prominent in private practice and a liberal professor at Harvard Law School. He was formerly an assistant U.S. attorney for New York and a founding member of the American Civil Liberties Union in 1920. He had assisted the appellate defense team following the infamous trial of Italian anarchists Nicola Sacco and Bartolomeo Vanzetti. Because of his association with this and other causes, he was labeled a "red" by critics and certain alumni sought his ouster from Harvard. Despite these challenges, Frankfurter enjoyed the confidence of influential politicians. At the time of his appointment, he was an advisor to Roosevelt and considered to be a member of his inner circle.[184] Notwithstanding these credentials, he did not align himself with the "liberal" justices on the Court. His philosophy of judicial restraint led him more often to side with and even lead the conservatives on the Court. He was also a strong supporter of states' rights. Many of his former civil libertarian colleagues felt betrayed by his support for, among other things, upholding the exclusionary order for Japanese Americans, *Hirabayashi v. United States* in 1943 and *Korematsu v. United States* in 1944, and the ruling which upheld the convictions of eleven members of the Communist Party for conspiring to overthrow the government of the United States, *Dennis v. United States* (1951). For much of his tenure on the Court, he was a leader and influential decision maker. But over time and with changes in composition of the Court, he lost influence with his colleagues. Illness forced him to retire in 1962.

Another opportunity to fill a seat on the Court came later in 1939 when Justice Louis Brandeis retired from the Court. Roosevelt nominated William O. Douglas, another member of Roosevelt's inner circle, to fill the seat. This son of a Presbyterian minister would rise from humble roots in rural Yakima, Washington, to teach law at Yale and Columbia and serve in a variety of federal positions, including chairman of the Securities and Exchange Commission in 1937. He was a reliable New Dealer and had been responsible for implementation of many of Roosevelt's reforms. At forty years of age, he was the youngest justice on the Court. He harbored broad political ambitions beyond the Court and was seriously being considered as Roosevelt's running mate in 1944 before Democratic Party leaders convinced Roosevelt to choose Senator Harry Truman instead.[185] Douglas's early tenure on the Court was characterized by support for progovernment, proregulation rulings, not the libertarian rulings he would later be known for. Still he would find himself voting frequently with the so-called liberals of the Court, Frank Murphy and Wiley Rutledge, rather than "conservatives" like Felix Frankfurter, Robert Jackson, and Harlan Stone. In all, Douglas would serve thirty-six years on the bench, the longest for any justice and one of the most controversial.

Frank Murphy was appointed an associate justice to the Court in 1940 by Roosevelt, replacing Pierce Butler. Murphy had served as an officer in the army and later as U.S.

attorney general and governor of Michigan. His appointment was fortuitously timed with the approach of war. He surprised many by his staunch defense of civil rights in wartime and criticism of the military tribunals instituted by Roosevelt. He remained on the Court until 1949.

By the time Roosevelt died in April 1945, he had appointed a total of nine justices to the Court, a record surpassed only by George Washington, who had the unique opportunity to appoint the first Court and over the course of his two terms appointed ten justices. That record is likely to stand since passage of the Twenty-second Amendment of 1951 limiting presidents to two terms.

**The Demise of Economic Due Process.** The Court sought to establish that it would not overturn acts of Congress based on mere disagreement with the policy but would instead rely upon justiciable standards by which to measure the constitutionality of provisions. In reality, it is hard to design clear, consistent justiciable standards that are easily distinguished from policy. In the 1938 case of *United States v. Carolene Products,* the Court upheld Congress's prohibition of interstate shipment of "filled milk." The Court rejected the appellee's claim that the legislation violated his Fifth Amendment due process rights. Justice Stone foreshadowed later civil rights litigation when he wrote in the now-famous footnote four:

> There may be a narrower scope for operation of the presumption of constitutionality when legislation appears on its face to be within a specific prohibition of the Constitution, such as those of the first ten amendments, which are deemed equally specific when held to be embraced within the Fourteenth Amendment . . . Nor need we enquire whether *prejudice against discrete and insular minorities* may be a special condition which tends to seriously curtail the operation of those political processes ordinarily to be relied upon to protect minorities, and which may call for a correspondingly *more searching judicial scrutiny.*[186] (emphasis added)

The Court accepted a rational basis test for economic regulation. Legislative findings that filled milk was injurious to public health was sufficient rational basis for the Court to uphold the law. The case turned the tables against economic due process and hinted at a return to the original intent of the Fourteenth Amendment. It represented a definite shift away from coverage of "economic" rights under substantive due process, coming full circle with the *Slaughter-House* cases of 1873.

**Civil Rights: Application of the Bill of Rights to the States via the Fourteenth Amendment.** In *Palko v. Connecticut* (1937), Justice Cardozo wrote for an 8-1 majority on the Court providing a test for application of the Bill of Rights to the states.[187] The case involved a statute which allowed state prosecutors to appeal unfavorable decisions in criminal cases. The defendant/appellant claimed this practice violated the Fifth

Amendment's prohibition against double jeopardy and consequently the due process clause of the Fourteenth Amendment. Cardozo's vague tests for constitutionality provided lawmakers with little practical guidance. He stated that certain rights, such as the First Amendment's freedom of speech and the right to peaceable assembly, are "implicit in the concept of ordered liberty." In other cases, one must ask whether the statute "subjected him a hardship so acute and shocking that our polity will not endure it. Does it violate those 'fundamental principles of liberty and justice which lie at the base of all our civil and political institutions?'"

In this case, Cardozo felt that the defendant did not meet the criteria; and the majority did not support the appeal. But this decision provided a basis for expanded application of constitutional rights to the states for future cases.

**Presidential Powers: Foreign Policy.** As American isolationism remained popular politically, President Roosevelt moved ahead with expansion of executive foreign policy powers, with surprising support from the Court. In the 1936 case of *United States v. Curtiss-Wright Export Corporation,* the Court upheld Congress's delegation of authority to the president to embargo U.S.-made weapons to countries at war.[188] The president had invoked the 1934 law to ban the sale of American weapons to Bolivia and Paraguay, then engaged in the Chaco War. Justice Sutherland rejected the allegation that the law was an unlawful delegation of legislative power to the executive. He distinguished the current case from those involving internal affairs where "the federal government can exercise no power except those specifically stated in the Constitution, and such implied powers as are necessary and proper to carry into effect the enumerated powers." Instead, the president is the government's "sole organ" in international affairs and does not depend upon a specific grant of power from the Constitution or from Congress.

The following year, the Court in *United States v. Belmont* upheld the president's power to make executive agreements with foreign states without the advice and consent of the Senate.[189] The specific case involved Roosevelt's 1940 agreement to provide fifty badly needed naval destroyers to Britain in exchange for the use of British bases for U.S. forces. Congress would in 1941 amend the Neutrality Act of 1925 through Lend-Lease legislation, authorizing the provision of military supplies to combatants. But constitutional scholar Edwin Corwin charged that the president had, in effect, usurped Congress's authorities, including the power to declare war.[190] The demise of the use of declarations of war after the Second World War would raise further questions about presidential and congressional powers in wartime in several later cases before the Supreme Court. The constitutional powers of presidents of both political parties were challenged in this regard.

## THE COURT OF THE NEW DEAL ERA (1936)

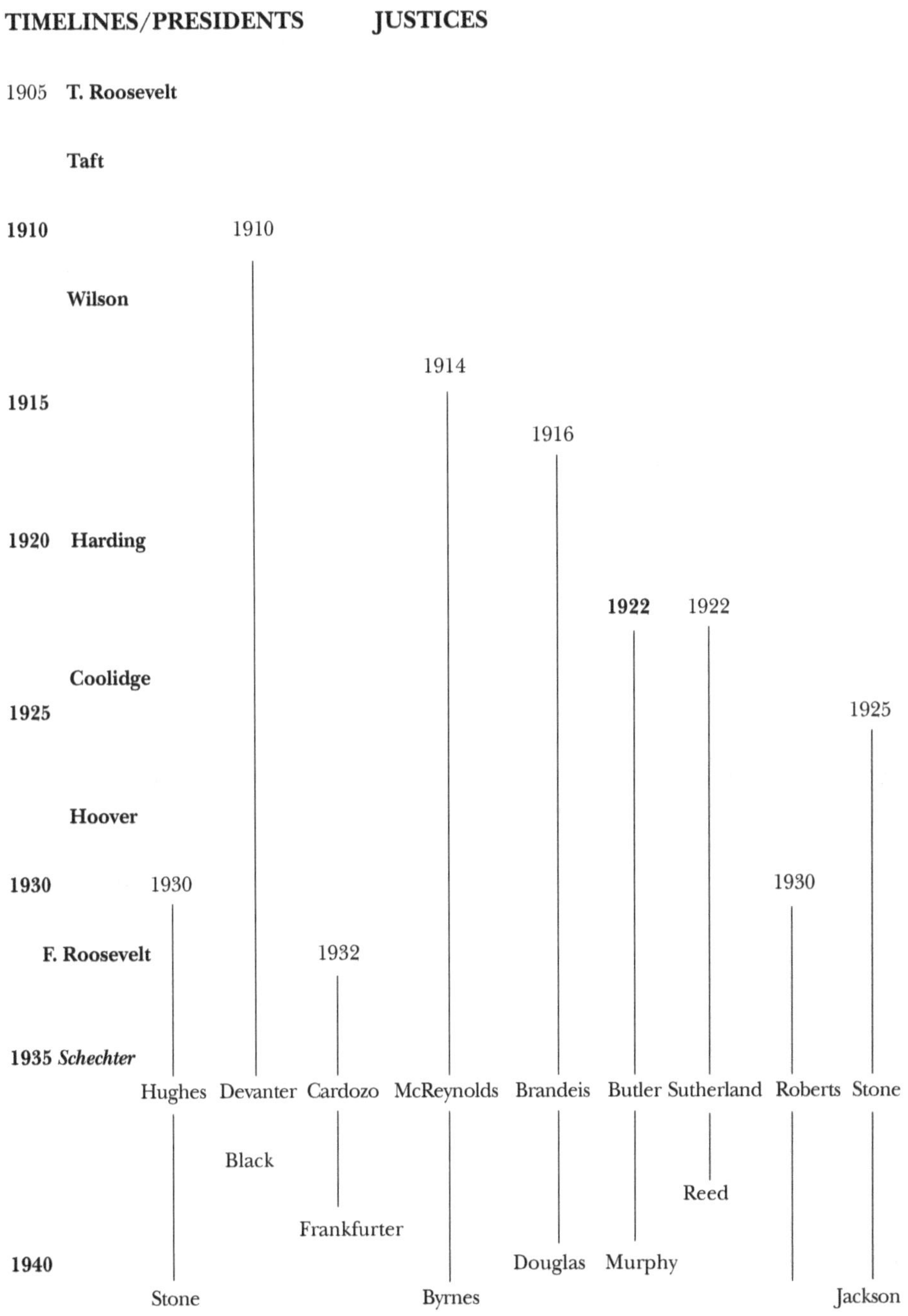

# CHAPTER 6

## THE COURTS OF STONE AND VINSON: 1941-1953

*Even where a president succeeds in substantially changing the makeup of the Supreme Court, such as Franklin Roosevelt who appointed a total of nine justices, he cannot be assured of a compliant, submissive Court. In an era when nominees were frequently selected from the political branches of government, with party affiliations well-known, Presidents Truman and Eisenhower would continue to be frustrated with appointments to the Court who would fail to follow party lines.*

**The Court during the Later Roosevelt Years.** The focus of the Roosevelt administration and ultimately Court shifted considerably from economic reconstruction to national security issues with war raging in Europe and the Pacific. Roosevelt nominated Harlan Fiske Stone to replace retiring Charles Evans Hughes as chief justice in 1941. This was a great disappointment to Attorney General Robert Jackson whom Roosevelt had led to believe would succeed Hughes as chief justice.[191] Instead, Roosevelt elevated Stone from his associate justice seat, where he had served since 1925, to be chief justice and appointed Jackson to the associate justice position vacated by Stone. With war seeming imminent, Roosevelt thought it more prudent to apply a bipartisan gloss to his appointments by choosing Stone, who had first been appointed to the Court by Republican President Coolidge.[192] The sixty-eight-year-old Chief Justice Stone, unlike his predecessor, was more tolerant of dissent. Consequently, the rates of dissents tripled, with a higher rate of dissent continuing throughout this period.[193] His time on the Court was cut short by his death in 1946, making it the shortest tenure as chief justice since Oliver Ellsworth left the Court in 1799.

Also in 1941, Roosevelt nominated Senator James Byrnes from South Carolina. He remained an associate justice on the Court for only a short time, resigning in 1942 to serve as head of the Economic Stabilization Board and, later, the War Mobilization Board. In 1945, President Truman appointed Byrnes secretary of state, where he served until 1947. He would go on to be elected governor of South Carolina, holding that office from 1951 to 1955.

When James Byrnes left the Court in 1943, Justice Frankfurter lobbied for the nomination of Learned Hand.[194] Roosevelt reacted negatively to this unsolicited advice and appointed Wiley Rutledge to the Court in 1943 instead. As dean of the University of Iowa School of Law, Rutledge filled Roosevelt's objective to strengthen Western representation on the Court. Rutledge would join Murphy and Douglas in an alliance of liberal interests on the Court.

**Civil Rights and Civil Liberties in Wartime.** The rise of New Deal liberalism on the Supreme Court did not result in liberal interpretation of civil liberties during World War II. Even before the formal declaration of war, freedom of speech was curtailed by the Internal Security Act of 1940, otherwise known as the Smith Act. This law made it a crime to "knowingly or willingly advocate, abet, advise, or teach the duty, necessity, desirability, or propriety of overthrowing or destroying any government in the United States by force or violence." The Espionage Act of 1917 was amended to increase penalties for violations. During World War II, approximately 160 people were convicted under this law. It would be used in 1948 to imprison leaders of the American Communist Party and in 1953 to convict and execute Julius and Ethel Rosenberg for espionage.

**Japanese American Internment.** After the Japanese attack on Pearl Harbor, significant security measures were adopted by the administration. On February 19, 1942, Roosevelt signed Executive Order 9066 authorizing the secretary of war to establish "military areas" from which "any or all persons" could be removed. Subsequently, 120,000 people of Japanese ancestry, including seventy thousand U.S. citizens, were interned in "relocation" camps. The Court upheld the curfew orders and exclusionary orders for Japanese Americans issued by the regional military commander under the authority of Roosevelt's executive order in *Hirabayashi v. United States* (1943) and *Korematsu v. United States* (1944).[195]

In the *Korematsu* decision, Justice Black wrote for a 6-3 majority that though compulsory exclusion is "inconsistent with our basic governmental institutions," the exclusionary order "was commensurate with the threatened danger" of hostile forces and war. He denied that the exclusion was the result of "hostility to (Korematsu) or his race." Surprisingly, Justice William O. Douglas, later noted for his defense of individual liberty, joined the majority in *Korematsu*. Douglas would later publicly regret that he withdrew his initial dissent in the case. He also concurred with the majority in *Hirabayashi*. ACLU cofounder Felix Frankfurter also concurred with the majority in *Korematsu*.

Justices Murphy, Roberts, and Jackson dissented in *Korematsu*. Justice Murphy stated that the exclusion "goes over 'the very brink of constitutional power' and falls into the ugly abyss of racism." The case did not meet his judicial test of an "immediate, imminent, and impending" public danger sufficient to justify the curtailment of "ordinary constitutional processes." In *Hirabayashi*, Justice Murphy, though concurring with the holding, admonished the Court to beware of "invasions upon essential liberties . . . accompanied by pleas of urgent necessity advanced in good faith by responsible men."

Nevertheless, the urgency of war swayed the majority of the justices. Unlike Truman during the later *Steel Seizure* case, Roosevelt had the benefit of war powers bestowed by Congress and legislative authorization to exercise certain emergency measures. Though Justice Black continued to defend the decisions for the remainder of his life, others in government felt otherwise. In 1976, President Ford rescinded the executive order, with apologies to Japanese Americans. In 1988, Congress awarded reparations to former internees and their survivors.

**The German Saboteur Cases.** In addition to issues regarding the treatment of U.S. citizens of foreign heritage, the war also raised questions about the treatment of foreign prisoners, particularly saboteurs captured on American soil. Eight Germans who had been transported to Amagansett Beach, Long Island, and Jacksonville, Florida, by a U-boat with the intent to carry out acts of sabotage against factories and bridges were captured and charged with violating the laws of war. They were tried by a secret military tribunal, commissioned by executive order of President Roosevelt in 1942. The charges were based upon the U.S. military's Articles of War, the predecessor of the current Uniform Code of Military Justice. Appointed military defense counsels, such as Army Colonel Kenneth Royall, vigorously attacked the commission as unconstitutional, foreshadowing later criticisms of similar military tribunals used against captured members of al Qaeda and the Taliban after terrorist attacks in New York City and Washington, D.C.[196] One German defendant unsuccessfully claimed U.S. citizenship by virtue of his birth. The seven-man tribunal found the defendants guilty and sentenced them to death. Roosevelt granted clemency to two of the men, including George Dasch, the leader of the Long Island group who turned himself in to the FBI and led U.S. agents to the seven other would-be saboteurs.

Chief Justice Harlan Stone denied habeas corpus petitions for the German saboteurs while accepting the Court's right to review jurisdiction of the tribunal.[197] In *Ex Parte Quirin* (1942), the high Court upheld the trial and conviction of the saboteurs. The Court agreed that constitutional guarantees did not apply to foreign combatants charged with war crimes. Congress, in promulgating the Articles of War, acted under, among other things, constitutional authority to "define and punish offenses against the law of nations." Justice Frankfurter, who did not hide his disdain for the saboteurs, argued for a unanimous decision as an imperative to preserve U.S. military morale. But the secrecy of the trial that ensured protection of intelligence sources and methods also allowed the process to proceed with little opportunity for effective appeal. The Supreme Court's judgment was rendered twelve weeks after six of the men had been executed. The process had been so expedited that the would-be saboteurs were put to death by the electric chair less than two months after their landing on U.S. shores.[198]

**War Crimes Trials.** Roosevelt's appointees were not uniformly supportive of his war measures. Much of the resistance came from unexpected members of the Court. Justice Murphy was one the few justices to challenge wartime measures that he felt went too far. He dissented, along with Justice Wiley Rutledge, in the case of *In re Yamashita* (1946), over the trial and conviction by a military commission of the Japanese general under whose command atrocities against civilians in the Philippines, military prisoners of war, and others were committed during World War II.[199] In criticizing the fairness of trial by a commission of five general officers without legal experience, Murphy stated, "By this flexible method a victorious nation may convict and execute any and all leaders of a vanquished foe, depending on the prevailing degree of vengeance and the absence of any objective judicial review." General Tomoyuki Yamashita claimed that he had no direct knowledge of activities in violation of the laws of war. Nevertheless, the Court upheld the conviction and sentence by a 6-2 majority. The Court's majority supported the tribunal's principle that as a field commander, the general would be held accountable for activities of troops under his command regardless of whether he had direct knowledge of them or not. Only eight justices were serving at the time, since Justice Jackson was on a leave of absence from the Court to serve as U.S. prosecutor for the International Military Tribunal in Nuremberg, Germany.

**Other War Cases.** Cases later decided concerning wartime matters portended a future shift in sentiment among certain justices who had in the past solidly supported expansive governmental power under New Deal programs. In 1950, the Court was called upon to decide upon the applicability of the right of habeas corpus to German agents. Lothar Eisentrager and twenty other Germans were convicted by a special overseas U.S. military commission of conducting wartime activities against the United States after the surrender of Germany while operating in a German intelligence office in Shanghai, China. In *Johnson v. Eisentrager*, a 6-3 majority ruled in favor of the commission, based upon Solicitor General Philip Perlman's argument that federal courts only had the authority to issue writs of habeas corpus within their respective jurisdictions in the United States. But Justices Black, Burton, and Douglas dissented, siding with the U.S. Court of Appeals which had held that the Constitution applies to the conduct of U.S. officials everywhere, not just on U.S. territory. This case would reemerge from obscurity in 2003 while the Court considered the constitutionality of the Patriot Act's powers to try foreigners as illegal combatants without the benefit of constitutional protections.[200]

**Growth of Substantive Equal Protection.** Despite Justice Stone's opinion in the *Carolene Products* case, the Court continued to give an expansive interpretation of the equal protection clause of the Fourteenth Amendment well beyond "discrete and insular minorities." In the 1942 decision of *Skinner v. Oklahoma*, the Court overturned a sterilization law for habitual criminals on the grounds that it was "uncivilized."[201] The Court retained the right to apply a more scrutinizing standard where "fundamental constitutional values" were at stake. The use of imprecise, nonjusticiable standards like "uncivilized" to strike down state statutes would later be criticized by Judge Bork because it would "embed in the Constitution the judge's notions of public policy."[202] Over time, a majority would emerge on the Court that supported broader interpretations of both the equal protection clause and the due process clause of the Fourteenth Amendment.

**The Early Truman Years: A Court Divided.** In 1945, Truman nominated Senator Harold Burton from Ohio to the Court to fill a vacancy left by Owen J. Roberts's departure. Burton would later be part of the majority supporting desegregation of public schools and transportation. He would remain on the Court until 1958, when replaced by Potter Stewart.

In the 1945 case of *Jewell Ridge Coal Corporation v. Local 6167, UMW*, the Court in a 5-4 vote upheld the United Mine Workers union's interpretation of the Fair Labor Standards Act.[203] In a petition for rehearing, lawyers for the mining company argued that Justice Black, who voted with the majority, should have recused himself from the case because the union case had been argued by a former law partner of Black's. Although there was general agreement of the justices on the Court to deny the petition, Justice Jackson (who had dissented in the original case) and Justice Frankfurter questioned the propriety of Black's sitting on a case for which he had a perceivable conflict of interest.[204] Without attention by the public, Chief Justice Stone attempted unsuccessfully to mollify differences between the justices who had sided with Justice Black and those who had sided with Justices Jackson and Frankfurter.

In 1946, Chief Justice Harlan Stone died. Truman nominated Frederick M. Vinson to replace him as chief justice. He had been a congressman from Kentucky who was later appointed to the U.S. Circuit Court of Appeals for the District of Columbia by Roosevelt. Vinson served on that court for five years. President Truman appointed him secretary of the treasury in 1945. Despite the conciliatory skills for which Truman selected him for the chief justice position, Vinson was unable to bridge the bitter personal and ideological divide on the Court following the *Jewell Ridge* case.[205] He presided over the Court until 1953.

Justice Jackson, who still harbored hopes of being elevated to the position of chief justice, was disappointed by Truman's selection of Vinson. The internal controversy over *Jewell Ridge* had ended Jackson's prospects for the post. At the time of Vinson's appointment, Jackson had already spent nine months away from the Court on a leave of absence to serve as the chief U.S. prosecutor to the Nuremberg trials in Germany. He returned to the Supreme Court for the term beginning in October 1946.

Douglas still entertained political ambitions but declined President Truman's offer to be his running mate in 1948. Douglas, with not-so-distant memories of Roosevelt's selection of Truman over himself in 1944, did not want to be "second fiddle to a second fiddle."[206] Douglas would undergo a personal transformation in the next few years, with the breakup of his first marriage and liberation from the immediate pursuit of political office. In cases dealing with prosecution of Communist Party members and wire surveillance, he began to deviate from his progovernment stance of the *Korematsu* era to defend individual civil liberties. He would often find himself allied with Justice Hugo Black on such cases.

In 1949, Truman nominated Attorney General Tom C. Clark and Sherman Minton to associate justice seats on the Court, replacing justices Frank Murphy and Wiley Rutledge. Clark had been appointed attorney general by Truman in 1945. But Clark would greatly anger Truman by siding against the president in the *Steel Seizure* case in 1952. Reflecting his disappointment, Truman later commented that "it isn't so much that he's a bad man. It's just that he's such a dumb son of a bitch."[207] Clark would serve on the Court until 1967. Minton served on the Court until 1956.

**Executive Powers: The *Steel Seizure* Case.** Even when a president has the benefit of a Supreme Court consisting of nine justices appointed by himself and his predecessor, of the same political party, he is not assured of prevailing in the Court. This was the case for President Truman in the *Steel Seizure* case of 1952. Truman's popularity waned with the rise of the McCarthy era, the fall of China to the communists in 1949, the emergent Red Scare, and the Korean War. In Truman's last full year as president, the Court's decision in *Youngstown Sheet & Tube Company v. Sawyer* represented a serious setback for presidential powers during wartime, as the Court ruled that Truman had usurped legislative authority when he ordered seizure of the steel mills during the Korean conflict. Although the president acted in the sincere belief that his action to bring an end to a labor dispute that crippled the industry was justified, six justices of the Court disagreed that the president had powers to seize industrial property without congressional approval. As evidence against these assumed powers, the Court took note of Congress's explicit rejection of such a power during the deliberations leading up to the passage of the Taft-Hartley Labor Relations Act. Truman had decided to ignore Taft-Hartley provisions allowing the president to impose a sixty-day cooling-off period in industrial disputes in order to postpone a strike. Truman's attorneys argued that in a national emergency, the president could do anything not explicitly prohibited by Congress or the Constitution. Writing for the Court, Justice Black declared that "the president's power to see that the laws are faithfully executed refutes the idea that he is to be a lawmaker."

The lack of an explicit congressional declaration of war or authorization of war powers was an added dimension of the issue of war powers. In the background was the debate over whether the conflict in Korea was a war, within the meaning of the Constitution and statutory law. The United Nations Charter embodied the philosophy of the Kellogg-Briand Pact of 1929 which "abolished" war as an instrument of national policy, at least as a matter of law. Congress had rejected a call for a declaration of war, referring to the United Nations response to North Korean aggression as a "police action." The nature of "war powers" in a "nonwar" situation without legislative authorization was one concern. Another issue, even accepting presidential powers to conduct a war, was the question of how far war powers extended. In essence, the Court reasoned that the steel mills were too far removed from inherent executive wartime powers such as applied to commander-in-chief authority over the military or negotiations with foreign governments. Like the Civil War case of *Milligan*, the Court ruled that presidential authority had extended too far from the battlefield to warrant constitutional validation. Franklin Roosevelt seized the North American Aviation plant at Inglewood, California, and property of Montgomery Ward. The latter seizure was overturned by the courts, albeit after the war was over. The Court continued to set a high bar for seizures of private property in wartime. Such actions were viewed by Justice Hugo Black as "suspect" and thus susceptible to a higher level of scrutiny, a standard that would later be applied to laws that curtailed the civil rights of specific groups or classes of people.

**The McCarthy Era and Civil Liberties.** Churchill's Fulton, Missouri, speech in 1946 on the descent of an "iron curtain" upon Eastern Europe, the fall of China to Mao Tse-tung's communists in 1949, and the Korean War in 1949 all heralded a new "red scare" in the United States, more virulent than the one following the First World War and the emergence of the world's first Communist state. Justice William O. Douglas would raise the ire of his fellow justices by granting a temporary stay of the executions of Julius and Ethel Rosenberg for passing nuclear secrets to the Soviets. California congressman Richard Nixon led an inquiry against a senior State Department advisor, Alger Hiss, who had been a law clerk to Oliver Wendell Holmes, for passing confidential diplomatic information to the Soviets. In pursuit of communists and sympathizers, aggressive tactics seriously challenged civil liberties and civil rights. Senator Joseph McCarthy used Senate hearings as a platform to launch accusations, often unfounded, against alleged communist sympathizers and infiltrators. But in 1954, McCarthy's momentum faltered when he accused the secretary of the army's office of assisting foreign espionage activities. The general counsel of the army issued a stinging rebuke. McCarthy was himself investigated on charges that he made threats against the army when it failed to provide preferential treatment for one of his former unpaid consultants who had been drafted. Though McCarthy was cleared of the charges, the Senate itself censured McCarthy for his tactics. He never regained his stature in the Senate and died in 1957.

One can perhaps see the rise and fall of McCarthyism in decisions of the Court, comparing for example the 1951 decision of *Dennis v. United States*[208] with the 1957 decision of *Yates v. United States.*[209] In *Dennis*, Eugene Dennis and ten colleagues of the Communist Party of the United States had been convicted under the Smith Act, which made it a crime to "knowingly or willingly advocate, abet, advise, or teach the duty, necessity, desirability, or propriety of overthrowing or destroying any government in the United States by force or violence." The convictions were upheld in a plurality decision written by Chief Justice Vinson, adopting a "clear and probable danger" test applied by Second Circuit Court of Appeals Chief Judge Learned Hand. As Chief

Justice Vinson stated in *Dennis*, "In each case (courts) must ask whether the gravity of the 'evil' discounted by its improbability justifies such invasion of free speech as necessary to avoid the danger."[210]

This new standard was less broad than Holmes's "clear and present danger" standard applied in the 1919 *Schenck* case, instead requiring an inquiry into the "gravity of evil" and its probability before justifying an abridgement of freedom of speech. Justices Black and Douglas dissented, critical of what in their view was the Court's plurality decision to uphold a conviction for mere advocacy of the overthrow of government without evidence of an actual attempt to carry it out.

But in *Yates*, the Supreme Court's majority sounded more like Black's and Douglas's dissent in *Dennis*. Though *Dennis* was not overruled, Harlan wrote for the Court that the words in question must be more than just abstract declarations "remote from concrete action" in order to uphold a conviction under the Smith Act. Instead, the words must be "calculated to 'incite' persons to action for the forcible overthrow of the government." In subsequent years, the Court increasingly distinguished between nominal and active membership in organizations advocating overthrow of the U.S. government. In *Scales v. United States* (1961),[211] a majority on the Court upheld the membership provision of the Smith Act, finding that the act impliedly required specific intent, conspiracy, or overt acts, rather than mere association or membership. But though the Court's interpretation of the Smith Act allowed the provision to stand, the Court stated that mere membership in an organization that advocated the violent overthrow of the U.S. government was not enough to sustain a conviction.

**In Retrospective: The Court's Role in War and the Cold War.** Presidents Roosevelt and Truman appointed justices intending them to be supportive of expansive governmental powers to enable the executive to act in the face of the Depression, war, and subversion. But ardent New Deal supporters, such as Black and Douglas, over time came to disagree with unrestricted governmental powers. When later joined by new justices on the Court, these dissenters would form the core of a new majority focused on protecting civil liberties.

# Chapter 7

## THE WARREN COURT: 1953-1969

*The Warren Court years demonstrate that after a president makes a nomination to the Supreme Court which is confirmed by the Senate, the chief executive has limited power to influence decisions of that justice. President Eisenhower was very disappointed with two appointments, one of whom had solid Republican credentials, albeit with bipartisan appeal. One of President Kennedy's appointments went on to be markedly conservative over the course of his long tenure on the Court. President Johnson's nominee to be chief justice, a close political affiliate and friend, would be forced to resign from the Court. Institutional separation would keep the Court in a different realm from the politics of the other branches of government.*

**Eisenhower Shapes the Court.** The election of Dwight Eisenhower to the presidency in the wake of the Red Scare and the Joseph McCarthy era ironically aided the development of civil rights and liberties. The death of Chief Justice Fred Vinson in 1953 gave Eisenhower his first appointment of five to the Court. He chose Earl Warren. Eisenhower would later describe the nomination as "the biggest damn fool mistake I ever made." But at the time of his nomination, Warren did not seem like a bad choice. He was an icon of the Republican Party, a popular governor of California, a former vice presidential candidate, and a key supporter of Eisenhower's presidential nomination.

Warren came with an unusual mix of qualifications for the role of chief justice. He was elected attorney general of California in 1938, with a solid crime-fighting reputation earned through his vigorous prosecution of racketeers in the state. He was elected governor of California in 1942 and reelected in 1946 and 1950 with substantial bipartisan support (with the unique circumstance of having nominations from both parties). But Warren's party upbringing differed from many Republicans. His formative years were influenced by the progressive Republicanism of California governor Hiram Johnson, who in 1910-11 championed direct democracy in that state through the innovative devices of initiative, referendum, and recall. Giving the citizens the right to initiate legislation, to revoke legislation, and to recall elected officials was a reaction against nineteenth-century California politics, where an oligarchy of powerful big business interests, such as the Union Pacific Railroad, dominated the legislative process at the expense of small business owners and workers. It was more akin to the Republicanism of Wisconsin governor Robert La Follette and President Theodore Roosevelt, who had fought corruption and the excesses of the large trusts, than to the Republicanism of William Taft, who was more friendly to big business interests. As governor, Warren championed many reforms in government, from hospital and prison administration to old-age and unemployment compensation. But Warren's apparent libertarianism and egalitarianism were absent when it came to his overt support for wartime measures for the relocation of Japanese Americans. That action stood in marked contrast to much of the rest of his government service.

In 1948, Warren ran for vice president as the running mate of New York prosecutor Thomas E. Dewey on the Republican ticket. At the 1952 Republican convention, the popular Warren threw his support behind Eisenhower for the Republican Party's presidential candidacy, assuring Eisenhower's place as the party candidate.

The Red Scare also inspired opportunists in Congress to change the composition of the Court. In 1953, a resolution was introduced in the House to impeach Douglas in response to his issuance of a temporary stay of the executions of Julius and Ethel Rosenberg, who had been convicted of spying for the Soviet Union.[212] The resolution failed to garner sufficient support. Douglas would survive to side with Warren in a series of cases significantly expanding civil liberties.

During Eisenhower's two terms in office, he would appoint, in addition to Warren, four other justices: John Marshall Harlan in 1955, William J. Brennan, Jr., in 1956, Charles Whittaker in 1957, and Potter Stewart in 1958, owing to the death of Robert Jackson in 1954 and the departures of Justices Minton, Reed, and Burton in that respective order. With the gradual change in composition of the Court, particularly the addition of Brennan to the Court in 1956, the Court brought more attention to the rights of criminal defendants and racial minorities, freedom of expression, and separation of church and state. Eisenhower was later surprised at the unexpected "liberality" of his appointments to the Court. When he was later asked if he had any regrets about his tenure as president, he was heard to say, "Yes, and both of them are sitting on the Supreme Court," referring to Warren and Brennan. Harvard professor Laurence Tribe, in support of his thesis of "the myth of the surprised president" in his book *God Save This Honorable Court,* argues that Eisenhower should not have been surprised by the performance of Warren considering his apparent record of "progressive views, independence of mind, and broad appeal to Democrats."[213]

Others are more forgiving of Eisenhower's genuine surprise by the performance of his appointments, since few would have predicted the turn the Court took toward civil rights and civil liberties. Warren's record prior to serving on the Court, especially his approval of the internment of Japanese Americans under his tenure as governor of California, was not consistently libertarian. Brennan, who was selected to boost Eisenhower's reelection bid with the workers and Irish Americans, reflected his modest working-class background. Brennan would eventually become an ally of Douglas in civil rights and civil liberties cases.

In all, the addition of Warren and Brennan aided the growth of civil liberties and civil rights that had already begun with the influence of two long-term FDR appointees: Hugo Black and William O. Douglas. Though they both supported the decision in *Korematsu,* they emerged over time as champions of civil liberties and civil rights. Together, all four justices would form the bulwark of a movement within the Court that would transform constitutional rights.

**Civil Rights: The *Brown* Decision and Desegregation.** By 1954, the political movement toward desegregation was well under way, though actual desegregation was decades away. African American veterans returning from service in World War II were less willing to accept degrading treatment, spurring renewed interest in desegregation. In 1946, NAACP attorney Thurgood Marshall secured a Supreme Court ruling that segregation in interstate travel was unconstitutional in *Morgan v. Commonwealth of Virginia.*[214] The NAACP, with Marshall's assistance, successfully challenged Texas's segregation of law schools in *Sweatt v. Painter* in 1950.[215] The course was set for a direct challenge to *Plessy.*

By 1949, Truman had ordered desegregation of the military through an executive order. Many federal schools were already desegregated, but Truman was reluctant to challenge segregation in local schools. Fresh in his memory was the "Dixiecrat" breakaway from the Democratic Party in 1948. Southern Democrats, unhappy with the civil rights portion of the Democratic Party's platform, walked out of the party's convention in Philadelphia and held their own counterconvention in Birmingham, Alabama. The States' Rights Democrats, as they came to be known, nominated then-South Carolina governor Strom Thurmond (a former U.S. senator and state circuit court judge), who carried much of the South. Thurmond nearly cost Truman the election to Republican Thomas Dewey (whose running mate was Earl Warren). Though Thurmond would later serve in the Senate again as a Democrat, he switched to the Republican Party in 1964, backing the presidential bid of Barry Goldwater.

With this background, the Court reached one of its greatest countermajoritarian decisions in the case of *Brown vs. Board of Education of Topeka (et alia)* in 1954, overturning public school segregation. The case had originally come to the Court in 1951 but was held past the 1952 presidential election and then consolidated with four other cases.[216] The unexpected death of Chief Justice Vinson in his sleep in 1953 and the arrival of Earl Warren broke the deadlock on how to proceed with the case. The Court had been divided up to that point, with Black and Douglas pressing most strongly for desegregation while Justices Stanley Reed and Robert Jackson were initially opposed. Warren may have lacked the scholarship credentials of many of his colleagues, but his personal persuasiveness, leadership ability, and talent at consensus building helped bring together a remarkably unanimous decision of the Court in *Brown.* It almost turned out differently. Reed, who hailed from Kentucky, had his clerks prepare a dissenting opinion for him; but Warren convinced him of the importance of solidarity of the Court on this subject.[217] Announcing the decision, Chief Justice Warren read,

> In approaching this problem, we cannot turn the clock back to 1868 when the (Fourteenth) Amendment was adopted, or even to 1896 when *Plessy v. Ferguson* was written. We must consider public education in the light of its full development and present place in American life throughout the nation . . . We conclude that in the field of public education, the doctrine of "separate but equal" has no place. Separate education facilities are inherently unequal.

Thus, the lone dissenter in *Plessy v. Ferguson,* John Marshall Harlan's grandfather and namesake, was vindicated. The Court had considered earlier cases litigated by the NAACP, including the 1938 decision in *Missouri ex rel. Gaines v. Canada,* where the Court had rejected state funding for African Americans to attend law schools outside the state rather than providing for law schools for African Americans in the state, and the 1950 decision in *Sweatt v. Painter,* where the Court held that the separate law school provided for Negroes in Texas violated the equal protection clause of the Fourteenth Amendment.[218] The Court in *Brown* went further by rejecting state efforts at equalization as a legitimate means to meet the requirements of the Constitution.

The unanimous decision of the Court did not bring about wide acceptance with the public. Nor did the Court's 1955 ruling that school boards use "all deliberate speed" in integrating schools hasten implementation. Border states complied within a few years, but segregation in the Deep South continued for decades after the decision. In 1956, ninety-six Southern members of Congress signed a "Southern Manifesto," protesting the *Brown* decision and foretelling official action to resist desegregation. Many states openly defied the Court. In 1962, Alabama's governor George Wallace, upon election with the largest popular vote in that state's history, defiantly proclaimed, "I draw the line in the dust and toss the gauntlet before the feet of tyranny, and I say, segregation now, segregation tomorrow, segregation forever." Associate Justice Hugo Black, the former senator from Alabama, would be shunned by his Southern colleagues and did not return to his college reunions for years afterward. Resistance to the Court's decision would continue for decades.

Though a majority of the American public came to accept the Court's decision over time, the Eisenhower and the Kennedy administrations resorted to force to gain compliance in selected cases, albeit reluctantly. Despite an initial decision not to use troops to enforce the *Brown* decision, Eisenhower changed his mind when it came to integration efforts in Little Rock, Arkansas, in 1957. Arkansas governor Orval Faubus mobilized the state's National Guard around Little Rock's Central High School to prevent integration.[219] With the governor threatening that "blood will run in the streets," with a student being turned away at bayonet point, with increasing violence, and with repeated pleas to the president from Little Rock Mayor Woodrow Mann (who accused Faubus of stirring up violent mobs), Eisenhower federalized the National Guard in Arkansas and ordered the 101st Airborne from Fort Campbell, Kentucky, to go to Little Rock.[220] The high school graduated its first black student in 1959, though subsequent fights in lower courts delayed further implementation of the Supreme Court's decision.

The struggle to enforce the *Brown* decision continued into the next administration. President John F. Kennedy came to office with a priority to keep the allegiance of increasingly alienated Southern legislators but was compelled to use troops to desegregate the University of Mississippi in 1962. By the tenth anniversary of the *Brown* decision, less than 10 percent of blacks in the Deep South went to integrated schools.[221] It became increasingly obvious that compliance with the Supreme Court's decision would require an approach more comprehensive than executive force applied through the use of troops. Legislation was needed to support and encourage integration. Such legislation, in the form of the Civil Rights Act of 1964, was initiated by the Kennedy administration but was skillfully shepherded through Congress by (former Senate majority leader) Lyndon Johnson, who succeeded to the presidency after the assassination of Kennedy. It provided authority to withhold federal funds from state and local institutions. Congress also passed the Voting Rights Act of 1965, effectively enfranchising blacks who had been denied the right to vote under ruses like literacy tests, despite the existence of the Fifteenth Amendment to the Constitution (1870) which gave former slaves the right to vote. There were follow-up decisions of the Supreme Court on related issues such as busing in *Swann v. Charlotte-Mecklenburg* (1971). It took twenty years after the decision until 90 percent compliance was achieved. Full compliance would continue to be elusive, as evidenced by the return of litigants to the Supreme Court questioning whether Topeka had actually desegregated, thirty-seven years after the *Brown* case.

In the end, the Court depended upon the other branches of government to enforce and implement its decision. It took the successive efforts of Presidents Eisenhower, Kennedy, and Johnson, as well as the support of Congress, over twenty years to prevail. Nevertheless, without the Supreme Court's decision in *Brown,* it is unlikely that desegregation would have happened as soon as it did. Truman's limited efforts at desegregation had nearly split the Democratic Party. Congress could have conceivably drafted a law under the Fourteenth Amendment but was equally reluctant. It would be ten years after *Brown* that Congress would pass the Civil Rights Act of 1964 and the Voting Rights Act of 1965. The Court led the way perhaps because of the failure of the other branches of government to deal with it, much like the issue of abortion in *Roe v. Wade* in 1973.

**The Kennedy Years.** When Senator John F. Kennedy received the Democratic Party's nomination for president in 1960, Justice William O. Douglas was disappointed. He had believed that Senate Majority Leader Lyndon Johnson, who also contended for the nomination, would have chosen him as his running mate had he secured the party's nomination. Though Douglas had turned down an earlier opportunity to run with Truman, he still had political ambitions, however unrealistic they might have been. But Douglas's belated recognition that no opportunity to serve in political office would be coming his way left him free to pursue his own agenda on and off the Court. On the Court, he would further expand upon individual rights and would promote environmental rights, a newly emerging area of law. Off the Court, he continued his prolific writing, promoting his personal causes. In the course of his lifetime, he would produce over thirty books.

Though as a senator and presidential candidate Kennedy was critical of Adlai Stevenson and his allied "liberals" in the Democratic Party who had twice lost to the Republicans,[222] Kennedy as president added to the new liberal trend on the Court that had already emerged under the Eisenhower administration. In 1962, Kennedy appointed Byron White and Arthur Goldberg to the Court. Both came from other positions within the Kennedy administration. White was the type of person Kennedy admired, a high-achieving scholar and athlete. Kennedy had first met White when the latter was a Rhodes scholar in the United Kingdom and the former resided at the Court of St. James with his father, Joseph Kennedy, U.S. ambassador to Great Britain prior to the Second World War. White had been an all-American football player from the University of Colorado and 1938 National Football League rookie of the year. He decided to forego a professional sports career in favor of a career in law. White served as deputy attorney general under Robert Kennedy at the Justice Department. Goldberg had been Kennedy's labor secretary. The appointments of White and Goldberg were a major turning point, leading to the heyday of the Warren Court.

**The Civil Rights Movement.** Civil rights continued to be a major issue. The Kennedy administration feared the kind of reprisals that Truman, the previous Democratic Party president, had experienced. Their reticence was criticized by NAACP Legal Defense and Education Fund (LDF) attorney Thurgood Marshall, who noted the administration's failure to propose any civil rights legislation in its first one hundred days.[223] He viewed both John Kennedy and his brother Robert, who had been appointed attorney general, as lacking a genuine commitment to civil rights.[224] But later in 1961, Robert Kennedy, recognizing Marshall's prominence as a civil rights lawyer, would offer Marshall a nomination for a seat on a federal district court. Marshall felt he deserved better and declined.[225] With an intense lobbying campaign by Louis Martin, the ranking African American at the Democratic National Committee, and the withdrawal of consideration by another potential nominee, Marshall was offered the nomination for the U.S. Second Circuit Court of Appeals in New York; and he accepted. President Kennedy made the nomination a week before the Senate Judiciary Committee went out of session, facilitating Marshall's being seated before opponents had a serious chance to challenge the appointment.[226]

In 1963, the Supreme Court ordered the University of Mississippi to admit African American student James Meredith. But Kennedy's cautious endorsement of the

Meredith decision led the new governor of Alabama, George Wallace, to defy Attorney General Robert Kennedy's integration orders for the University of Alabama.[227] The president and his brother were not enthusiastic supporters of Martin Luther King's 1963 civil rights rally in Washington, asking the leaders not to march.[228] They feared it would cause race riots and told the leaders that the march would endanger the civil rights bill pending in Congress. Yet Kennedy continued to back the legislation that would eventually become the Civil Rights Act of 1964, mandating integration of public accommodations. It would take the legislative skill and arm-twisting of his successor and former senate majority leader, Lyndon Johnson, to get the controversial legislation through Congress. After Kennedy's assassination, Marshall was more forgiving and favorable in his assessment of the late president.[229]

**Civil Rights: Criminal Law.** The early sixties witnessed increased constitutional scrutiny in the area of criminal law and procedure. The Court unanimously upheld the right to counsel for indigent defendants in *Gideon v. Wainwright* (1963).[230] The case involved a rare grant of certiorari in response to an in forma pauperis petition from a prisoner. The Court in *Mapp v. Ohio* (1961)[231] applied the exclusionary rule, excluding evidence (criminal obscenity charges) seized in violation of the Fourth Amendment, to the states via the Fourteenth Amendment, which applied the requirement of "due process" to the states. In *Miranda v. Arizona* (1966),[232] the Court by a 5-4 vote required the advisement of rights by law enforcement officials before questioning suspects in criminal cases. These rights included the right to the assistance of counsel during questioning and the right to remain silent. Such decisions, which required creative interpretations of the Constitution, led to heavy criticism of the Court by Congress and the public.

**Federalism and State Issues.** In *Baker v. Carr* (1962),[233] the Court was called upon to consider the manner in which the size and shape of representational districts would be determined, an issue with large political implications. Voters in Tennessee had filed a federal class action lawsuit, alleging malapportionment in the drawing of legislative districts, resulting in more representation for certain districts with fewer people. A 6-2 plurality held in favor of the plaintiffs. In an opinion written by Brennan, the Court articulated the principle of "one person, one vote" for the restructuring of state governments, based upon the equal protection clause of the Fourteenth Amendment. Among others, Chief Justice Warren had strong feelings about the inequities of districts he was familiar with in his native California.

Justices Frankfurter and Harlan dissented, with the former accusing the majority of "asserting destructively novel judicial power" beyond that sanctioned by the Constitution. Applying the political question doctrine in support of states' rights, he decried the Court's inserting itself into "political entanglements" that remain the province of state legislatures to resolve. He stated that since this type of apportionment was not practiced by states at the time of the Fourteenth Amendment, the Court could not later insert such a requirement into the Constitution. He pointed out that Article IV, Section 4 only guarantees a "republican form of government," not specific methods of apportionment. Bork commented that a consequence of this decision was not help for inner cities as intended but increased the representation for the suburbs instead.[234] Bork's position on *Baker v. Carr* later became a basis for criticism by senators during his confirmation hearings. Members of Congress who were angry with the Court's decision sponsored a bill in 1964 that proposed to remove federal jurisdiction over state legislative apportionment. The bill passed the House but foundered for lack of support in the Senate. States felt the pressure of increasing federal scrutiny in the area of criminal law as well. In the course of several cases, Justice Black with the assistance of like-minded colleagues on the Court would attempt to apply all of the Bill of Rights to the states via the due process clause of the Fourteenth Amendment. The effort could be seen in the area of criminal law, with *Mapp v. Ohio* (1961)[235] applying the exclusionary rule applied to states. Increasingly in the minority, Justices Harlan, Frankfurter, and Whittaker dissented, critical of the lack of "the sense of judicial restraint."

**Church and State: School Prayer.** At the intersection of religion, politics, and federalism, lay the issue of school prayer. The issue would prove to be divisive both on and off the Court. In particular, the states resented efforts to apply the establishment clause of the First Amendment to local schools and governmental activities. That amendment states that "Congress shall make no law respecting an establishment of religion or prohibiting the free exercise thereof." Though the amendment does not use the terminology "separation of church and state," that interpretation was popularized by Thomas Jefferson, the author of Virginia's statute for religious freedom and a fighter for church-state separation.[236] Jefferson was not always a strong secularist, but exposure to French anticlericalism and political barbs from New England ministers solidified his feelings about the necessity to separate religion from politics.[237] In *Engel v. Vitale* (1962), the Court ruled by a 6-1 vote that public schools may not require students to recite a state-composed school prayer.[238] The New York Board of Regents' policy had provided for public schools to begin each day with children to voluntarily reciting a generic prayer. Justice Black wrote for the majority that "in this country, it is no part of the business of government to compose official prayer." Justice Potter Stewart dissented, maintaining that the practice had not "established an 'official religion' within the meaning of the establishment clause" of the First Amendment. The next year, the Court banned Bible reading and the reciting of the Lord's Prayer in the public schools of Pennsylvania and Maryland in the companion cases of *Abington School District v. Schempp* (1963)[239] and *Murray v. Curlett* (1963).[240]

Congress attempted to overcome the Court's objection by sponsoring a constitutional amendment. This school prayer amendment failed in the Senate in 1966 and 1984, as well as in the House in 1971. The amendment process is difficult with two-thirds of each house required along with three-quarters of the states. In 1979, a bill to remove jurisdiction over school prayer also failed. During his 1980 presidential election campaign, Ronald Reagan called upon Congress to revive the school prayer amendment but did not succeed in getting congressional action.

**The Johnson Years.** Before President Johnson could move forward on his Great Society programs, he had to deal with issues as a result of events during the previous administration. In 1963, President Johnson selected Earl Warren to head the investigation into the assassination of President Kennedy because of Warren's reputation for integrity and bipartisan support. Warren was still sitting as chief justice when appointed to the commission, despite the potential for conflict between the roles. The report produced by the Warren Commission concluded the assassination was the work of Lee Harvey Oswald working alone and not part of a broader conspiracy. The report has been much criticized; and many questions surrounding the assassination and the investigation remain unanswered, despite a congressional reinvestigation of the matter in the 1970s. Attacks on the validity of the report aside, the use of sitting justices to conduct investigations that could lead to criminal charges and potential appeals to the Supreme Court is dubious. Like John Jay's role in the production of the unpopular Jay Treaty or Robert Jackson's role as U.S. prosecutor in the criticized international tribunal at Nuremberg, such nonjudicial assignments for sitting justices away from the Court, even under the cloak of a temporary "leave of absence," seldom inure to the benefit of the Court's reputation for independence, nonpartisanship, and fairness.

Justice Goldberg left the Court in 1965 to accept Johnson's nomination to be U.S. ambassador to the United Nations and would unsuccessfully run for the office of governor of New York State in 1970. He was replaced by longtime Johnson confidant Abraham "Abe" Fortas, who continued the liberal trend and perhaps represented its high-water mark. Fortas was a widely known Washington attorney who had successfully represented Earl Gideon in the landmark decision of *Gideon v. Wainwright* concerning the right to counsel. He had been and would continue to be a close advisor to President Johnson. But Fortas's nomination for the chief justice seat would become his undoing in 1968 when conflict of interest allegations were raised.

One undisputed legacy of President Johnson was his commitment to civil rights. The former Texas senator was instrumental in the passage of the Civil Rights Act of 1964, the Voting Rights Act of 1965, and the Fair Housing Act of 1968. In 1967, Associate Justice Tom C. Clark stepped down from the Court in order to allow his son Ramsey to take the post of attorney general with the Johnson administration. According to one account, Johnson engineered this shift of Clark family positions not only because Johnson favored Ramsey, the well-educated, liberal Texan, as attorney general over the incumbent Nicholas Katzenbach, but also because he wanted to open up a vacancy in order to place an African American on the Court by 1968.[241]

Johnson had for a long time considered nominating Solicitor General Thurgood Marshall, a star NAACP attorney and successful advocate in the *Brown* case, to sit on the Court. Marshall held a near-legendary status as a civil rights attorney, with three decades of litigation experience fighting segregation, including in the Deep South, where his life had been threatened on several occasions.[242] He had been the key architect of the successful NAACP litigation effort and strategy to end segregation in a series of cases leading up to the *Brown* decision, challenging segregation's legal basis methodically and incrementally. In 1961, President Kennedy appointed him to the U.S. Second Circuit Court of Appeals. Johnson appointed Marshall solicitor general in 1965. The first African American solicitor general was confirmed by the full Senate without debate.[243] By the time of his nomination for the Supreme Court, he had argued thirty-two cases before the Court, including fourteen cases as solicitor general.[244] Unlike White, Goldberg, and Fortas, who each went from nomination to confirmation within fourteen days or less, Marshall's confirmation would take seventy-eight days.[245] Johnson used his ample skills in maneuvering the nomination through the Senate, despite much lingering resistance on Capitol Hill. Senators Sam Ervin, Strom Thurmond, James Eastland, and John McClelland led a six-hour "mini-filibuster" against the nomination.[246] But in a cleverly devised strategy, Johnson persuaded twenty senators not to vote at all, rather than vote against his nominee. Marshall was confirmed as the first African American on the U.S. Supreme Court by a Senate vote of 69-11.

**Civil Rights: Voting.** The Court dealt with the issue of poll taxes in the case of *Harper v. Virginia State Board of Elections.* [247] Douglas said the right to vote was a "fundamental interest" like the right to procreate in *Skinner.* Such fundamental interests were subject to close scrutiny. As such, taxes on voting activity was deemed an impermissible limitation on the right to vote. Douglas went on to state that "notions" of equality under the Fourteenth Amendment "do change." Justices Black, Harlan, and Stewart dissented.

In *Katzenbach v. Morgan* (1966), the Court reviewed the federal Voting Rights Act of 1965 which declared that the right to vote could not be denied to anyone based on inability to speak English (if they completed sixth grade in Puerto Rico).[248] It invalidated a New York state law which required an ability to speak and write English without conditions. Justice Brennan, writing for the majority, stated that the federal statute "had redefined the meaning of Fourteenth Amendment equal protection." Critics of the decision, such as Justice Harlan, who dissented, and later observers like Robert Bork, argue that the Constitution Article I, Section 2 provides states with the authority to set requirements for voting and that the Court is, in effect, upholding Congress's power to change the Constitution by statute.[249] The Court, however, found that Congress had a basis on which to conclude that the New York literacy requirement was invidiously discriminatory and therefore had the authority to invoke the law under existing interpretations of the Fourteenth Amendment. The debate would continue over the Court's and Congress's authority to put new meaning into parts of the Constitution.

**Civil Rights: A Constitutional Right to Privacy?** In the 1965 decision of *Griswold v. Connecticut,* the Court overturned a state statute under which Estelle Griswold and Dr. C. Lee Buxton, the executive director and medical director of Planned Parenthood

League respectively, were convicted of providing information and medical advice on the use of contraceptives to married persons.[250] Reminiscent of the "right to be left alone" mentioned by Justice Brandeis in his dissent in *Olmstead v. United States,* Justice Douglas described a "zone of privacy" implicit within the First, Third, Fourth, Fifth, and Ninth Amendments to the Constitution. Writing for the Court, he declared that

> The First Amendment has a penumbra where privacy is protected from governmental intrusion. In that context, we have protected forms of "association" that are not political in the customary sense but pertain to the social, legal, and economic benefit of the members . . . cases suggest that specific guarantees in the Bill of Rights have penumbras, formed by emanations from those guarantees that help give them life and substance.

He provided a disclaimer that "we do not sit as a superlegislature." Justices Goldberg, Brennan, Harlan, White, and the chief justice concurred. But his usual judicial soul mate, Black, joined by Stewart, wrote a spirited dissent, reflecting his textualist disposition: "I like my privacy as well as the next one, but I am nevertheless compelled to admit that the government has a right to invade it unless prohibited by some specific constitutional provision." Stewart as well could "find no such general right of privacy in the Bill of Rights, in any other part of the Constitution, or in any case ever before decided by this Court." Even Professor Tribe described the Court as having first determined to find a right of privacy and then found a rationale, having little basis in accepted modes of legal interpretation. Later in *Eisenstadt v. Baird* (1972), the Court extended the *Griswold* right to use contraceptives to unmarried couples.[251] The *Griswold* decision would also form a foundation for the right to abortion expressed in the later case of *Roe v. Wade.* Later justices such as Ruth Bader Ginsburg would be troubled by the existence of a general right of privacy, using Fourteenth Amendment equal protection instead, to support the *Roe* decision.

**Civil Rights: Miscegenation.** The Court continued to invalidate state laws in accordance with a broader view of the Fourteenth Amendment equal protection clause. In *Loving v. Virginia* (1967), [252] the Court invalidated a Virginia statute prohibiting interracial marriage. The Court rejected the state's argument that because the law was applied equally to all races that it complied with Fourteenth Amendment guarantees of equal protection of the laws. Instead, any statute based upon race has been subject to a "very heavy burden of justification" as Chief Justice Warren wrote. At the time of the decision, sixteen states prohibited interracial marriages.

**Civil Liberties: Freedom of Speech.** The Court was less inclined to give deference to local laws and policies restricting political expression, even when applied to nonverbal symbolic acts. In the 1969 case of *Tinker v. Des Moines Independent Community School District,* the Court held that the First Amendment protected certain activities of public high school students.[253] John Tinker, his sister Mary Tinker, and Christopher Eckhardt wore black armbands to school in protest of American support of war efforts in Vietnam. School policy decreed that students would be suspended until they agreed to remove the armbands. The Court reversed a lower court's ruling that the policy was reasonable based upon concerns that wearing the armbands would cause a disturbance. Writing for the majority, Justice Abe Fortas found that the act of wearing the armbands was very close to "pure speech" within the purview of the First Amendment and that the "mere desire to avoid discomfort" caused by unpopularity of the viewpoint expressed was not sufficient justification to warrant prohibition of the expression itself.

**The End of the Warren Years.** The retirement of Chief Justice Earl Warren in 1968 left a vacancy for the Johnson administration to fill. Warren had served on the Court for fifteen years and nine months, second only to Warren Burger as the longest-serving chief justice in the twentieth century.[254] President Johnson nominated Associate Justice Abraham Fortas, who remained a confidant and advisor to Johnson even after he took a seat on the Court, to replace Warren. Associate Justice Fortas's failure to entirely disclose his business affiliations and questions about his acceptance of fees from businesses derailed his nomination for chief justice. Abe Fortas was a symbol for the strong liberalism of the Warren Court. Southern Democrats opposed the nomination and used a filibuster to block a vote in the Senate. Additionally, the Republicans anticipated the election of a Republican president who would take office the following year. The Johnson administration withdrew his nomination in the face of growing opposition. The Court's top position remained vacant for over a year. The failure of this nomination opened the way for the incoming Nixon administration to nominate Warren Burger.

Many are critical of the Warren Court's activism. According to historian Arthur Schlesinger, the "Black-Douglas wing" settled cases according to their own "social preconceptions." Former circuit court judge Robert Bork described the Warren era as surpassing other Courts in "making policy."[255] He was critical of the Court's attempt to apply parts of the Constitution intended for application to the federal government to the states. Yet years later, even Chief Justice Rehnquist would uphold fundamental rulings of the Warren Court, such as *Miranda,* because they had become accepted standards of law.

# THE WARREN COURT ERA

**TIMELINES/PRESIDENTS JUSTICES**

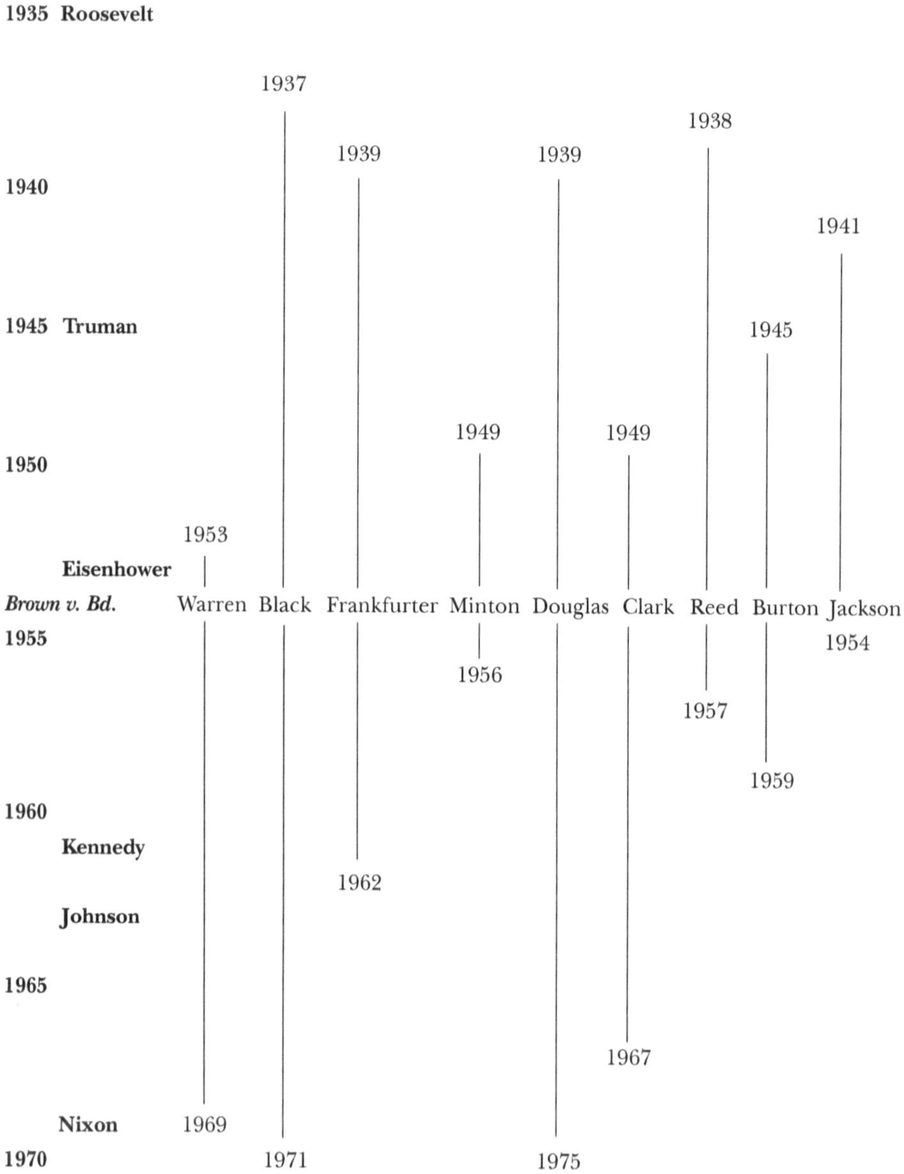

# CHAPTER 8

## THE BURGER COURT: 1969-1986

*The Burger Court era demonstrates, once again, that the constitutional independence of the judiciary means that loyalty to the nominating president or any previous political party affiliation can take a back seat to the independent consideration of cases by each justice. This independence limits the influence of the political branches on the Court, sometimes to the great frustration of the president and Congress.*

**Nixon Shapes the Court.** Richard Nixon campaigned as the Republican candidate for president in 1968 with a law-and-order theme targeting the Warren Court.[256] He pledged to appoint justices who would be more supportive of law enforcement activities. This theme resonated with traditional conservatives who viewed with dismay the sometimes violent protests against the Vietnam War, the civil rights movement, the rise in drug abuse, and social disintegration. The 1968 election was a historic realignment of parties, with much of the South swinging away from the Democratic Party and voting for independent candidate George Wallace. Nixon capitalized on divisions within the Democratic Party and a prevailing conservative mood of voters. As a young congressman from California, Nixon had combined his interests in law enforcement and anticommunism. He had led the effort that convicted suspected spy Alger Hiss of perjury before the House Un-American Activities Committee. Hiss was a senior State Department official who had previously served as a law clerk to Justice Oliver Wendell Holmes. Nixon's aggressive role as congressman earned him a place as Eisenhower's running mate and, ultimately, the vice presidency. His run for the presidency in 1960, despite his loss to John F. Kennedy, solidified his credentials as a Republican conservative.

The demise of President Johnson's nomination of Abe Fortas left Nixon the opportunity to name U.S. Court of Appeals judge Warren Burger to succeed Earl Warren as chief justice in 1969. For the next twenty-three years, Republicans dominated nominations to the Court. Nixon's selection of Burger echoed his law-and-order campaign theme. Burger had been a vocal opponent of many of the Warren Court's "liberal" rulings in the area of criminal law.[257] Nixon would later call on Burger for advice, even after his seating on the Court, much as Johnson consulted Fortas. Burger lobbied in the Senate for the confirmations of Carswell, Haynsworth, and Blackmun, succeeding only in the latter case.[258]

Yet it would be incorrect to characterize the Burger era as a thorough retrenchment of the old judicial order. The Court made "liberal" rulings on busing, abortion, sex discrimination, flag burning, and death penalty. Republican changes to composition of the Court were incremental and subject to Senate approval, which served as a partial check on the quality and character of the nominees. Much as conservative groups helped defeat Abe Fortas's nomination for chief justice in 1968, labor and civil rights groups, as well as prominent attorneys, helped defeat Nixon nominations of appellate court judges Clement Haynsworth, Jr. in 1969 and G. Harrold Carswell in 1970. Haynsworth was accused of unethical conduct in the form of financial conflicts of interest. The AFL-CIO opposed him because of several antiunion rulings. The NAACP opposed the nomination because of his stance of civil rights. Other liberal Democrats were angry over the rejection of Fortas's nomination for chief justice and sought revenge. As a result, Haynsworth was defeated in a 45-55 vote. Carswell's segregationist views drew opposition from civil rights groups. His competence to serve on the Court was questioned, and he was defeated by a vote of 45-51.

Following the defeat of the Haynsworth and Carswell nominations, Nixon nominated Harry A. Blackmun. Blackmun fulfilled Nixon's objective to nominate someone who had a reputation for being strong on law and order, then a major conservative issue. Like Burger, Blackmun was a native of Minnesota. Friends since childhood, Blackmun served as best man at Burger's wedding.[259] The two would become known as the Minnesota Twins because of their personal similarities and like-minded opinions on many cases. Despite Burger's early endorsement, Blackmun would eventually disappoint conservatives with many decisions, especially the case of abortion rights in *Roe v. Wade.*

The challenge to the composition of the Court came not only from liberal circles within Congress. In 1970, in apparent retaliation for the rejection of two of Nixon's nominees, Congressman Gerald Ford from Michigan sought to impeach Justice William O. Douglas on the basis of alleged conflict of interest and for inciting rebellion.[260] The former charge was based upon his acceptance of payments from private foundations.[261] The latter charge was based upon his 1970 book, *Points of Rebellion,* and publication of excerpts of that book in a left-oriented magazine. He remained outspoken on political issues from the war in Cambodia to the environment, authoring more than thirty books in his lifetime. By the moral climate of the time, his divorcing and marrying three times while on the Court was considered scandalous.[262] His reputed philandering while serving on the Court did not help.[263] But the House Judiciary Committee, which was controlled by a Democratic majority, found insufficient grounds for impeachment. Like the 1953 attempt at his impeachment, this effort also failed. Douglas would remain on the Court until disabled by a stroke in 1975, the longest-serving justice in history. Yet Ford did not suffer this loss in vain, as his efforts to impeach Douglas gained the favorable attention of Richard Nixon, who would later select Ford to replace Vice President Spiro Agnew.

Two vacancies were opened on the Court by the departures of Hugo Black and John M. Harlan in 1971. Nixon saw an opportunity to continue his efforts to strengthen his standing in the South.[264] He offered to nominate Senator Howard Baker, the ranking Republican from Tennessee, but Baker declined. Nixon then nominated eminent Richmond lawyer Lewis Powell to the Court. As a Southerner and a Democrat, Powell faced much less opposition with the Democratic majority in the Senate.

**Rehnquist Joins the Court.** In 1971, Nixon also nominated Assistant Attorney General William Rehnquist to the Court. Rehnquist served with the Army Air Corps in North Africa in World War II. After the war, he graduated first in his class at Stanford Law School. Justice Sandra Day O'Connor was third in the same class. He clerked for Justice Jackson during the 1951-2 judicial term. During this time, he wrote a controversial memo to Jackson on *Plessy* in preparation for the decision in *Brown v. Board of Education* that was to haunt him later.[265] As it turned out, Jackson ignored his clerk's recommendation to uphold *Plessy* and voted with the majority in *Brown.* Rehnquist later practiced law in Arizona, establishing ties to Republican Party regulars and assisting the Barry Goldwater presidential election campaign in 1964 as a poll watcher, speechwriter, and legal advisor.[266] Rehnquist was a believer in limited government and judicial restraint. He was a vocal opponent of integration, testifying against a Phoenix public accommodations ordinance which banned discrimination in shops and restaurants.[267] Arizona Republican Party chairman Richard Kleindienst went on to a senior post at the Department of Justice in the Nixon administration, later replacing John Mitchell as attorney general when Mitchell resigned in 1972. Kleindienst hired Rehnquist to head the Office of Legal Counsel, as an assistant attorney general at the Department of Justice. While there, Rehnquist urged Nixon to oppose the ill-fated Equal Rights Amendment (ERA). Rehnquist was forty-seven years old when he was nominated in 1971 and would be one of the longest-serving justices in the history of the Court.

President Nixon described both Powell and Rehnquist as "two hard-right conservatives," predicting that Rehnquist would draw the most opposition.[268] Through his positions on many cases, Rehnquist had attracted the ire of civil rights groups. Though he had an excellent academic record and a good record of service at the Department of Justice, he lacked any prior judicial experience. Rehnquist was not alone but rather one among many Supreme Court justices who never held a judicial post before joining the Court. Of thirty-three justices appointed between 1937 and 1994, only sixteen had been appellate judges.[269] The American Bar Association had provided unenthusiastic "qualified" assessments of Nixon's earlier nominees, but this time Nixon chose not to ask for the ABA's "clearance" prior to submitting the nomination. After the nomination fights over Haynsworth and Carswell, the Democratic-dominated Senate was exhausted and not ready for another confirmation fight. Rehnquist was confirmed by a vote of 68-26 on December 10, 1971.[270] In the ensuing years as an associate justice, he quickly established a conservative voting record in cases involving abortion, separation of church and state, and criminal law.

**Executive Powers: The Pentagon Papers and Watergate.** The president and the executive branch lost two major cases in the Burger Court. In the first case, conservatives were disappointed by the Court's decision in *New York Times Co. v. United States* (1971) a.k.a. the Pentagon Papers case.[271] The federal government sought to bar the *New York Times* from publishing classified documents contained in a study on the Vietnam War provided by ex-State Department employee Daniel Ellsberg.

In an unusual effort to expedite the process, the Court reached a decision on June 30, only five days after it had agreed to hear the case. In a 6-3 ruling based on the First Amendment, the Court ruled that any request for prior restraint on the press bore "a heavy presumption against its constitutional validity." Justice Black, writing for the Court, set a high standard for justification of a prior restraint against freedom of speech. It limited such measures to where disclosure "will surely result in direct, immediate, and irreparable damage to the nation or its people."[272]

The language of the First Amendment is quite clear, "Congress shall make no law . . . abridging the freedom of speech, or of the press." Thus, the "liberal" result of this case was delivered via a conservative textualist approach. But such a strict textual approach was not inconsistent with Associate Justice Hugo Black's approach in other decisions, such as the *Steel Seizure* case. Chief Justice Burger dissented, protesting what he considered to be the haste of the decision and the absolutist application of First Amendment. Justices Harlan and Blackmun also dissented.

The Nixon administration was not pleased with the Court, though the Pentagon Papers were of primarily historic interest, chronicling the events leading to the Kennedy and Johnson administrations' increased involvement in Vietnam. Nor did the Court's decision bar prosecution of Ellsberg, since he had violated separate laws related to his obligations to protect classified information as a federal employee. But Ellsberg was lucky, since the federal officials were accused of burglarizing his psychiatrist's office and the case was consequently dropped on grounds of prosecutorial misconduct.

The Nixon administration was soon disappointed by another decision of the Court. President Nixon lost significantly and personally in *United States v. Nixon* (1974) where the Court rejected a presidential claim of absolute executive privilege with regard to withholding the infamous Watergate tapes subpoenaed by Special Prosecutor Leon Jaworski.[273] The tapes were believed to contain conversations implicating the president and others in the White House in involvement in the 1972 break-in of the Democratic National Headquarters at the Watergate Hotel. The Court voted against the president 8-0, with Associate Justice Rehnquist withdrawing himself from the case because of his former service to Nixon as assistant attorney general. Chief Justice Burger wrote the opinion upholding federal district court judge John Sirica's order for the president to produce the tapes. Burger wrote that "to read the Article II powers of the president as providing an absolute privilege as against a subpoena essential to enforcement of criminal statutes . . . would upset the constitutional balance of 'a workable government' . . . and cut deeply into the guarantee of due process." Justice Brennan attempted but failed to get a unanimous decision on his key points concerning executive privilege. Yet a majority agreed that executive privilege exists in a form that must be balanced with legislative and judicial prerogatives. After the Supreme Court's decision, the House Judiciary Committee voted to recommend impeachment of President Nixon. Fifteen days after the Court's decision, Nixon resigned as president.

**Capital Punishment.** The Court continued its challenges to state criminal laws, applying broad interpretations of the Eighth Amendment's ban on "cruel and unusual punishment." In *Furman v. Georgia* (1972), a 5-4 Court ruling struck down Georgia's death penalty law and by implication the death penalty statutes of other states.[274] A major part of the rationale for the Court's striking down the death penalty was its disproportionate application to minorities as demonstrated by statistical evidence. But the decision produced five concurring opinions rather than a majority, providing little guidance for the states on the precise situations when the death penalty was unconstitutional. All four Nixon appointees (Burger, Powell, Blackmun, and Rehnquist) dissented. Not until 1976 did the Court provide clarification.

In *Gregg v. Georgia,* Justices Stewart, Powell, and Stevens formed a centrist core that affirmed that the death penalty could be constitutional provided state procedural safeguards to guide juries in their deliberations to prevent arbitrary and capricious sentencing.[275] After that decision, thirty-eight states adopted new capital punishment laws. But almost half of the new laws removed "capricious" jury discretion by mandating the death penalty for certain crimes.[276] Stewart, Powell, and Stevens viewed this development as a large step backward.[277] The Court would later make clear that consistency in sentencing was not the only criteria of concern. In the 1978 case of *Lockett v. Ohio,* the Court asserted the right of those convicted of capital crimes to present mitigating circumstances during sentencing proceedings as evidence that death would not be appropriate in that particular case. Over the next decades, majorities would continue to evolve on various death penalty cases coming to the Court.

**Civil Rights: The Right to Privacy and Abortion.** The right to privacy articulated in *Griswold* was taken a step further in *Eisenstadt v. Baird* (1972).[278] In *Baird,* the Court invalidated a Massachusetts statute regulating the distribution of contraceptives. The Court based its decision upon the equal protection clause of the Fourteenth Amendment and an implicit right of the individual to be free from government intrusion.

*Griswold* and *Baird* laid the groundwork for the historic decision regarding abortion in *Roe v. Wade* (1973).[279] Where the Court in the former cases recognized a right to privacy in the distribution and use of contraceptives, the *Roe* case dealt with extension of the right to privacy to a woman's choice to terminate her pregnancy. Jane Roe, who was unmarried and pregnant, challenged Texas law which prohibited abortion except when necessary to save the life of the mother. Dr. James Hallford, a physician charged with performing abortions, intervened in the action seeking relief from the same statute.

Writing for a plurality rather than a majority, Justice Blackmun referred to "zones of privacy" mentioned in *Griswold,* though acknowledging that there is no explicit right of privacy in the Constitution. He argued that such a right was implicit in the zones of privacy within the First, Fourth, Fifth, and Ninth Amendments of the Constitution. Until this time, the issue of abortion had been considered a state question. Chief Justice Burger and Associate Justices Douglas and Stewart wrote separate concurring opinions providing differing rationales for the decision, leaving the true meaning and extent of the decision vague and confusing. Investigative reporter Bob Woodward suggests that Chief Justice Burger cynically joined the majority so he could assign the opinion writing to his friend Blackmun and thereby limit the "mandate" of the decision.[280] The choice of Blackmun was not without merit, as he was the justice with the strongest credentials on medical issues, having served as general counsel for the Mayo Clinic for ten years. In research for his opinion, Blackmun immersed himself in medical literature. Consequently, his opinion focused on medical determinations regarding the viability of the fetus. He would permit abortions only up to the point of viability of the fetus or when the woman's health is in danger.

Justices White and Rehnquist dissented, failing to find a constitutional basis for such an expansive right to privacy. White could "find nothing in the language or history of the Constitution to support the Court's judgment." Rehnquist, invoking Holmes's dissent in *Lochner,* accused the majority of "applying substantive due process standards to economic and social welfare legislation . . . The decision here . . . partakes more of judicial legislation than it does of a determination of the intent of the drafters of the Fourteenth Amendment."

The plurality of the decision would be the cause of much subsequent debate and litigation regarding the precise meaning and impact of the decision. Blackmun was shocked and dismayed by the outrage the decision stirred in the growing right-to-life community. Additionally, his rigid trimester-based standards would be questionable given scientific and medical advances, permitting earlier survival of premature infants and detection of heart and brain activity.

The *Roe* decision, written by a "law-and-order" justice nominated to the Court by a conservative Republican president, would become a legal rallying cry for social conservatives for decades thereafter. Even Chief Justice Burger's lifelong friendship with Blackmun suffered as a result of the decision.

**Civil Rights: Desegregation.** The Court led by Chief Justice Burger surprised conservatives again when it went beyond the *Brown* decision and supported busing as a necessary measure to achieve desegregation in *Swann v. Charlotte-Mecklenburg Board of Education* (1971).[281] In a decision that took nearly eight months to write, Chief Justice Burger stated that busing was necessary to overcome de facto segregation. The result was as unpopular as *Brown*, with consequences reaching into not merely the South but northern cities where school districts reinforced separation of the races in residential areas. In 1979, Congress attempted to reverse this decision through a proposed constitutional amendment. This antibusing amendment failed in the House by 75 votes.

**Civil Rights: Voting.** Congress continued its expansive enactment of laws that bound states. But the Supreme Court would not simply rubber-stamp such federal laws. The attorneys general of Oregon and Texas sought to enjoin the federal government from enforcing a federal law allowing eighteen-year-olds to vote in state elections. The Court agreed and overturned the statute in *Oregon v. Mitchell* (1970), finding congressional power to set qualifications to vote only in federal elections as opposed to state elections.[282] But Congress initiated a constitutional amendment which was subsequently ratified by the states and enacted as Amendment XXVI on July 21, 1971, thus guaranteeing eighteen-year-olds the right to vote in state elections. In effect, the Court was reversed, but through constitutionally permissible means.

**Civil Rights: Employment and Affirmative Action.** In the 1970s, the civil rights movement put new efforts into integrating the workplace and remedying past injustices. Affirmative action, which consisted of hiring and promotion preferences, became a hot political issue. The Court provided a mixed review of affirmative action cases. In *Griggs v. Duke Power Co.* (1973), the Court invalidated an employer's requirement for a high school diploma and an intelligence test score for certain jobs.[283] Justices Brennan, Marshall, Douglas, Burger, Stewart, Powell, and Black voted in favor of affirmative action, with Justices Rehnquist and White dissenting. According to the majority opinion, neither job requirement was shown to "bear a demonstrable relationship to successful performance of the jobs" and both had a disparate racial impact. This, coupled with evidence of past discrimination, was enough for the Court to decide in favor of affirmative action. Chief Justice Burger limited the impact of the ruling by stating that it was the intent of Congress in Title VII of the Civil Rights Act of 1964 to proscribe "discriminatory preference for any group, minority or majority." Despite his words, this case foreshadowed later cases furthering more aggressive forms of affirmative action.

**The Ford Years.** The resignation of Richard Nixon in 1974 resulted in the elevation of the unelected vice president Gerald Ford to the presidency to complete the Nixon term. His lone appointee to the Supreme Court was John Paul Stevens in 1975, who replaced the aging William O. Douglas who had suffered a disabling stroke. The stroke accomplished what Ford could not as a congressman who had sponsored an attempted impeachment of Douglas. Ford chose Stevens over the more visible and controversial solicitor general Robert Bork, wishing to avoid Nixon's confirmation fights and knowing that Stevens's confirmation by the Senate would be almost assured. During World War II, Stevens had served as an intelligence officer in the navy, helping to crack Japanese military codes. He had gone to Northwestern Law School and graduated in only two years while ranking at the top of his class. He clerked for Supreme Court Justice Wiley B. Rutledge during his 1947 term. In 1970, Nixon appointed him to the Seventh Circuit Court of Appeals. His nomination to the Supreme Court was confirmed by a unanimous vote of the Senate. On the Supreme Court, he came to be viewed as a frequent but independent member of a liberal voting block. On some issues, such as flag burning, he voted with the conservatives. On the issue of the 2000 presidential election, he voted with the liberals supporting a recount of votes.

**Federalism.** In the 1975 ruling in *Fry v. United States,* the Court upheld the Nixon administration's wage and price controls program to curb inflation against a challenge by the states.[284] The lone dissenter was Nixon appointee Rehnquist, who argued that the states have an "affirmative constitutional defense" based upon the intent of the framers of the Constitution. This was a direct challenge to the Court's position for nearly four decades of New Deal-style federal authority over the states through the commerce clause as well as the even longer-standing position on the application of federal authority via the Fourteenth Amendment. Rehnquist's dissenting opinion in favor of states' rights over federal power would come to represent a trend of the Court upon which Rehnquist would eventually preside.

**The Carter Years.** President Carter, who assumed the presidency in 1977, was the first president in over one hundred years to lack an opportunity to nominate a justice to the Court and the only president in history to serve a full term without doing so.[285] During Carter's years, the Court in key cases restricted the application of affirmative action under the Fourteenth Amendment but arguably expanded freedom of expression and freedom of the press under the First Amendment.

**Limits on Congressional Power.** The executive branch was not alone in the Court's curtailment of its authority by the Burger Court. In *Buckley v. Valeo* (1976),[286] the Court struck down limits on candidate spending as a violation of First Amendment rights to free expression while upholding some limits on campaign contributions. This case set back campaign finance reform many years.

**Civil Liberties.** The Court in *Richmond Newspapers v. Virginia* (1980)[287] allowed the press (and the public) to sit in pretrial proceedings, effectively reversing the decision in *Gannett v. DePasquale* (1979).[288] It may be an indication that criticism by the press can influence the Court's decision.[289]

**Civil Rights: School Admissions and Affirmative Action.** Burger's view on affirmative action prevailed in *Regents of the University of California v. Bakke* (1978) where a 5-4 majority overturned the selection preference for minorities by the University of California at Davis Medical School.[290] Alan Bakke was a white male who was denied admission though his Medical College Admission Test scores and his grade point average were better than several of the minority students admitted under a policy that set aside sixteen out of one hundred places for blacks, Asians, Latinos, and Native Americans. Writing in the plurality decision, Justice Lewis Powell stated that though the state has a compelling interest to achieve diversity in its medical school and that race can be one criteria among many for admission, the use of a rigid quota system for admissions is impermissible. This was one of the first cases of "reverse discrimination." The Court did not rule out all forms of affirmative action. Such programs were viewed as a fitting remedy where there had been an established pattern of discrimination in the past. Powell pointed to the Harvard approach, which considered minority status as one among many factors to be considered during the admission process, as a permissible means to promote minority representation in schools. Justice Rehnquist concurred with the result but dissented from Powell's opinion. He argued that Congress had outlawed *all* discrimination, including affirmative action, through the Civil Rights Act of 1964. Chief Justice Burger and Justices Stewart and Stevens agreed. Dissenting were Justices Brennan, Marshall, White, and Blackmun, who found no statutory or constitutional violations by the set-aside policy. For the next twenty-five years, this case served as guidance for permissible affirmative action programs: those committed to individual consideration for all applicants with a goal of achieving diversity of all types (including geographic and economic) without the use of quotas or separate admission pools.[291]

**Civil Rights: Employment and Affirmative Action.** In *United Steelworkers of America v. Weber* (1979), Burger's view on affirmative action became the minority. Brennan wrote for a 5-4 majority to uphold "voluntary affirmative action." The case involved a collective bargaining agreement plan that reserved 50 percent of the spaces in a plant training program for blacks. Burger dissented, declaring that the majority opinion was contrary to explicit language of the Civil Rights Act of 1964.

**The Early Reagan Years.** President Ronald Reagan came to office with a pledge to appoint justices to federal courts who would use "original intent" as their primary method in interpreting the Constitution and who would overturn "liberal" decisions on abortion and federalism.[292] He would be the first president to appoint a woman to the Supreme Court. In 1981, during Reagan's first year in office, he nominated Sandra Day O'Connor to replace Potter Stewart. She was Chief Justice Rehnquist's classmate at Stanford Law School, ranking third in her class. Despite her scholastic excellence, pervasive gender discrimination at the time of her graduation denied her employment opportunities with the major West Coast law firms. She later worked as an assistant state attorney general in Arizona. She was appointed to fill a vacancy in the state Senate in 1969. Subsequently, she was elected to two additional terms in the Senate and rose to the position of (Republican) majority leader in 1972. Politically, her legislative record was mixed.[293] She voted against busing for school integration, voted to give hospital employees the right to not participate in abortions, and opposed gun control. On the other hand, she supported bilingual education, supported the federal Equal Rights Amendment, and opposed state aid to private religious schools. She also voted against a ban on state-funded abortions for poor women and against a ban on abortions at the University of Arizona hospital. She had served as a state trial judge. Governor Bruce Babbitt, a Democrat, appointed her to the Arizona Court of Appeals. The Justice Department recommended her nomination, but antiabortion groups tried to defeat the nomination because of her legislative record opposing restrictions on abortion in Arizona. However, the Justice Department, aided by a memo of support from a young employee named Kenneth Starr, continued to recommend her nomination.[294] Opposition never materialized in the U.S. Senate. Her nomination to the Supreme Court was confirmed by unanimous vote in that body.

**School Prayer.** In 1982, President Reagan had asked Congress to introduce a constitutional amendment that would permit prayer in public schools. Despite the change in composition of the Court, the justices declined to overturn its earlier rulings on the subject, such as *Engel v. Vitale* prohibiting state sponsorship of school prayer. In the 1985 case of *Wallace v. Jaffree*, the Court reviewed a 1981 Alabama law requiring public schools to begin each day with a one-minute period of silence for "meditation or voluntary prayer."[295] Although meditation was allowed, silent prayer was found to have crossed the line in promoting religion in violation of the establishment clause of the First Amendment. Writing for the majority, Justice Stevens found the record to indicate the purpose was to endorse religion rather than to advance any secular purpose. White, Burger, and Rehnquist dissented. Again, the president and Congress reacted verbally but were unable to garner sufficient support for a constitutional amendment.

**Other Separation of Church and State Issues.** In the 1984 decision of *Lynch v. Donnelly*, the Court held that a government-sponsored Nativity scene during the Christmas season did not violate the establishment clause.[296] In a sharply divided 5-4 decision, Chief Justice Burger wrote for the majority that the crèche in the Christmas display did not impermissibly advance religion, finding that the celebration of the holiday was a national tradition serving a legitimate secular purpose. Justice O'Connor's separate concurring opinion provided two tests for judging religious displays: "excessive entanglement with religious institutions, which may interfere with the independence of the institutions, give the institutions access to government or government powers not fully shared by nonadherents of the religion, and foster the creation of political constituencies defined along religious lines . . . (or) government endorsement or approval of religion." Justices Brennan, Marshall, Blackmun, and Stevens dissented.

Justice O'Connor's pivotal vote in this case would foreshadow her growing role as an influential decision maker and tiebreaker over the next twenty-one years on the Court. The ability of justices like O'Connor to decide cases independently and on her own terms would become a source of frustration for social conservatives.

**Congressional Powers.** In the 1983 case of *Immigration and Naturalization Service (INS) v. Chadha,* the Court invalidated a provision of law enabling Congress to reverse decisions of the Immigration and Naturalization Service after the fact. Under the provisions of the 1952 Immigration and Naturalization Act, the House voted to deport a Kenyan student who overstayed his visa but had received permission from the INS to stay. The Court by a 7-2 vote ruled that once a power was delegated to the executive branch by law, Congress could not then attempt to second-guess executive action. Writing for the majority, Chief Justice Burger argued that this was, in effect, the exercise of a *legislative veto* in violation of the separation of powers principles embodied in Articles I and II of the Constitution. More specifically, the presentment clause of the Constitution, Article I, Section 7, confines the role of Congress to presenting legislation to the president for signature or veto without allowing for any residual right to withdraw authorities once delegated to the president or the executive branch. Justice White dissented, pointing out that since delegation of substantial authority from the legislature to the executive branch that began with the New Deal era, it would be unwise to deny Congress the power to oversee the exercise of those authorities. The ramifications of *Chadha* were far-reaching, impliedly invalidating similar provisions in other laws, such as the War Powers Act where Congress asserted the right to withdraw authority for foreign deployment of U.S. forces even after the president had deployed forces overseas. But when the Court had the opportunity to decide whether *Chadha* went that far during the Gulf War of 1991, it declined to hear the case. More significantly, since the *Chadha* decision, Congress has challenged the ruling by passing more than two hundred new laws with legislative veto provisions. The executive branch has even provided de facto recognition of legislative vetoes for certain actions through informal agreements with Congress.[297] But absent a case and controversy presented to it, the Court could not simply overturn such legislation or executive agreements. The Court's power was limited by jurisdictional mandates wholly different than those of the political branches of government.

**The End of the Burger Era.** Burger was seventy-nine years old when he left the Court in 1986 to head up the U.S. Constitution Bicentennial Commission. He had spent sixteen years and nine months as chief justice. His was the longest term of a chief justice in the twentieth century. Burger's tenure was considered a disappointment by conservatives because, despite his credentials as a law-and-order judge and strict constructionist, the Court under his stewardship approved citywide busing, struck down the death penalty, legalized abortion, and upheld affirmative action preferences for minorities, among other things. But Burger's tenure did mark a significant slowing of the Court's activism in the area of civil rights and liberties, presaging further changes in the direction of the Court.

# CHAPTER 9

## THE EARLY REHNQUIST COURT: 1986-2000

*Even with changes in composition to the Supreme Court as a result of appointments by the Republican administrations of Presidents Nixon, Ford, and Reagan (President Carter had no opportunity to make an appointment), the Court was slow to reverse precedents set by the Warren Court. The nomination process would become very politicized, with political interest groups exercising considerable clout. The Senate's central role in the nomination process was reaffirmed with the rejection of Judge Robert Bork. Both political branches of government would continue to be disappointed by decisions of the Court, from flag burning to abortion, with limited ability to affect or reverse the outcome.*

**Reagan's Legacy for the Court.** In 1986, Associate Justice William Rehnquist was nominated by President Ronald Reagan to succeed Warren Burger as chief justice. Rehnquist who had been first appointed to the Court by President Nixon in 1971 became the Court's sixteenth chief justice. Reagan had been swept into office along with the first Republican majority in the House of Representatives since the Eisenhower administration. The so-called Reagan revolution capitalized on disaffected Democrats ("Reagan Democrats") who were opposed to the agenda of the "liberal social revolution" and the Court's alleged role as an engine thereof.

The more conservative elements of the Republican Party were disappointed with the failure of Presidents Nixon and Ford to name "true" conservatives to the Court. The performance of Justices Powell and Blackmun were particularly disappointing, in their view. Therefore, the stage was set for the Court to be recast in a new mold. Rehnquist had a solid record as an associate justice and was a logical choice to succeed Burger. Senior Justice Department officials William Bradford Reynolds and Charles Cooper, former associates of Rehnquist, lobbied Reagan's attorney general Edwin Meese hard for his support of the nomination.[298]

At the age of sixty-one, Rehnquist had already served on the Court for over fourteen years before his nomination to be chief justice. Rehnquist's confirmation to the position of chief justice was by no means assured. Controversy emerged over Rehnquist's involvement with the Goldwater presidential campaign and alleged voter harassment in the 1960s. When the vote came, Rehnquist was confirmed by the Senate with a vote of 65 in favor and 33 opposed, the highest negative vote for the post in history. At the time, the Republicans controlled the Senate and senior senator Strom Thurmond chaired the Judiciary Committee. A few months later, the Republicans lost the Senate to the Democrats, which hurt the already-limited chances of Bork to gain a Senate confirmation.

The appointment of Rehnquist to the chief justice seat also left an opening for a new associate justice. The choices to fill this seat came down to Robert Bork and Antonin Scalia. Bork was dismissed at the time as too controversial, though he was nominated for Lewis Powell's seat the next year. "Nino" Scalia was chosen for a number of reasons. He would be the first Italian American nominated for the Court. Scalia's conservative Catholic values and judicial record jibed with the Reagan administration's agenda. He was an avowed "originalist," believing in following the original intent of the drafters of the Constitution. He attended a Jesuit school in Manhattan, followed by Georgetown University. He graduated from Harvard Law School in 1960, serving on the school's *Law Review*. He later taught at the University of Virginia Law School. He then worked consecutively with the Nixon administration, the American Enterprise Institute, the Hoover Institute, and the University of Chicago. Scalia's 1986 nomination was confirmed by unanimous vote of the Senate, benefiting from the lion's share of attention focused on Rehnquist's nomination.

**Brennan's Twilight Years.** At the time of Scalia's nomination, William Brennan was the recognized leader of the so-called liberal wing of the Court. With his tenure on the Court stretching from his appointment during the Eisenhower administration and his established record in persuading other justices to his point of view, he exercised considerable influence. He was able to carry majorities with him even through the era of Burger. He believed it was the Court's duty to enforce the rights of the low and disenfranchised members of society. Some denounced him as a radical egalitarian. He actively fought to apply the entire Bill of Rights to the states via the Fourteenth Amendment. But he was losing a fight against time and the tide of growing conservative composition of the Court. The retirements of Powell in 1987 and Brennan in 1990 changed the overall balance on the Court, though their replacements, Kennedy and Souter, would often come to defy categorization as "conservatives."

**Challenge to Congressional Authority.** In the 1986 case of *Bowsher v. Synar*, the Court struck down the provision of the Gramm-Rudman-Hollings Deficit Control Act of 1985 that mandated automatic spending cuts when allocations exceeded maximum allowable deficit levels through procedures executed by the comptroller general.[299] Congressman Mike Synar petitioned the Court to set aside the law as an unconstitutional realignment of budgetary powers between the executive and the legislative branches.

Chief Justice Burger, writing for the majority, held that the act was an intrusion into executive powers and a violation of the constitutional separation of powers where it assigned executive functions to the comptroller general. Since Congress retained removal powers over the comptroller general, the Court viewed that official as "an officer of the legislative branch" who "may not be entrusted with executive powers." Justice White was the lone dissenter, finding Congress's delegation of authority for purposes of deficit reduction to be "necessary and proper." Though this decision does not easily fit into either a "liberal" or "conservative" political categorization, it engendered resentment from members of Congress whose powers to deal with the budget deficit were curtailed.

**Civil Liberties: Sodomy Laws.** In *Bowers v. Hardwick* (1986), the Court upheld a Georgia statute criminalizing sodomy by a 5-4 vote. [300] The police had discovered the activity when they entered the premises lawfully. There had been no prosecutions under the statute for decades. Writing for the majority, Justice White found that nothing about homosexual conduct qualifies for protection under the Constitution and that proscriptions against homosexual conduct "have ancient roots." He criticized previous opinions as "facetious" which recognized rights with "little or no textual support in the constitutional language" such as Justice Cardozo's writing in *Palko v. Connecticut* (1937)[301] where he supported the protection of rights "implicit in the concept of ordered liberty" and *Moore v. East Cleveland* (1977) referring to principles "deeply rooted in this nation's history and tradition." In a spirited dissent, Blackmun, who was joined by four others, defended "the right most valued by civilized men, the right to be let alone," highlighting the "moral fact that a person belongs to himself and not others nor to society as a whole." He wrote that the state should not be allowed to outlaw such a victimless activity. This holding would not be the last word on the subject of homosexual rights, as this deeply divided Court would have the opportunity to struggle with various aspects of issues affecting the gay community.

**Civil Rights: Affirmative Action.** In the 1987 case of *Johnson v. Transportation Agency*, the Santa Clara, California, transportation agency used an affirmative action program to promote a female to the position of road dispatcher over a male with a higher test score.[302] The male, Paul Johnson, filed suit, alleging discrimination in violation of Title VII of the Civil Rights Act of 1964. Justice Brennan wrote for the majority that it was not unreasonable to consider gender as one factor in promotion, provided there was no quota or absolute bar to the promotion of men. He stated that the measure was necessary to eliminate the vestiges of discrimination in the workplace. Chief Justice Rehnquist and Justices Scalia and White dissented. Again, a sharply divided Court would have more opportunities to decide issues regarding affirmative action in the future.

**The Bork Confirmation Fight.** Court dynamics were changing because of evolving views within the Court, which was narrowly divided on many key issues. Byron White over time became more conservative, particularly on criminal law matters. Harry Blackmun also evinced more conservative views on some decisions, such as on the death penalty. With the retirement of Nixon appointee Lewis Powell in 1987, President Reagan nominated U.S. Court of Appeals justice Robert Bork. But a growing role for interest groups would forever change the nature of confirmation fights. Reagan's announcement of the nomination before the Senate's summer recess provided time for diverse opposition groups to unite to defeat the nomination. A coalition of 185 nongovernmental interest groups, including the National Organization for Women (NOW), the National Abortion and Reproductive Rights Action League (NARAL), and the Alliance for Justice, coordinated efforts and spent an estimated $12-15 million to defeat the nomination. Bork, a former solicitor general and professor of law at Yale, was not attacked on grounds of competence but rather because of his substantive views on civil rights and liberties, especially abortion, affirmative action, and the death penalty. He had a controversial political track record, where as solicitor general in 1973 Bork carried out Nixon's order to fire Special Prosecutor Archibald Cox, who was investigating alleged White House involvement in the 1972 break-in of the Democratic National Headquarters at the Watergate Hotel, after Attorney General Elliot Richardson and his deputy, William Ruckelshaus, resigned in succession rather than obey Nixon's order.

During five days of Senate questioning broadcast on national television, Bork provided a spirited defense, clarification, and explanation of his views. Senator Kennedy led the opposition in the Senate which held a Democratic majority. Bork's views were well-known because of his extensive writings frequently critical of liberal judicial activism on the Court. His anticipation of serving on the Court as an "intellectual feast" did little to comfort his detractors. Despite (or perhaps because of) a twenty-five-year record of service in government and academia, ten members of the ABA's Committee on the Federal Judiciary rated him "well qualified," four members rated him "unqualified," and one voted "not opposed."[303] Bork was defeated by a 58-42 vote, the widest margin of defeat for a nomination in Supreme Court history.[304] He was the twenty-eighth nominee for the Court but only the fourth in the twentieth century to be rejected by the Senate.[305] The Bork nomination was evidence of a larger Republican vs. Democrat fight for control of the Court. All but eight senators voted along party lines. The results were not altogether surprising as historically presidents have had an 89 percent success rate with their nominees when their party controls the Senate versus 61 percent when opposition party controls.

After Bork's defeat, Reagan nominated Harvard professor Douglas H. Ginsburg. His nomination was withdrawn when allegations surfaced about his use of marijuana and alleged conflicts of interest while he worked in the Department of Justice.[306] It was not until Ninth Circuit U.S. Court of Appeals justice Anthony Kennedy was nominated that an acceptable "moderate conservative" successor was found.[307] He was confirmed by a unanimous vote of the Senate. As in many cases before him, the supposed political categorization of this nominee proved to be a poor predictor of his performance on the Supreme Court.

**The Administration of George H. W. Bush.** In January 1989, George Herbert Walker Bush took office as president. Having served as vice president for two terms under President Ronald Reagan, he sought to continue Reagan's agenda on the Court, favoring individuals who believed in "original intent" in interpreting the Constitution.[308] Though Bush served only one term, he had the opportunity to name two justices to the Court. Like Reagan before him, he faced resistance from a Democratic majority in the Senate; but, unlike Reagan, all of his primary nominees would be ultimately confirmed. During Bush's presidency, the Court would hear controversial cases from flag burning to abortion. Despite successive appointments to the Court by four Republican presidents, "conservative" results would not be guaranteed.

**Civil Liberties: Flag Burning.** The Court stunned conservatives by consistently striking down state and federal flag-burning laws. In 1989, the Court by a 5-4 decision written by Brennan in *Texas v. Johnson*[309] overturned a Texas state flag-burning law on the grounds of First Amendment freedom of expression. Though the statute purported to prohibit conduct rather than speech, Justice Brennan, writing for the Court, applied the long-standing recognition that expressive conduct is protected under the Constitution, not just verbal or written expression. He found that Gregory Lee Johnson's object was political expression (he had burned the flag outside the 1984 Republican national convention in Dallas) and was unconvinced by arguments that the ordinance was justified in order to prevent a breach of the peace. The justices recognized the unpopularity of these types of decisions, despite the importance of maintaining independence from public opinion when exercising their constitutional duties. Reflecting mixed feelings, Justice Kennedy, who concurred with the decision, referred to these kinds of cases as "decisions we do not like." Chief Justice Rehnquist and Justices White, O'Connor, and Stevens dissented. At the time of the decision, forty-eight states had enacted prohibitions against flag burning.

The "conservative" reaction to the Court's decision was determined and swift. Subsequent to the *Texas v. Johnson* decision, Congress attempted to accomplish what the Court said states could not do by passing the Federal Flag Protection Act of 1989, making flag burning a federal crime. Again, the Court was compelled to overturn the law in *United States v. Eichman* (1990).[310] Congress tried to push through a constitutional amendment to accomplish what they could not do through a statute. But constitutional amendments require approval of a two-thirds majority in both the House and Senate, in addition to ratification by two-thirds of the states. A proposed anti-flag burning amendment in 1989 was defeated in the House by 34 votes and the Senate by 9 votes. Since 1985, the House approved a flag-burning amendment by well over the two-thirds majority required in four separate votes; but the Senate, voting on the issue twice, fell a few votes short of the two-thirds majority required.[311] In 2000, another congressional flag-burning amendment was voted down by Congress. Another initiative garnered a 298-125 vote in the House on 17 July 2001.[312] Forty-nine of fifty states have passed resolutions asking Congress to outlaw flag burning. But in the absence of an amendment to the Constitution, the current interpretation prevails.

But conservatives are not always of one mind on the issue of flag burning, as Scalia's vote with the majority in *Johnson* indicates. Social conservatives have less problem with curtailing the application of the First Amendment than do conservatives of the libertarian persuasion, who place high value on individual liberties. Indeed, even many erstwhile liberals of the Court, such as Stevens, who had strong feelings about the flag dating back to his days of military service, joined Chief Justice Rehnquist in dissent. Such cases, once again, evidence the frequent futility of political labels for the justices.

**Civil Rights: Affirmative Action.** By the late 1980s, the changing composition of the Court had a major impact on support for affirmative action. Back in 1971, a majority consisting of Justices Brennan, Marshall, Douglas, Burger, Stewart, Powell, and Black voted in the *Griggs v. Duke Power* case to limit affirmative action programs, with Justices Rehnquist and White dissenting. But by 1989, Black, Douglas, Stewart, and Powell had departed the Court. The change could be seen in *Richmond v. J. A. Croson Co.* (1989). The Court in a 5-4 decision struck down the city's program to set aside 30 percent of certain contracts for minorities. Writing for the majority, Justice O'Connor found the program applied hard quotas in violation of the equal protection clause of the Fourteenth Amendment. Brennan, Marshall, and Blackmun dissented.

The trend against affirmative action continued in *Wards Cove Packing Co. v. Antonio* (1989). The majority consisting of Justices O'Connor, White, Rehnquist, Kennedy, and Scalia voted against affirmative action striking down a law mandating affirmative action where a limited statistical racial imbalance is shown. According to the Court, there can be no automatic inference that discrimination is the cause nor that affirmative action is required for a remedy. Nor can employers be expected to have proportional representation of every ethnic group in every occupation. Justice White stated that this approach meant that employers could be hauled into court anytime there was an imbalance, with the burden to show justification for job requirements. Justices Brennan, Marshall, Blackmun, and Stevens dissented in favor of affirmative action. The decisions of *Croson* and *Wards Cove* met with the public outcry of civil rights activists and the media. As time would tell, these decisions would not be the final word on affirmative action. A deeply divided Court would not succumb to simply deciding "for or against" affirmative action but would seek out more explicit criteria for the acceptability or unacceptability of policies intended to address past discrimination. Again the Court defied simple political categorization.

**Civil Rights: Private Sector Discrimination.** In *Patterson v. McLean Credit Union* (1989), the Court was called upon to decide whether Section 1981 of the Civil Rights Act of 1866, which banned discrimination in the making and enforcement of contracts, went so far as to cover workplace harassment.[313] The 1976 opinion of *Runyon v. McCrary* already accepted the application of Section 1981 to discrimination in the making and enforcement of private contracts.[314] In *Patterson,* Kennedy appeared ready to cast the deciding vote in favor of Patterson's claims of discrimination but as a committed textualist disagreed with Brennan's intentionalist approach, delving into the legislative history of the Reconstruction Congress of 1866 and the intent of the legislators. In the midst of the exchange of briefs, Kennedy withdrew his support from Brennan, declaring that Section 1981 did not cover conduct after the formation of the employment contract. Former Blackmun clerk Edward Lazarus attributed the switch to the work of a new clerk to Justice Kennedy, who had formerly worked for Scalia and launched a personal mission to convert Kennedy.[315] The narrow defeat of civil rights advocates met with a strong reaction from congressional liberals. With the urging of Senator Kennedy, Congress amended civil rights legislation, passing the Civil Rights Act of 1991. The new law effectively reversed *Patterson* and *Wards Cove,* allowing for legal action on conduct after formation of the employment contract. Changing the law worked for Democrats so long as they maintained working majorities in the House and Senate. The dynamics on Capitol Hill would change with the composition not long thereafter.

**Abortion.** Changes in the composition of the Court began to have an effect in the area of abortion. In 1973, Justices Blackmun, Marshall, Douglas, Brennan, and Stewart formed a majority in favor of the right to an abortion. At the time, a minority consisting of Rehnquist, White, and Burger dissented. By the time Rehnquist became chief justice, Douglas and Stewart had left the Court. The retirement of Powell in 1987 was thought to have meant the loss of the five-vote majority for *Roe.* That left Brennan, Blackmun, Marshall, and Stevens forming a minority in favor of the right to an abortion. But O'Connor and Kennedy declined the opportunity to overturn the *Roe* decision in *Webster* in 1989 and in *Casey* in 1992.

In *Webster v. Reproductive Health Services* (1989), a 5-4 majority consisting of Justices White, Scalia, Rehnquist, Kennedy, and O'Connor upheld a Pennsylvania law requiring a physician to determine the viability of fetus before performing abortions on women over twenty weeks pregnant. Scalia in his concurring opinion stated that *Roe* should be overruled. Indeed, the "rational relations" standard (for validity of state conditions on abortion) applied by Justices Rehnquist, White, and Kennedy would have overruled *Roe* had there been one more vote in their favor. But O'Connor's opinion upheld state limitations on the right to abortion without expressly overturning *Roe,* using an "undue burden" test. There was overwhelming public interest on both sides of the issue, as over eighty amicus briefs were filed for over four hundred interest groups, two hundred fifty members of Congress, and one thousand state legislators and officials.

As it turned out, the decision was not the reversal of Roe that many had expected. The net effect of these decisions was simply to give states more leeway in regulating conditions of abortions and to convert the issue to one for state legislatures rather than federal courts.

In *Planned Parenthood of Southeastern Pennsylvania v. Casey* (1992), the Court ruled on a Third Circuit judgment effectively challenging the continued legitimacy of the "strict scrutiny" test of *Roe*, applying instead O'Connor's "undue burden" standard proffered in *Webster.*[316] Pennsylvania required "informed consent" in the form of a package of risks of abortion, alternatives, and descriptions of human features of abortion followed by a twenty-four-hour waiting period. In most cases, husbands were to be notified; and in all cases, parents of minors would be notified. The addition of Souter and Thomas to the Court, replacing Brennan and Marshall respectively, caused many to think that *Roe* was doomed. In this highly visible and politicized case, some have suggested that the chief justice delayed the certiorari vote in order to postpone the decision until after the fall 1992 elections, fearing a voter backlash.[317] Where Chief Justice Rehnquist and Justices White, Scalia, Kennedy, and Thomas were initially ready to uphold the entire state statute, O'Connor and Souter objected to parts of the Pennsylvania law. But ultimately Kennedy abandoned the conservatives and joined the latter justices, coauthoring an opinion upholding the essential ruling of *Roe* while striking down the spousal notification provisions of the state law. The personal papers of Harry Blackmun, made public after his death in 2004, indicate that Justices O'Connor and Souter lobbied Kennedy hard to leave the would-be majority.[318] O'Connor's undue burden test was applied. As expected, Justices Blackmun and Stevens concurred with the three others, giving them a clear majority. In his dissent, Scalia declared that he was "appalled by" the reasoning contained in the opinion that overturning *Roe* would "subvert the Court's legitimacy" by succumbing to "political pressure."

But the results left many on both sides of the abortion issue disappointed. Supporters viewed *Casey* as gutting the essential holdings of *Roe* by letting stand state restrictions on abortions. The antiabortion challengers felt they had been cheated of a victory. Legal practitioners were left with a vague standard for adjudication. Yet it is a remarkable statement about the independence of the Court that the combined efforts of Presidents Ronald Reagan and George H. W. Bush to reconstruct the Court through five appointments did not result in the reversal of *Roe.*

**Capital Punishment.** The frequently divided Court faced many cases involving the death penalty. As a frequent tiebreaker on the Court, Justice O'Connor played a pivotal role in the review of capital cases. In the 1988 case of *Thompson v. Oklahoma,* O'Connor joined a 5-4 majority striking down the death penalty for juveniles under the age of sixteen.[319] But in the 1989 case of *Stanford v. Kentucky,* she helped form a majority upholding the constitutionality of death sentences for sixteen- and seventeen-year-olds.[320] In the latter case, she noted that in the thirty-seven states that had the death penalty, a majority of those states allowed it only for defendants sixteen years and older.

Justice O'Connor sided with the law-and-order conservatives in a 1989 review of a Texas case, *Penry v. Lynaugh.*[321] In the case, also known as *Penry I,* a 5-4 majority on the Court held that the execution of mentally retarded persons did not necessarily violate the Eighth Amendment. She questioned whether all mentally retarded people could be considered to lack the ability to reason to such an extent to warrant capital punishment. She observed the lack of a national consensus against such executions, since at the time only two states, Georgia and Maryland, prohibited the execution of mentally retarded persons. Chief Justice Rehnquist and Associate Justices Scalia, Kennedy, and White joined O'Connor for this point. But Justice O'Connor also wrote in *Penry* that the jury must be given the opportunity to make a "reasoned moral response" as evidence of mental retardation. The Court ordered a retrial. Justices Brennan, Marshall, Blackmun, and Stevens joined O'Connor's opinion for this point.

In the 1989 per curiam decision of *Powell v. Texas,* the Court reversed a capital sentence for murder based upon the conduct of a psychiatric examination on "future dangerousness" without the assistance of counsel in violation of the Sixth Amendment.[322] Many lower courts were unhappy with this decision, ensuring that similar issues would return to the Court in future cases.

Despite more conservative composition on the Court, there would be many reversals of lower court decisions on issues concerning criminal procedure. On the whole, the Court narrowly interpreted criminal rights under the Constitution but overturned few of its previous decisions in favor of rights of defendants. Nevertheless, changes were already in the making on the Court. Justices O'Connor and Blackmun would have the opportunity to revisit their positions on the death penalty in future cases, and their decisions would surprise many observers.

**Civil Rights: The Right to Die.** In 1990, a 5-4 majority on the Court upheld the Missouri Supreme Court's reversal of a lower court's order to remove the feeding tube for a woman who had been comatose for six years following an automobile accident. In the absence of clear and convincing evidence of her desire to terminate artificial life-support systems, Chief Justice Rehnquist wrote in *Cruzan v. Missouri Health Department,*[323] the Court could not support such an order. The state had a legitimate interest in the preservation of life. Right-to-life groups hailed the decision as a victory.

**David Souter's Nomination.** In 1990, President Bush nominated New Hampshire Supreme Court justice David Souter to replace William Brennan. With an abundance of caution from the experience of previous nominees, White House counsel C. Boyden Gray advised against answering questions from the Senate Judiciary Committee about specific decisions of the Court.[324] Unlike Bork, Souter did not publish extensively; and relatively little was known about him, in spite of his service on New Hampshire's highest court and his time as state attorney general. Pundits jokingly referred to him as the stealth candidate, able to undermine potential opposition by eluding detection on their "radar" screens. He had worked as an assistant to New Hampshire Attorney

General Warren Rudman, who later was elected to the Senate. Senator Rudman was a Republican who was well respected by both parties in Congress. His support was a plus. When he was governor of New Hampshire, John Sununu appointed Souter to the state supreme court. Though Sununu was unpopular in his notoriety as President Bush's chief of staff, that alone provided little ammunition for the opposition, who complained about the dearth of background information on Souter. After his confirmation, Souter became a noted swing voter on the Court. His performance would disappoint many conservatives. Over time, he consistently sided with "liberal" justices, even voting against a pro-Republican result in *Bush v. Gore.*

**The Thomas Nomination.** In 1991, President Bush nominated U.S. Court of Appeals justice Clarence Thomas as the "best qualified" individual to replace Thurgood Marshall. Marshall, the first African American on the Supreme Court, was a near-mythic litigator on behalf of the NAACP in early civil rights cases. Consequently, Marshall's Supreme Court "seat" held great symbolic as well as political significance. Thomas came from a very different background. Born poor in rural Georgia, he attended Catholic schools. During his college years, he was known for his admiration of Malcolm X; but at some point he changed his philosophical course and became enamored with the views of libertarians Thomas Sowell and Ayn Rand. Thomas graduated from Yale Law School and had spent eight years as the chief of the Equal Employment Opportunity Commission (EEOC). While at the EEOC, he was noted for his opposition to affirmative action plans for minorities.[325]

The nomination of a decidedly conservative African American presented a particular challenge to the coalition of diverse groups that had successfully fought Bork's nomination. Unlike the Bork case, the ABA's Committee on the Federal Judiciary gave Thomas a "qualified" rating, the lowest rating short of "unqualified."[326] Two members rated him "unqualified." This was a lukewarm endorsement from a group that gave "highly qualified" ratings to most nominees. Thomas had only served for a short fifteen months as a judge on the U.S. Circuit Court of Appeals for the District of Columbia. The Alliance for Justice attempted to rally the forces that had defeated Bork, boasting prematurely that they were going to "Bork" Thomas.[327]

Though both Thomas and Bork were known conservatives, there were significant differences with the environment surrounding the nominations. In Thomas's case, Attorney General Thornburgh and White House counsel C. Boyden Gray coordinated the administration's effort on behalf. Conservative interest groups were mobilized in advance to counter opposition.[328] Senate leaders like John Danforth, a moderate Republican for whom Thomas had worked for briefly as an aide, and Strom Thurmond rallied support behind Thomas. The Senate hearings, chaired by Senator Joseph Biden, began with a focus on the nominee's ideological orientation, similar to the Bork hearings. But this approach was not fruitful to opponents of the nomination since Thomas did not have the prolific trail of writings that Bork did. Thomas's belief in natural law theory drew a curious eye from many jurists and academics who considered such views to be outdated, but this was not a topic that resonated with the public at large.

On the fifth day of the confirmation hearings, the Thomas hearings took on a decidedly personal ad hominem tone concerning the nominee's integrity. The opposition raised allegations of sexual harassment by a former EEOC colleague, Anita Hill, who was at the time a professor at Oral Roberts School of Law in Oklahoma. Thomas responded with a vitriolic attack on the opposition's tactics of launching a "high-tech lynching" of his character. The opposition was also hindered in its efforts by the handicap of a usually reliable member of its team. Senator Ted Kennedy was in a weakened position to attack Thomas when shortly before the hearings his nephew, William Kennedy Smith, faced highly publicized rape charges in West Palm Beach, Florida, and Kennedy's own conduct in general came under scrutiny. Senators Arlen Specter and Orrin Hatch aggressively questioned Hill, contributing to an already highly charged atmosphere.[329]

The African American community was not a unified source of opposition to Thomas's nomination. Though it appeared that a majority in the African American community would have preferred a candidate with more liberal credentials, opposition to Thomas was divided. Lacking solid opposition in the Senate, Thomas was confirmed by a narrow vote of 52-48. But the acrimonious nature of the confirmation left participants of both parties, including the nominee, with a bitter taste for the politicization of the process. Once on the Court, Thomas did not emerge as an influential, consensus-building force. Nor did he tip the balance in favor of a working "conservative" majority or coalition on the Court. Instead, he frequently wrote separate opinions supported by few if any of the other justices.

**School Prayer.** The addition of Scalia, Kennedy, Souter, and Thomas to the Court was expected to bring about a change in the Court's rulings on prayer in public schools. Yet a thin majority chose to uphold *Engel* and its progeny in *Lee v. Weisman* (1992). The case involved the invocation of God and prayer at graduation ceremonies. The Bush administration filed an amicus brief asking the Court to reject its earlier rulings and allow such a "noncoercive ceremonial acknowledgment."[330] Kennedy, who cast the deciding vote, found the situation can result in indirect "compulsion" in violation of the establishment clause. Only three years earlier in *County of Allegheny v. ACLU,* Kennedy dissented in part from a decision written by elder justice Blackmun for a majority prohibiting a Nativity scene on the steps of the Allegheny County Courthouse in Pennsylvania.[331] Kennedy, who concurred in the result but not the reasoning of Blackmun in this case, accused his colleague of an "unjustified hostility to religion."[332] Again, the divided Court made political pigeonholing an endeavor fraught with failure.

**The Clinton Years.** President William Jefferson Clinton brought to an end to fourteen years of Republican domination of judicial appointments to the Supreme Court. By the time Clinton took office in 1993, the Republican administrations of Presidents Nixon,

Ford, Reagan, and Bush had replaced all but one of the appointments by Democratic presidents to the Court. There were no vacancies during the previous Democratic administration of Jimmy Carter, depriving that president of the opportunity to make appointments to the Court. Byron White, a Kennedy appointee, remained the sole justice appointed by a Democrat. Yet the Supreme Court could not be categorized as a conservative or even Republican court when assessing its holdings.

The years out of power left the Democrats with somewhat of a handicap in nominating candidates for key legal posts. The inexperience of the Clinton administration's selection team contributed to the failure of President Clinton's first two nominations for attorney general in 1993.[333] Clinton's search for nominees for the Court would not be a smooth road either, though his ultimate nominees would be confirmed by wide margins.

His first opportunity came after only two months in the office when Justice White announced his retirement. Clinton expressed a desire to nominate someone with a "big heart" and real world experience.[334] During a three-month search for a successor to White, Clinton considered widely known politicians including New York Governor Mario Cuomo, Maine Senator George Mitchell, and Interior Secretary Bruce Babbitt. But in the end, the president nominated U.S. Court of Appeals (District of Columbia Circuit) justice Ruth Bader Ginsburg to replace him. Prior to her judgeship, she was an attorney for the ACLU. She was confirmed by a vote of 96-3.

Clinton's second opportunity was not long to follow. Harry Blackmun stepped down in 1994. To replace him, Clinton named another U.S. Court of Appeals justice, Stephen G. Breyer. Prior to his judgeship, he was a professor at Harvard and chief counsel to the Senate Judiciary Committee. He had clerked for Justice Goldberg during the 1964 term. Breyer was confirmed by a vote of 87-9. Both Ginsburg and Breyer had the unanimous support of the ABA's Committee on the Federal Judiciary for a rating of "highly qualified" for the Supreme Court. Clinton was also assisted by the good fortune of timing, as the Democrats held a majority in the Senate when both Ginsburg and Breyer were nominated to the Court. Indeed, the Senate would confirm over three hundred seventy-five of his judicial nominees overall.[335] But the 1994 elections gave the Republicans a majority in the Senate. The Republicans maintained their majority through the next six years of the Clinton administration. The absence of a Supreme Court vacancy for the remainder of Clinton's tenure as president forestalled fights between a Republican Senate and the chief executive over composition of the Court.

Despite the success of the Clinton administration's judicial nominees, political blunders in the early years left the Democratic Party unpopular with a large segment of the voting population. The administration mismanaged and lost congressional support for a national health care plan, fumbled nominations to key executive posts, backed away from a campaign pledge to openly integrate gays in the military, and was blamed for failure of a major military operation in Somalia. Consequently, the Democrats lost control of both the House and the Senate in the 1994 midterm congressional elections. As Congressman Newt Gingrich from Georgia took the reigns as Speaker of the House, he spearheaded his new Republican agenda known as the Contract with America, championing states' rights, school prayer, opposing abortion, and other "conservative" causes. It foreshadowed the rise of and eventual domination of Southern Republicans in both the House and Senate, a trend that would continue long after Gingrich's departure from the House. Though Clinton would be handily reelected in 1996, the Republicans persisted in pressing their agenda in legislatures and courts. Tocqueville's observation about the propensity of political questions to become judicial issues would be borne out in the ensuing years.

**Federalism.** Over the course of his long tenure on the Court, Chief Justice Rehnquist had championed states' rights, but not always with the support of a majority. But in 1995, his view prevailed. In *United States v. Lopez*, a 5-4 majority on the Court struck down the Gun-Free School Zones Act of 1990, a federal law banning the possession of a gun within one thousand feet of a school since it was viewed as too remotely related to interstate economic activity to warrant federal intervention in the traditional state function of law enforcement.[336] This case was evidence of Rehnquist's growing influence on the Court regarding state sovereignty, where in earlier cases, such as the *Fry* case concerning wage and salary controls in 1975, he was the lone dissenter with strong views on the intent of the framers regarding distribution of powers between the states and federal government.[337] But the chief justice had gained the support of many justices joining the Court since that decision, including O'Connor and Kennedy. Justices Stevens, Souter, Breyer, and Ginsburg dissented. But a states' rights victory in this case did not signify a clear conservative triumph, at least as concerns many law-and-order or social conservatives, who placed a higher value on tougher treatment of criminals than protecting "obscure" jurisdictional prerogatives for states. But the case did demonstrate a resurgence of states' rights perspectives and a reincarnation of the values of Jeffersonian Republicans and Jacksonian Democrats, albeit with different names attached.

**Civil Liberties.** The Court defied easy political categorization in the area of free speech. In 1997, Justice Stevens wrote the majority opinion striking down the Communications Decency Act which sought to outlaw "indecent" or "patently offensive" material over the internet.[338] In *Reno v. ACLU/ALA*, the Court attempted to balance the government's interest in protecting minors from indecent material against the right of adults to provide and receive the material, finding that the law overly restricted the latter group's rights. The balancing test most often prevailed on the Court when it considered cases concerning multiple speech interests and new technologies.[339]

But Justice Stevens was in the minority in a later free-expression case. In 2000, the Supreme Court upheld the city of Erie's ban on nude dancing in bars.[340] Justice O'Connor, writing for a divided Court, upheld the ordinance as a content-neutral regulation with a restriction "no greater than is essential to the furtherance of the government's interest." This reflected the traditional "categorical approach," where predetermined rules are applied based upon certain categories of speech and associated restrictions, such as content-neutral regulations; restrictions on time, place, and manner of the speech; commercial speech; fighting words; and prior restraints, based upon a body of law developed by the courts over time. Justices Stevens, Ginsburg, and Souter dissented in part in this case.

The Court when dealing with free speech issues was not always neatly divided along political lines. The proponents of the balancing test, Justices Stevens, Souter, and Breyer, often provided "illiberal" results based upon subjective valuations when balancing interests, such as flag burning where Stevens would accord the national symbol a unique status requiring higher protection. On the other hand, the proponents of the categorical approach, such as Scalia and Kennedy, were generally more protective of controversial speech when categories such as prior restraint applied.[341] They were less likely to allow regulation of speech based upon the offensiveness of the speech or the speaker.

**The Right to Die.** In 1997, the Court denied the right to physician-assisted suicide in *Vacco v. Quill* and *Washington v. Glucksberg.*[342] The cases involved a challenge by terminally ill individuals and physicians to the laws of the states of New York and Washington that criminalized assisted suicide. These decisions signaled an unwillingness of the Court to accept expansive interpretations of due process liberties, especially those that lacked an established tradition of support. The Court found the state had a rational interest in banning the activity and that assisted suicide was inconsistent with medical tradition and practice in preserving life. But the Court was not of one mind on the subject and would revisit the issue with different results later.

**Redistricting.** Since the *Baker v. Carr* decision evoked charges of unwarranted meddling of the judiciary into areas best left to the political branches of government, many on the Court were reluctant to deal with the politically hypersensitive area of legislative districting. But, as in the case of *Baker,* serious charges of malapportionment cried out for a review of state practices in light of the Constitution. In 1995, a 5-4 majority on the Court struck down an electoral redistricting plan for Georgia that relied too heavily on race in the case of *Miller v. Johnson.*[343] The redistricting was the result of a 1990 census. Consequently, African Americans were elected from three of the eleven congressional districts in Georgia. Those districts held black majorities. A number of white voters challenged the redistricting on the basis of Fourteenth Amendment equal protection. But Justice Kennedy, writing for the majority, rejected the use of race as a redistricting criteria in the absence of a compelling governmental interest.[344] Dissenters such as David Souter objected, pointing out that past redistricting had been used for the benefit of Irish, Italian, and Jewish groups.

**The Line-Item Veto.** In the 1998 case of *Clinton v. City of New York,* a six-justice majority struck down the Line Item Veto Act. The case concerned President Clinton's exercise of the line-item veto to negate a tax break associated with the Medicaid program and to eliminate a capital gains tax provision for farmers' cooperatives. Like the *Chadha* case, the Court relied upon the presentment clause of the Constitution, Article I, Section 7, which assigns the power of presenting bills to Congress and the power to either sign or veto to the president. But unlike *Chadha*, which denied Congress's right to "veto" certain executive actions, this decision worked against executive power. Justice John Paul Stevens wrote that the law had attempted to provide the president with the power of "partial repeal" of bills, a power not contemplated or allowed by the Constitution. Ironically, though the ruling took away from a Democratic president's power, the political movement to kill the act resided with powerful Democratic legislators, led by Senator Robert Byrd from West Virginia.[345] The act had been the product of a Republican Congress in 1996 with the purported intent of ending wasteful pork barrel projects tucked into legislation that the president was not likely to veto. The Republicans also backed this legislation in the hope to reclaim the presidency in the 1996 elections, but Clinton's reelection dashed their plans.

**Executive Privilege: Presidential Immunity.** Allegations of misconduct would haunt Clinton throughout his presidency. In the 1997 case of *Clinton v. Jones*, the Court rejected the president's claims of immunity to thwart a sexual harassment lawsuit brought by former Arkansas state employee Paula Jones. Even the argument that civil lawsuits would disrupt the important conduct of the chief executive's business was not enough to convince a majority of the need for presidential immunity. Echoing an earlier era, the justices reinforced the idea that the presidency should be subject to the rule of law being "a government of laws, not men." Independent counsel Kenneth Starr built on this precedent to remove immunity from key presidential aides and compel them to testify against the president. This paved the way for impeachment hearings the following year.

**Impeachment Hearings of President Clinton.** As James Madison advised, the Constitution divides the powers of impeachment among the two houses of the legislature. By the terms of the Constitution, the House is charged with the authority to impeach (i.e., presents charges or indicts) and the Senate is charged with the authority to convict (or acquit) based upon the charges. In December 1998, the House approved two articles of impeachment for President Clinton: one for lying under oath to a federal grand jury (i.e., regarding his relationship with White House intern Monica Lewinsky) and one for obstruction of justice in the *Paula Jones* civil case.

But the 1998 midterm elections cost Republicans five seats in the House, narrowing their majority to 233 to 211 and leaving their lead in the Senate at fifty-five to forty-five.[346] Though the elections preserved their lead, Republicans took the results hard, surprised that President Clinton's foibles did not translate into electoral gains for Republicans. Many believed that "extremist" politics of Gingrich were out of touch with the American people. Subsequently, Newt Gingrich gave up not only his post as Speaker of the House but his seat in Congress. The Gingrich revolution which began in 1994 was over. Though the Republican majority in Congress remained, prevailing with the effort to impeach and remove the president was not assured.[347]

As a result of the timing of the elections, the Senate of the 106th Congress would have to hold hearings on and vote on charges presented by the House of the105th Congress. In accordance with the Constitution, Chief Justice Rehnquist presided over the Senate hearings, which ultimately resulted in the president's acquittal in February 1999. The trial of a sitting president was a procedure not witnessed in the country since Andrew Johnson was impeached in 1868. Johnson escaped conviction by one vote in the Senate. President Nixon's resignation in 1974 after the House committee voted to recommend impeachment prevented the full House from conducting a voting to impeach him and the Senate from conducting a trial.

**Summary of the Early Rehnquist Era.** As can be said about the Burger Court, it would be incorrect to characterize the Rehnquist era as a thorough retrenchment of the old judicial order, since the latter Court made "liberal" rulings on sex discrimination, flag burning, abortion, and the death penalty. Where the Court had the opportunity to reverse previous rulings on abortion and affirmative action, the Court more often limited the application of previous rulings without overturning them. As in previous eras, political categorizations and simplistic labels for the justices provided little in the way of useful guidance for predicting decisions of the Court.

# THE BURGER AND REHNQUIST ERA

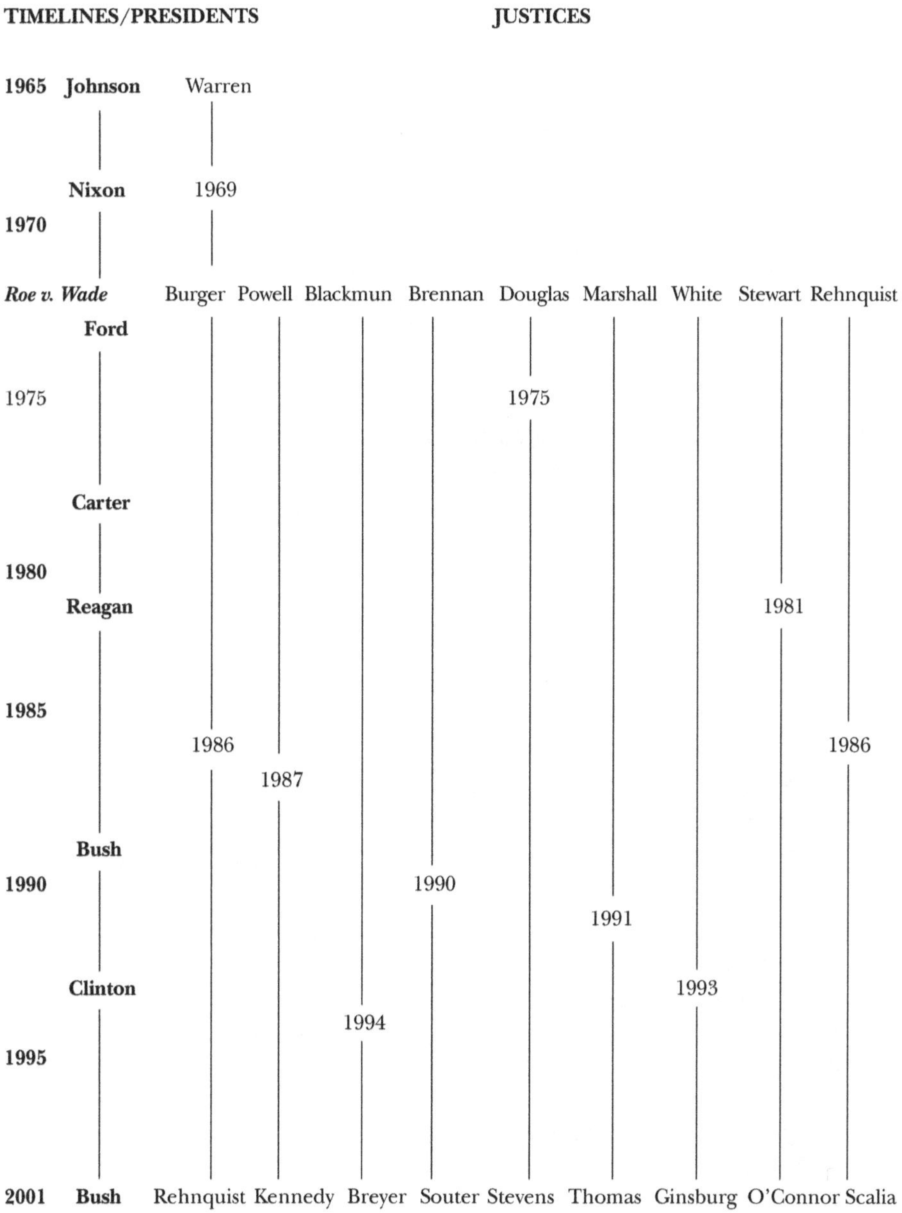
TIMELINES/PRESIDENTS
JUSTICES
1965 Johnson
Warren
Nixon
1969
1970
Roe v. Wade
Burger Powell Blackmun Brennan Douglas Marshall White Stewart Rehnquist
Ford
1975
1975
Carter
1980
Reagan
1981
1985
1986
1986
1987
Bush
1990
1990
1991
Clinton
1993
1994
1995
2001 Bush
Rehnquist Kennedy Breyer Souter Stevens Thomas Ginsburg O'Connor Scalia

# CHAPTER 10

## THE LATTER REHNQUIST ERA: 2000-2005

*The period between the nomination of Stephen G. Breyer to replace Harry Blackmun in 1994 and the seating of Chief Justice John Roberts following the death of William Rehnquist in 2005 marked the longest period in history when the Court was without a change in its composition since 1823.*[348] *The Court was called upon to decide cases with significant political implications, including the election of 2000. With stakes high, vitriolic fights over nominations and consequent "control" of the Court are imminent. But despite determined efforts to change the direction of the Court and collateral attacks on the Court by legislators and talk show hosts, the Court's independence continues to defy the political branches of government.*

In July of 2005, President George W. Bush nominated circuit judge John Roberts to replace Associate Justice Sandra Day O'Connor. Less than two months later, Chief Justice Rehnquist, who suffered from thyroid cancer, died, prompting the president to nominate Roberts as his replacement instead of O'Connor's. Since O'Connor's resignation was not effective until a replacement was confirmed, a swift confirmation of Roberts ensured the Court convened on schedule with nine members in October 2005. According to some reports, both Rehnquist and O'Connor had been delaying retirement plans until a Republican presidency was assured.[349] Even O'Connor had long denied plans to leave the Court.[350] The oldest member of the Court, Stevens maintained good health and showed no inclination to retire.[351] His vigorous dissent in *Bush v. Gore* (2000) put him at odds with Rehnquist, Scalia, and Thomas, continuing Stevens's already-established trend away from the right. He may prefer to stay on the Court until a more moderate successor can be assured. President Bush's selection of ideological choices for key law enforcement and judicial posts, such as former Missouri senator John Ashcroft as attorney general, replaced by White House counsel Alberto Gonzalez in 2004, may mean that some liberals and moderates on the Court will try to outlast the Bush administration. Justice Ginsburg, like O'Connor, recovered from a bout with cancer and enjoys good health.

The 2000-2001 term witnessed the departure of President Bill Clinton and the arrival of President George W. Bush. The Court decided eighty-five cases during this term, a period distinguished by cases of unusual legal and political significance. The cases included decisions on the 2000 presidential election, campaign finance reform, and immigration, subjects the Court may have been expected to leave for the political branches of government to decide.[352] Despite decisions which met with much criticism, such as *Bush v. Gore,* the public's approval rating of the Court was 72 percent favorable.[353] Justices O'Connor and Kennedy continued their pattern of swing votes, joining conservative 5-4 majorities fourteen times and liberal 5-4 majorities eight times.[354] The Court was in a transition period, as the number of close cases increase and the Court was poised to overturn long-standing decisions on issues like the execution of mentally retarded adults. Statistically, there were more 5-4 decisions (33 percent) this term than at any time in the previous ten years.[355] This divided Court continued to defy simplistic political categorization.

**Abortion.** Abortion opponents found themselves thwarted in attempts to outlaw partial birth abortions. In *Stenberg v. Carhart* (2000), a 5-4 majority overturned a Nebraska statute that criminalized partial birth abortions.[356] Writing for the majority, Justice Breyer held that the law placed an "undue burden" on a woman's decision to have an abortion and was therefore unconstitutional. The law contained no exception for such procedures based upon considerations of health of the mother. The determination of necessity of such procedure depends upon "appropriate medical judgment" (language borrowed from *Casey)* regarding the health of the mother. Chief Justice Rehnquist and Justices Scalia, Thomas, and Kennedy dissented. Though pro-choice liberals could accept this case as a victory, the Court's inconsistent track record in striking down restrictions on abortion brought no guarantees in future rulings, leaving both pro-choice and pro-life groups dissatisfied.

**Environment: Federalism.** The Court faced a string of cases that challenged the federal government's power to regulate activities within states, with a presumption that noneconomic activities are nonfederal matters. In *Solid Waste Agency for North Cook County v. U.S. Army Corps of Engineers,* the Court upheld the power of twenty-three local municipalities in northern Illinois to convert a wetlands area into a garbage dump despite federal objections.[357] The local governments challenged federal authority to block the project based upon the Clean Water Act and the presence of migratory birds. The wetlands and pond under consideration in this case were not connected to any interstate waterway. The Clean Water Act's jurisdiction over "navigable waterways" had been unquestioningly applied to waters that were neither navigable nor connected to interstate waterways for decades. This was not unlike the long-standing application of the interstate commerce clause to economic and commercial activities only remotely related to interstate commerce. But the Court appears to have drawn a line for the application of federal powers over noncommercial activities. Chief Justice Rehnquist's long-standing views on Federalism once again prevailed.

**Federalism: Criminal Law.** A divided Court continued to cull federal power when it struck portions of the Violence Against Women Act of 1994. In *United States v. Morrison* (2000), a 5-4 majority on the Court struck down a federal law that had permitted victims of rape and domestic violence to sue their attackers.[358] Writing for the majority, Chief Justice Rehnquist wrote that neither the commerce clause nor the Fourteenth Amendment provides Congress with the authority to prescribe federal civil remedies for acts of private parties. Justices Souter, Breyer, Stevens, and Ginsburg dissented.

**Criminal Law: A Reexamination of Miranda.** After years of whittling down the application of the *Miranda* decision, the Court had the opportunity to overturn the case in *Dickerson v. United States* (2000).[359] Among those filing amicus briefs was the Fraternal Order of Police, the largest national police association, who backed a concerted effort to overturn the 1966 *Miranda* decision. In the *Dickerson* case, law enforcement officials asserted application of an erstwhile ignored 1968 federal statute that purported to allow the use of confessions even without the Miranda warnings so long as the confession was voluntary. The Fourth Circuit Court of Appeals held that the Miranda warnings were not constitutionally required but were rather just one approach to enforcing the Fifth Amendment guarantee against self-incrimination. But Chief Justice Rehnquist, writing for the 7-2 majority, reaffirmed the constitutional basis for the original *Miranda* decision. In his opinion, the chief justice deferred to the Court's thirty-four-year-old ruling which had become an accepted part of the law. Although Rehnquist had long been a critic of the *Miranda* decision, he wrote the opinion supporting its continued use, based upon long-standing precedent or stare decisis. The decision had become an "embedded" legal tradition and legal right, he wrote. Notably, the Justice Department did not defend the 1968 statute, maintaining that Congress had no right to pass it in the first place.[360] Once again, a "conservative" justice (in this case the chief justice) defied political categorization by reaching a "liberal" result. But conservatives had larger issues of concern to care about, such as who would become the next chief executive.

**Presidential Election of 2000.** For the first time since the disputed election of Rutherford B. Hayes over Samuel J. Tilden in 1876, the Supreme Court was called upon to deal with disputed presidential election results in two separate decisions. Similar to 1876, vote counts in Florida were contested. In the exceedingly close November 7, 2000, election, Democratic presidential candidate Al Gore had over five hundred thousand more of the popular vote in the United States overall but would nevertheless carry fewer electoral votes if Florida went to Republican candidate George W. Bush.[361] Therefore, Florida's twenty-five electoral votes would be decisive, with the winner of that state's electoral votes taking the presidency.[362] The Florida Supreme Court decided in favor of extending the deadlines for manual recounts of votes. At this time, every member of the

Florida Supreme Court had been appointed by Democratic governors.[363] Knowledge of the composition of the Florida Supreme Court prompted Bush's campaign manager, James Baker, to enlist the aid of Theodore Olson (later to be named President Bush's solicitor general) to file suit in federal court. With the U.S. District Court and the Eleventh Circuit Court of Appeals failing to enjoin the recount, Olson appealed the Florida ruling to the U.S. Supreme Court.[364] On December 4, 2000, in *Bush v. Palm Beach County Canvassing Board*, the Court unanimously set aside the decision of the Florida Supreme Court.[365] The decision was made only four days after the Court decided to hear the case, one of the most expedited decisions in the history of the Court. The Court directed the Florida court to clarify the reasons for its ruling. The decision of the U.S. Supreme Court effectively returned the state vote tally to 930 votes in favor of George W. Bush, ahead of the narrower 537-vote lead after the recount.

The first issue was whether the Florida Supreme Court had usurped the state legislature's power to regulate the conduct of presidential elections, granted by Article II, Section 1 of the Constitution. It was unclear if the Florida court, dominated by appointees from Democratic governors, had based its decision on the Florida state constitution's guarantee of the right to vote in order to override the legislature's desires (the latter being dominated by Republicans). The second issue was whether the Florida court had considered a federal law enacted in 1887 which prohibits changing the rules for presidential elections after election day. The seven-page decision was issued a mere seventy-two hours after oral argument. The Court reached unanimity by avoiding a direct decision that would have handed the presidency to either Al Gore or George Bush and remanding the case, allowing the Florida Court the opportunity to reestablish the legitimacy of its ruling.

On December 12, a divided Supreme Court handed down its second decision in *Bush v. Gore*.[366] In a 5-4 ruling, the Court reversed the Florida Supreme Court order for hand recounts of votes ruling that the state court had violated the equal protection clause of the Fourteenth Amendment.[367] A 7-2 majority found that there were constitutional problems with the Florida Supreme Court's order to recount votes. Winning Florida gave Texas governor George W. Bush 271 electoral votes and left Vice President Al Gore with 267 votes. Gore advisors speculated that if the recount had proceeded, the vice president would have won Florida's electoral votes and the presidency. No doubt historians will ponder this for some time to come.

In an unsigned opinion, the majority ruled that because federal law prevents challenge of electors selected by December 12 and because the Florida legislature had appointed the electors by that date, the Florida Supreme Court's decision violated Article II powers designated to the state legislature. Rehnquist, Scalia, and Thomas agreed with the majority view but wrote a separate opinion. They recognized that principles of "comity and respect for federalism compel us to defer to decisions of state courts on issues of state law" but that this case was one of those "exceptional cases where the Constitution imposes a duty or confers a power on a particular branch of a state's government," referring to Article II's assignment of responsibility for choosing electors to the state legislatures. The Court ruled by a 5-4 majority that there wasn't time for Florida election officials to do a constitutionally correct recount.

In her dissent, Justice Ginsburg argued that the Court should defer to the Florida Supreme Court's decision, respecting federalism and our system of dual sovereignty. Souter and Breyer recognized problems with the Florida court's order for a recount but felt that the order should have been allowed to proceed prior to the December 12 deadline, referring to the U.S. Supreme Court's issuance of a stay for the recount on December 9. Breyer wrote that the Court risked "undermining the public's confidence in the Court itself."

In his strenuous dissent, Justice Stevens wrote, "Although we may never know with complete certainty the identity of the winner of this year's presidential election, the identity of the loser is perfectly clear. It is the nation's confidence in the judge as an impartial guardian of the rule of law." The decision lent "credence to the most cynical appraisal of the work of judges throughout the land."

All members of the 5-4 majority were appointed by Republican presidents. But was this a purely political decision of those justices appointed by Republican president's versus those appointed by Democratic presidents? Of the dissenting votes, Ruth Bader Ginsburg and Stephen Breyer were appointed by Democratic president William Clinton. On the other hand, David Souter was appointed by Republican President George H. W. Bush and John Paul Stevens was appointed by Republican Gerald Ford. The closeness of the vote tells us that this holding cannot be wholly explained by political affiliation.

**The Presidency of George W. Bush: Beneficiary of a Conservative Court?** With the Bush administration's inaugural in January of 2001 made possible by the Supreme Court, the judiciary would maintain high visibility. Indeed, a chief litigator in the legal fight, Theodore B. Olson, was awarded the coveted post of solicitor general. Yet the Court continued to defy rigid categorization as a "conservative" body. Conservatives were disappointed by key decisions in the 2002-3 term, such as on the death penalty and affirmative action. On a Court divided on significant issues, Justice O'Connor established her dominance as "kingmaker." In all thirteen of the term's 5-4 decisions, she was in the majority and wrote the decision in many.[368] More often than not, she was joined by Justices Stevens, Souter, Ginsburg, and Breyer. The nine justices on the Supreme Court, prior to the departure of Rehnquist and O'Connor, had been in place longer than any other group of justices since 1823.[369]

**Campaign Finance Reform.** First Amendment challenges to campaign spending limits were no longer successful, as Republicans found out. In *Federal Election Commission v. Colorado Republican Federal Campaign Committee* (2001) the Court held that federal election law may limit coordinated political party expenditures on specific candidates.[370] O'Connor cast the deciding vote in the 5-4 decision. Chief Justice Rehnquist and Justices Scalia, Thomas, and Kennedy dissented.

**Environmental Law.** In *Whitman v. American Trucking Associations* (2001), the Court held that the Environmental Protection Agency may set new and tougher clean-air standards without considering their implementation costs.[371] Justice Scalia wrote for the Court holding that Congress through the Clean Air Act had properly delegated power to the Environmental Protection Agency to set air quality standards but that the EPA had no authority to consider economic impact in setting those standards. There were no dissents in this case. Scalia disappointed conservatives by not availing himself of this opportunity to attack the doctrine of legislative delegation, not to mention his rendering a rather "unconservative" result that favored environmentalists.[372]

**Criminal Law: Search and Seizure.** In *Illinois v. McArthur* (2001), the Court ruled that police can impede a resident's access to a private home while they seek a search warrant.[373] Justice Breyer, writing for an eight-member majority, held that the action of the police was reasonable when they feared destruction of the evidence if the suspect reentered his home without their supervision and refrained from searching until a warrant was obtained. Justice Stevens dissented, objecting to police power to intrude into the "sanctity of the ordinary citizen's home" to prosecute a "petty offense."

In a decision surprising to many observers, Justice Scalia wrote for a 5-4 majority decision in *Kyllo v. United States* (2001) holding that the use of a thermal imaging device to detect heat from high-intensity lamps used for growing marijuana indoors violates the Fourth Amendment's protection against illegal searches.[374] Police acquired a search warrant partially based upon the detection of heat emanating from the walls and garage roof of the defendant's house as well as tips from informants. Scalia, joined by Souter, Thomas, Ginsburg, and Breyer, found that the thermal imaging technology took law enforcement officials beyond the "degree of privacy against government that existed when the Fourth Amendment was adopted." Scalia has proclaimed himself an "originalist" who looks to construing the constitution as the words were used and understood at the time they were adopted.[375] In a turn of the tables, Justice Stevens, joined by Rehnquist, O'Connor, and Kennedy, accused the majority of abandoning judicial restraint in not applying the well-accepted "in plain view" rule and overturning the Ninth Circuit Court of Appeals.

In *Indianapolis v. Edmond,* the Court struck down drug-search roadblocks set up by metropolitan law enforcement officials in high-crime areas.[376] In a 6-3 decision written by Justice O'Connor, the Court held that the tactic was an unreasonable search and seizure in violation of the Fourth Amendment because it intruded on the privacy of the motorist without probable cause or even reasonable suspicion. The method, conducted six times in 1998, involved stopping cars and examining drivers' licenses while drug-sniffing dogs circled the car. The practice was challenged by two drivers who were stopped but not arrested. Justices Rehnquist, Scalia, and Thomas dissented, with the former arguing that the practices served a legitimate state interest with a minimal intrusion on the privacy of motorists. O'Connor distinguished this case from a 1990 ruling upholding drunk-driving checkpoints set up on highways because it served the independent purpose of public safety, not merely law enforcement's objective to ferret out criminals.

In a 6-3 vote, the Court struck down the nonconsensual use of drug tests administered to pregnant women by a public hospital. Positive results were forwarded to police. Writing for the majority in *Ferguson v. City of Charleston*,[377] Justice Stevens stated that testing patient's urine for cocaine at the Medical University of South Carolina in Charleston, South Carolina, amounted to an unconstitutional police search without a warrant. Scalia dissented, joined by Chief Justice Rehnquist and Justice Thomas.

**Criminal Law: Capital Cases.** An unexpected siding of Scalia with the liberal justices could be seen in *Rogers v. Tennessee* (2001).[378] The Court faced the question of whether a state could retroactively abrogate the "year and a day" rule, under which an offender could only be charged with attempted murder if the victim dies within 366 days of infliction of injury. Wilbert Rogers was convicted of murder upon the death of a man fifteen months after Rogers had stabbed him. A five-to-four majority on the Court voted to uphold the conviction, but Scalia dissented, joined by Breyer and Stevens. Thomas also joined Scalia. Reflecting his "originalist" approach, Justice Scalia wrote that it is widely understood that a court "cannot make murder what was not murder when the act was committed." Thus, the application of conservative judicial methodology would have rendered an opinion supporting a liberal result.

Capital punishment remained a contentious issue on and off the Court. The advent of DNA testing and subsequent acquittals of a number of death row inmates stirred a new examination of death penalties in the United States. Such concerns motivated Governor George Ryan of Illinois to announce on 31 January 2000 a moratorium on the death penalty. He was spurred by the publicity surrounding the case of Rolando Cruz, who had spent ten years on death row in Illinois prior to his exoneration via DNA tests. The popularity of the death penalty has declined in recent years. According to one poll, 66 percent of the American public supported the death penalty in 2000, down from 80 percent in 1994.[379] In 1997, the ABA called for a moratorium on executions in the United States.[380] Allegations of racism, the original basis for the legal challenge of the death penalty, persisted. As of April 1, 2000, death row inmates were 46 percent white, 43 percent black, 9 percent Hispanic, 1 percent Asian, and 1 percent Native American.[381]

In 2000, Alaska, the District of Columbia, Hawaii, Iowa, Maine, Massachusetts, Michigan, Minnesota, New Hampshire, North Dakota, Rhode Island, West Virginia, and Wisconsin did not allow the death penalty.[382] Additionally, the states of Connecticut, Kansas, New Jersey, New Mexico, New York, and South Dakota allowed the death penalty but carried out no executions. The death penalty issue has even become an issue of foreign policy, as European Union states rigorously oppose capital punishment. The European Court of Human Rights in Strasbourg, France, and nongovernmental organizations like Amnesty International have taken strong stances against the death penalty. In one well-known case, the government of the Netherlands refused to extradite a U.S. soldier accused of brutally killing and dismembering his wife until assured that U.S. military prosecutors would not seek the death penalty.

The death penalty became an issue during the presidential elections of 2000. Texas governor George W. Bush effectively used the issue against then-incumbent governor Ann Richards in 1994. Consequently, Texas led the nation in the number of executions. Yet presidential candidate Bush found himself under considerable pressure to request a halt to the execution of Gary Graham, though the Texas governor has no direct clemency powers. George Ryan, the Republican governor of Illinois, ordered a moratorium on executions in his state after thirteen people on death row were exonerated for crimes they had been convicted of.[383] DNA tests led to five of the exonerations. Senator Russ Feingold (D-Wisc.) and Rep. Jesse L. Jackson, Jr., (D-Ill.) introduced bills in both houses of Congress calling for a moratorium.

As in the *Penry I* case, Justice O'Connor continued to play the pivotal role on the Court. Johnny Paul Penry was retried in 1990. He was again convicted of rape and murder and sentenced to death. When the case reached the Supreme Court, *Penry v. Johnson (Penry II)*,[384] the death sentence handed down in the retrial was overturned.[385] Justice O'Connor wrote for a 6-3 majority that the judge's instructions "provided an inadequate vehicle for the jury to make a reasoned moral response to Penry's mitigating evidence." This evidence included a measured intelligence equivalent to a seven-year-old and severe abuse as a child. By the time of the decision in 2001, eighteen states (of thirty-eight allowing the death penalty) prohibited the execution of the mentally retarded.[386] Justices Thomas, Rehnquist, and Scalia dissented.

Facing an onslaught of worldwide criticism, the Texas legislature approved a bill to ban executions of mentally retarded persons. But in June 2001, Texas governor Rick Perry vetoed this legislation, reaffirming his belief that sufficient safeguards were in place to protect mentally retarded defendants. Nevertheless, reconsideration about the death penalty continued in other states. After disclosures that thirteen death row inmates had been wrongly convicted in Illinois, Governor George Ryan declared an indefinite moratorium on state executions pending a three-year review of state procedures. He ultimately commuted the sentences of all 167 inmates with death sentences as his term neared its end in January 2003.[387] Governor Ryan did so with the urging of former South African president Nelson Mandela, Reverend Desmond Tutu, and Mexican president Vicente Fox. Justice O'Connor later remarked that serious questions of the death penalty are being raised in light of statistics such as the exoneration of at least ninety death row inmates since 1973.[388] O'Connor also questioned the adequacy of assistance of counsel citing statistics that defendants with court-appointed counsel were 28 percent more likely to be convicted than those who hired their own attorneys and 48 percent more likely to get the death penalty.[389] Senate Judiciary Committee chairman Patrick Leahy sponsored a bill for the Innocence

Protection Act which would guarantee access to DNA evidence and provide assistance to capital defendants.

In *McCarver v. North Carolina* (2001),[390] the Court was called upon to reexamine the issue of whether the application of the death penalty to a mentally retarded man violated the Eighth Amendment's prohibition of cruel and unusual punishment. Ernest McCarver was an inmate in North Carolina's death row who had an IQ of 67. Public momentum had gathered on the issue, but the Court dismissed the case as moot after North Carolina outlawed the execution of the mentally retarded. With America's death row population burgeoning to over three thousand inmates and with DNA evidence reversing convictions in remarkable numbers, unqualified popular support for the death penalty appeared to be on the wane.

The Court had the opportunity to face the issue again in 2002, in the case of *Atkins v. Virginia.*[391] In that case, the Court banned executions for mentally retarded adults altogether, overturning the 1989 decision of *Penry v. Lynaugh (Penry I).* Stevens wrote for the 6-3 majority. Since that latter case was decided, the number of states prohibiting capital punishment for mentally retarded adults increased from sixteen to thirty. The Court's recognition of society's "evolving standards of decency" guided the majority to reach a ruling reversing its previous decision.

In the 2003 case of *Wiggins v. Smith,*[392] Justice O'Connor wrote for a 7-2 majority overturning the death sentence for Maryland inmate Kevin Wiggins because of ineffective assistance of counsel in violation of his Sixth Amendment right, where the defense failed to investigate or raise mitigating evidence about Kevin Wiggins's severe childhood abuse and borderline mental retardation. Scalia and Thomas dissented.

The trend limiting the death penalty continued in the 2005 case of *Roper v. Simmons,* where a 5-4 majority held that the Eighth and Fourteenth Amendments forbid the execution of defendants under the age of eighteen when the offense was committed. Writing for the majority, Justice Kennedy echoed *Atkins* notion of "evolving standards of decency" and a new "national consensus." The Court reversed the 1989 decision of *Stanford v. Kentucky,* which had allowed the death penalty for sixteen- and seventeen-year-olds.

Chief Justice Rehnquist and Associate Justices Scalia, O'Connor, and Thomas dissented. Justice Scalia strongly criticized Kennedy's use of foreign and international law and international proclamations in support of the Court's decision, such as the United Nations Convention on the Rights of the Child and the International Covenant on Civil and Political Rights. But Kennedy was hardly original in citing international law, which is mentioned in at least seven different sections in the Constitution. In the 1900 case of *Paquette Habana,* Associate Justice Horace Gray stated explicitly that "international law is part of our law."[393] Ignoring foreign and international law will often mean ignoring our own legal traditions and history. One significant piece of foreign law, the English Magna Carta, has been cited in at least fifty opinions.[394]

**Criminal Law: Noncapital Cases.** A unanimous Court struck down state laws allowing the use of marijuana for medical purposes in *United States v. Oakland Cannabis Buyer's Cooperative.*[395] Justice Thomas wrote for the majority that federal laws outlawing the growing or selling of marijuana allowed for no "medical necessity" exception. He pointed out that legal alternatives, such as the synthetic form tetrahydrocannabinol, exist. Justice Breyer recused himself from participating in the decision because his brother was the federal judge who issued an injunction against the marijuana cooperative. Justices Stevens, Souter, and Ginsburg concurred with the result but refused to accept a blanket ruling against the application of medical necessity in cases of extraordinary suffering.

In *Atwater v. Lago Vista,* a 5-4 majority on the Court upheld the arrest and detention of a Texas woman for not buckling her children's seat belts. The detention was challenged on the basis that it was not warranted for a minor offense that was normally only punishable by a fine. In an unusual alignment of the Court, Souter and Kennedy joined Rehnquist and Scalia in the majority while Thomas and O'Connor joined the dissent, who argued that allowing full custodial arrests for minor offenses could lead to police abuses and racial profiling.

**Civil Rights: Employment.** As a sign of the times, more civil rights cases concerning gay rights reached the Court for resolution. In *Circuit City Stores v. Adams,* the Court in a 5-4 decision ruled that an employer can force a worker to adhere to an arbitration agreement signed as a condition of employment where the employee alleges discrimination.[396] A gay former employee had sued the store over alleged harassment that occurred at the workplace. The Court had previously held in *Gilmer v. Interstate/Johnson Lane Corp.*[397] that an arbitration clause foreclosed litigation for a stockbroker. The Ninth Circuit Court of Appeals in the *Adams* case held that a provision in the 1925 Federal Arbitration Act (which made such arbitration clauses binding as a matter of federal law) excludes coverage for "contracts of employment of seamen, railroad employees, or any other class of workers engaged in foreign or interstate commerce."[398] John Paul Stevens dissented stating that it was never intended that this law would apply to employment contracts.

In *Boy Scouts of America v. Dale* (2000), the Court upheld the Boy Scouts' ban on gay men serving as scoutmasters.[399] Under the application of the principles of federalism to private associations, Rehnquist writing for the majority struck down the New Jersey public accommodations law as a violation of the Boy Scouts' First Amendment right to "expressive association."

Rights of the disabled cases also found their way to the Court. The Court in *University of Alabama v. Garrett* (2001) ruled that employees cannot recover damages from states for noncompliance with the Americans with Disabilities Act in the absence of unequivocal intent by Congress to overcome state immunity as provided in the Eleventh Amendment.[400] Nor did the Court find a pattern of discrimination which violates the Fourteenth Amendment. One plaintiff, Patricia Garrett, was a director of nursing at the University of Alabama who lost her job because of time off for treatment of breast cancer. Failing to convince the Court that the state's discrimination was incongruent and disproportional made it incapable of overcoming the state's sovereign immunity. Justice Breyer dissented, joined by Justices Stevens, Souter, and Ginsburg. The ACLU had filed an amicus brief noting the extensive *Congressional Record* indicating the intent of the legislators to allow such suits.

**Affirmative Action.** Affirmative action for school admissions faced its greatest challenge since the 1978 *Bakke* decision in two major decisions involving the University of Michigan. In a 6-3 ruling in *Gratz v. Bollinger,* the Court struck down the undergraduate admissions system that awarded the equivalent of a full grade point for applicants from certain racial groups.[401] Chief Justice Rehnquist wrote for the majority, striking down the bonus point system, which granted 20 points for minorities (100 generally assured admission), resembled an inflexible quota.

By contrast, in a 5-4 ruling, the Court in *Grutter v. Bollinger* upheld the University of Michigan Law School's program which based its admissions upon a "holistic review" of each individual record, including consideration of race as one among many factors, rather than a rigid point or quota system.[402] O'Connor wrote for the majority in *Grutter* arguing that there was a compelling state interest in achieving diversity, echoing Justice Powell's opinion in *Bakke* twenty-five years earlier. She looked to the three hundred briefs from corporations, unions, and nonprofits institutions, as well as statements from military leaders about the benefits of diversity in the workplace and the dependence of the workplace upon the educational system to achieving such diversity.

But justices on both sides of the issue, found it hard to distinguish between the two methods of admission.[403] Justice Scalia dissented in the *Grutter* case, calling the majority's opinion "a sham to cover a scheme of racially proportionate admissions." Justice Souter dissented in *Grutter,* arguing that the undergraduate school "simply does by a numbered scale what the law school accomplishes in its 'holistic review.'" Justice Ginsburg, who dissented in the *Gratz* case, predicted that institutions of higher learning would now resort to "camouflage" as well as "winks, nods, and disguises." Justice Thomas, dissenting in the *Grutter* case, echoed his long-held theme that racial preferences "demean us all."

**Criminal Law: Sodomy.** At the end of the term in June 2003, a 6-3 majority of the Court struck down the antisodomy statutes of Texas and, by implication, those of twelve other states in the case of *Lawrence v. Texas.* The case involved consensual sex in a private home. The Court's majority in a decision written by Justice Kennedy based its decision upon a "zone of privacy" implicit in the Constitution. In overturning the Court's own decision of *Bowers v. Hardwick,* Kennedy challenged the basis of the 1986 decision stating that "there is no long-standing history in this country of laws directed at homosexual conduct as a distinct matter." The sodomy statute in question was enacted in 1973. Kennedy continued, "When homosexual conduct is made criminal by the law of the state, the declaration is in and of itself an invitation to subject homosexual persons to discrimination in both the public and the private spheres" and therefore violates the Fourteenth Amendment's equal protection clause. Thus, state laws criminalizing homosexual conduct were declared unconstitutional.

Scalia and Thomas dissented, with the former pointing to twenty prosecutions and four executions for homosexual conduct during colonial times as evidence that the framers of the Constitution never intended protection for such activities. In his vituperative criticism of the majority's decision that exceeded the usual bounds of comity between the justices, Scalia warned that the opinion by implication "calls for the end of all morals legislation" and would result in "a massive disruption of the social order." In the wake of the decision, the movement for homosexual marriage burgeoned from California to Massachusetts.[404] Social conservatives were outraged. It did not take long for lawmakers to seek ways to reverse the Court's ruling. Within days of the Court's decision, Senate Majority Leader Bill Frist proposed a constitutional amendment to ban gay marriages.[405]

**Criminal Law and the War on Terrorism.** The ostensibly conservative Court surprised the Bush administration by its plurality opinion written by Justice Sandra Day O'Connor ruling against holding Yaser Esam Hamdi, captured in Afghanistan in 2001, indefinitely as an "enemy combatant." Hamdi's father filed a writ of habeas corpus in 2002 on his son's behalf. O'Connor was joined by Chief Justice Rehnquist, Kennedy, and Breyer. The Court in *Hamdi v. Rumsfeld* (2004) upheld the right of the government to hold Hamdi for trial by military tribunal as a result of authority conferred by Congress, but not without limitations on the length of time held, as well as the right to present evidence on his behalf (concerning his status as an enemy combatant), the right to habeas corpus, and the right to consult counsel.

> We have long since made clear that a state of war is not a blank check for the president when it comes to rights of the nation's citizens . . . Any process in which the executive's factual assertions go wholly unchallenged or are simply presumed correct without any opportunity for the alleged combatant to demonstrate otherwise falls constitutionally short.[406]

Although Hamdi's fight in U.S. courts was assisted by his U.S. citizenship (by virtue of his birth in the state of Louisiana), the implication of the ruling applied to all "enemy combatants." Thus, the case called into question the nature of the detention of hundreds of prisoners at Guantanamo Bay, Cuba. Justices Souter and Ginsburg joined the plurality on the right of Hamdi to offer evidence that he is not an enemy combatant but maintained that the detention was unauthorized. Justice Scalia, joined by Stevens, dissented. Justice Clarence Thomas filed a separate dissenting opinion as the only justice persuaded by the government's argument of "inherent" presidential powers under Article II of the Constitution. In another case concerning detention of a U.S. citizen, the Court in *Padilla v. Rumsfeld* (2004) avoided constitutional decisions by its holding against jurisdiction of the U.S. District Court for the Southern District of New York over Jose Padilla. In *Rasul v. Bush* (2004), the Court held that aliens held at Guantanamo Bay had the right to petition for habeas corpus, regardless of their location outside the jurisdiction of any federal court. On a related note, Congress included a provision in the 2004 National Defense Authorization Act that sets a policy against the use of torture for prisoners in U.S. custody.[407]

**Federal Sentencing Guidelines.** Two landmark cases decided in January of 2005 resulted in challenging the results of over four hundred criminal sentences. The Court in the cases of *United States v. Booker* and *United States v. Fanfan* held that the practice (as mandated by the federal sentencing guidelines) of adding time to a criminal sentence based upon facts found by a judge alone is unconstitutional. In one exemplary case to be reconsidered by lower courts, an individual, Mohamad Hammoud, had been sentenced to 155 years in prison for smuggling cigarettes. Though the smuggling conviction would normally carry a fifty-seven-month sentence, Mr. Hammoud's intent to use the profits to support the terrorist group Hezbollah resulted in 150 years added to the sentence.[408] But district court judges would still have much discretion in sentencing, as the Court kept intact the use of the federal guidelines in an "advisory" capacity provided that the sentences are "reasonable."

**"Takings" under the Fifth Amendment.** In one of the last cases of the 2004-2005 term, the Court upheld the power of government to take property for purposes of development. In *Kelo v. City of New London*, a 5-4 majority on the Court found a legitimate "public purpose" of taking privately owned properties for the development of a new business district, with shops, restaurants, and hotels. Chief Justice Rehnquist and Justices Scalia, O'Connor, and Thomas dissented, questioning the expansive finding of a public purpose, which appeared to be without limit. "The specter of condemnation hangs over all property," O'Connor wrote.

But was this a victory for *liberals* seeking to expand government power at the expense of private landowners? Certainly the result was an expansion of the government's power of eminent domain, but the motivation appears to be less an ideological quest for domination on the part of the majority Democratic City Council of New London, Connecticut, than the desire for economic development spurred by private sector developers in pursuit of profit. With the private developers, the real victors in this case, standing to gain millions of dollars as a result of the decision, calling this a "liberal" victory is a shrill, untenable spin on the Court's decision.[409] The unusual division of the Court indicates once again that not all decisions fall squarely along ideological lines.[410]

**The Rehnquist Court in Retrospect.** The death of William Rehnquist in 2005 meant the end of the longest period of stability of the Court's composition. There were no new appointments to the Court after the appointment of Stephen Breyer in 1994 until 2005, when Judge John Roberts became chief justice. Rehnquist witnessed many changes since he first joined the Supreme Court in 1972. As for him and the other justices sitting on the Court for over thirty years (including John Marshall, Roger Taney, Oliver Wendell Holmes, and William O. Douglas), the world inside and outside the Court that existed at the time of their departure was very different from that of the time when they began. In the 1970s, the influence of Chief Justice Earl Warren could still be strongly felt. He and like-minded justices had vectored the institution in a direction that vastly strengthened the Court's role in individual liberties, civil rights, and federal power over the states. Changing course over the next decades was incremental, often dependent upon the individual departures of members of the Warren Court as well as the evolution of views of individual justices on specific issues.

Yet many are perplexed that a Court with seven Republican appointees has not reversed "the Warren Court revolution."[411] Was this the result of a division on the Court between "old Republicans" (i.e., Rehnquist) versus "new Republicans" (i.e., O'Connor and Souter) as some have suggested?[412] Such a division based upon age makes no sense, since O'Connor graduated from Stanford Law School the same class as Rehnquist. Even Rehnquist moderated his views enough to support upholding the *Miranda* decision, albeit in the interest of consistency and stare decisis. Later appointees, such as Scalia, are certainly more conservative but will frequently surprise us with "liberal" results on cases concerning flag burning and warrantless searches. It is inescapable that political generalizations and categorizations of the Court do not always work well, especially when evaluating the performance of individual justices.

If a case can be made for a consistent political theme for the Court, especially regarding the influence of Chief Justice Rehnquist, it could be made on the subject of federalism. [413] In the view of some, the theme is the product of the Court's deliberate selection of specific cases with federalism issues, not the result of a shift in the litigation environment.[414] The trend can be seen in a shift from the Court's review of predominantly "social" issues, such as freedom of speech, abortion, school prayer, and affirmative action, to issues more focused on federalism.[415] Contrary to the meaning in the days of John Marshall, federalism in this context has come to mean the recognition of power for states, local government, and private associations as opposed to the aggregation of power in the central government in Washington. Indeed, the Court struck down over thirty-one federal statutes since 1995. The types of cases the Court reviews have changed in part because of more power the Court has in cases that come before it. With the removal of much of the Court's mandatory appellate jurisdiction by Congress, the Court has been able to concentrate on cases of its own choosing. Nevertheless, Rehnquist's views on federalism, once a minority viewpoint on the Court, now represent the views of a working majority.

Other commentators see the trend as more focused on dismantling antidiscrimination laws, with federalism often used as a cover.[416] The Court's rulings in *Boy Scouts of America v. Dale* and affirmative action cases seem to bear this out. The *Boy Scouts* case, where the doctrine of federalism was used to strike down the New Jersey public accommodations law is a good example.

Subject matter of cases aside, the manner of decision making on the Rehnquist Court is worthy of comment. Some observers accuse the chief justice of having an ipse dixit approach to decision making (translated from Latin as "he himself said it" but meaning "it is so because I say so").[417] This style is exemplified by "preemptive" opinions not known for deep reasoning, showing little deference for the opinions of other colleagues and discouraging internal discussion within the Court. In an era when the Court is under a political microscope, much media and interest group attention is focused on the result rather than the reasoning. But, as will be argued later, it is often the reasoning that distinguishes the judiciary from the political branches of government. In the complex world of constitutional law and statutory interpretation, it is not unusual for conservative reasoning to lead to liberal results and vice versa.

Notwithstanding great public attention to the institution, the Court remains sharply divided on many issues. The number of 5-4 decisions has gradually increased through the 1990s and was up to 31 percent of the Court's decisions in the 2000 term.[418] In more than half of those decisions, Chief Justice Rehnquist was joined by Justices Scalia, Thomas, O'Connor, and Kennedy.[419] Recent Court rulings on affirmative action and sodomy statutes demonstrated the limits of Rehnquist's hold on the Court.

In the end, the Rehnquist Court was hard to categorize politically, frustrating both ardent liberals and conservatives, with divided rulings reflecting diverse composition and independent approaches to the cases and issues before it. The Court's continued independence from the political branches of government makes it a target for those with specific agendas for the judiciary.

# Chapter 11

## THE COURT AS A CHANNEL FOR POLITICS

*The Supreme Court has long differentiated itself from the so-called political branches of government, eschewing decision making based upon explicitly political grounds. But that does not excuse the Court from having to decide cases with political implications, notwithstanding the "political questions" doctrine. In this vein, political issues are "channeled" through legal "cases and controversies" with parties possessing standing via injury-in-fact or other legal status cognizable by law. These legal channels may lead to seemingly contradictory results. In practice, conservative methodology in deciding a case does not necessarily guarantee a conservative result any more than liberal methodology will guarantee a liberal result.*

Political scientists are fond of *models* that can "describe, explain, and predict" organizational behavior. In the case of the Supreme Court, a notional model would begin by looking at institutional inputs and outputs in the context of the judicial process. *Inputs* include jurisdiction (controlled to an extent by the legislative branch), judges (including the selection and confirmation process), legislation (statutory lawmaking), and the public (including media and interest groups). The fundamentally important inputs are the cases and controversies themselves, with associated counsels' written and oral briefs, amicus curiae material, and internal judicial discussions. But, as mentioned previously, inputs can be more limited than for the other branches. Justice Douglas aptly used the "oyster analogy" to describe how cases come to the Court. As such, the Court has no choice but to wait for an actual case and controversy to come to the Court, much as an oyster must wait for a grain of sand in order to generate a pearl. The Court lacks the unfettered discretion to reach out and grab issues as do the executive and legislative branches.

*Outputs* of the judicial process consist of judicial decisions, which include not only cases adjudicated by the Court but even those cases where the Court denies certiorari, effectively letting the lower court decisions stand. The Court is limited to the relatively few cases it hears, an average of 84 a year. In reality, the Court's decision is rarely the final word on any given issue. Most often, final resolution of the issue depends upon action taken by other bodies, such as the lower courts, the executive branch, the legislature, and/or the states. These cases and other inputs are channeled through a decision-making process that is different from the executive and legislative branches. The judiciary has its own procedural methodology and rules of interpretation, guided or limited by defined and traditional roles of the Court. This is discussed in more detail later.

**An Inherent Duality: The Supreme Court as Both a Legal and Political Institution.** As Alexis de Tocqueville saw it in 1835, "scarcely any political question arises in the United States that is not resolved, sooner or later, into a judicial question."[420] By David Easton's definition of politics, the "authoritative allocation of values in society," there are very few legal causes of action that will be lacking in implications of political import. Whether the case concerns property rights, abortion, civil rights, or the powers of Congress, there will be political consequences to decisions. Where societal values are affected, certain groups may be pleased or displeased with the results. Those displeased with results of the Court's decisions will often attack the institution itself. Critics, such as Professor David O'Brien, believe that the Court is too much a political institution and "wields an antidemocratic power and is rarely held accountable for its decisions."[421] One must take a comprehensive look at the Court over the course of its history, however, before making conclusions about its political nature and power in relation to the other branches of government. As Lawrence Baum describes it, the Supreme Court is *both* a political and a legal institution neither wholly insulated from politics nor free to make decisions outside of the legal framework.[422] This requires further examination.

John Marshall was not altogether successful in his attempts to insulate the Supreme Court from politics.[423] As an integral part of government, the judiciary cannot help but be subject to political influences from within and without the Court, including, as Baum describes them, the following: the contentious appointment process, the input of interest groups, the prior political activity of justices, the justices' political values and their perceptions of public and congressional opinion, the impact of the Court's controversial decisions on government and elections.[424] Current Court aside, many justices have held political office; and many had no judicial background. In fact, forty-one Supreme Court justices, including eight chief justices, had no prior experience as a judge.[425] These include, among others, John Marshall, Roger Taney, Louis Brandeis, Felix Frankfurter, Hugo Black, Earl Warren, Byron White, William Rehnquist, and Lewis Powell. Appointees over the last twenty-five years, however, including Roberts, Breyer, Ginsburg, Kennedy, O'Connor, Souter, Thomas, Scalia, Roberts, and Alito have all had judicial experience. This appears to be coming at the expense of judges with political experience. But with the departure of O'Connor, the Court no longer has a member with prior experience as a state legislator or other elected office. The last federal legislator to sit on the Court was former senator Hugo Black, who retired in 1971.

But the Court differs in its nature from the other branches of government, particularly in the way that it decides which cases it will review and how it deals with the issues. Of approximately eight thousand petitions received every year, the Court will only hear arguments for about eighty or roughly 1 percent.[426] The Certiorari Act of 1925 gave the Court much discretion to choose which cases it hears. Supreme Court Rule 10 provides that the Court should choose cases that involve rulings of federal circuit courts of appeals that conflict with each other, rulings of circuit courts that conflict with decisions of state courts of last resort, rulings that conflict with a prior decision of the Supreme Court, rulings of state courts of last resort which conflict with decisions of other state courts of last resort or a circuit court, among other cases. But in the 1970s, Justice Powell proposed that the preparation of the "cert memo" upon which the justices would decide whether or not to grant jurisdiction be delegated to clerks, on a rotational basis.[427] Justices Powell, Blackmun, Rehnquist, and White agreed. But Justices Marshall and Brennan opposed this "cert pool" system because it put so much influence in the hands of a single clerk. Despite initial resistance, over time the cert pool system prevailed. Consequently, by this process, the Court clerks and justices methodically screen the cases before deciding to take them on.

When it accepts cases, the Court is charged with approaching the issues as a distinctly legal institution, making decisions within a framework of the law, relying upon principles of legal interpretation. In carrying out these functions, it benefits from a certain degree of insulation from the political process. The institutional independence of the Supreme Court, ensured by appointments for "good behavior," furthers a measure of separation from the majoritarian politics of the other branches and fortifies its role in safeguarding the Constitution and rights thereunder from legislative and executive encroachments. As Hamilton stated in "Federalist No. 78," "the judiciary, from the nature of its functions, will always be the least dangerous to the political rights of the Constitution."

**The Court as a Policy Maker with Limitations.** Because of the unique nature of the judiciary, the predispositions of individual justices cannot be applied arbitrarily or openly to cases in the name of politics but must be articulated in terms of judicial principles and rules of interpretation. The Court is intended to function as a "forum of principle" rather than a mere political body.[428] That is not to say that justices never allow a political result to prevail over judicial principle in decisions, but the degree to which that is done depends upon the particular justice. Prior political leanings of justices are not *always* a good predictor of decisions in specific cases. This is often the case where presidents are disappointed in their appointments to the Court, such as Theodore Roosevelt's dismay at Holmes's dissenting vote where the Court upheld antitrust laws in the *Northern Securities* case.

The Supreme Court is an institution designed to be countermajoritarian, at least where necessary to ensure independence of judgment and adherence to the Constitution, free from popular prejudice and the influence of the political branches of government. Alexander Hamilton advocated lifetime terms for the justices to reduce their dependence on public opinion and their subjugation to policy makers. But, as David Savage points out, the existence of unelected officeholders with life terms makes the Court an odd institution in a democratic society.[429] Sometimes older long-serving justices may represent the values of a different era, a time lag of a sort, such as Taney's states' rights views during the Civil War or the opponents of New Deal legislation in 1936.

Admittedly, the Court can never be entirely insulated from popular pressures and sentiment. Political scientist Robert Dahl pointed out that policy views dominant on the Court are never for long out of line with policy views dominant among lawmaking majorities in United States.[430] Similarly, Robert Bork observed that the Court cannot stand forever against a strong and persistent political movement, such as Franklin Roosevelt's New Deal legislation.[431] In short, judicial independence is tempered by political pressures in the larger context of decision making, but measured independence remains.

**Inputs of Interest Groups.** Interest groups may have substantial influence on who is nominated and whether or not the Senate will confirm the nomination. They pressure the Court to render specific results on specific cases with great political ramifications. *Liberal interest groups,* such as the Alliance for Justice, a coalition of liberal groups led by Nan Aron, spearheaded successful efforts to defeat the nomination of Robert Bork, with the assistance of the National Association for the Advancement of Colored People (NAACP) and the National Organization for Women (NOW). In addition to confirmation fights, interest groups support political candidates, litigate select causes of action, fund litigants, or file amicus briefs, such as the American Civil Liberties Union (ACLU), the Sierra Club, the Environmental Defense Fund, Planned Parenthood, and the National Abortion and Reproductive Rights Action League (NARAL). The focus of the groups range from broad-based legal causes such as the Coalition for a Fair and Independent Judiciary and People for the American Way, to more narrowly focused groups, such as Americans United for Separation of Church and State. *Conservative interest groups* will similarly fund both legal and political activism, with a high degree of success in recent years, such as when they pressured President Bush to withdraw the nomination of Harriet Miers as a replacement for Sandra Day O'Connor. The political clout of groups like Progress for America, a conservative advocacy group that spent $45 million on George W. Bush's reelection campaign, is apparent.[432] They have a contact list of 8.7 million e-mail addresses from which they can mobilize supporters. The issue of O'Connor's replacement has been of interest to other groups, such as the Committee for Justice, set up by C. Boyden Gray, former aide to President George H. W. Bush, and the Judicial Nomination Network. The religious right has dramatically increased its presence on the legal and political fronts. In recent years, considerable influence has been wielded by groups like Focus on the Family, a Washington affiliate of the Family Research Council, founded by Dr. James Dobson and directed by Tony

Perkins. Other religious-oriented groups vying for attention include the American Center for Law and Justice, an advocacy group founded by evangelist Pat Robertson; the Becket Fund for Religious Liberty; and the Home School Legal Defense Association. Other groups have broader focus, such as the Independent Women's Forum and the Federalist Society. In all, interest groups remain a factor in the composition of and conduct of the Court. But as in the case of the influence of the president and the Senate, once a justice is confirmed, the power of interest groups to effect a specific result is inherently limited.

**The Historical Role of the Court: Providing Stability to Democracy**. Another benefit of the Supreme Court's independence from the other branches of government and insulation from electoral politics is the degree of stability and continuity in the development of the body of common law. As the final arbiter of the law, the Court's role is paramount in a governmental system based upon laws and a written constitution. In order for law to play a fundamental role in democratic society, it must have an element of predictability and reliability.[433] Therefore, the importance of principles of decision making, providing for consistency in application of the law, cannot be overstated. The common law principle of stare decisis commands that precedent be followed, whether it leads to a liberal or a conservative result. Put simply, it means similar treatment for similar cases. It follows from an imperative in Western judicial systems for predictability of the law. In other words, subjects should have fair warning as to actions and consequences in regard to the law. The Court also contributes to democratic stability by moderating the excesses of majoritarianism.

**The Role of a Countermajoritarian Judicial Institution in a Democracy.** When the French lawyer, Alexis de Tocqueville, toured America in 1831 conducting research on the U.S. penal system, he discovered larger truths about the nature of democracy and about American political culture. During the course of his study, he met with Associate Justice Joseph Story, President Andrew Jackson, and former president John Quincy Adams, among others. His first volume of *Democracy in America* was published in 1835, noting the societal importance of values like equality and liberty and the potential for conflict between the two. He observed that Americans particularly valued individualism as an essential component of liberty. At the same time, the Jacksonian era witnessed egalitarian advances such as the expansion of the franchise beyond the wealthy property-owning classes to all white males. Yet Tocqueville feared tyranny of majoritarianism, a characteristic feature of "egalitarian democracy."[434] The execution of royalists like his maternal great-grandfather and aunt as well as mistreatment of his parents and other relatives at the hands of the sansculottes during the French Revolution left him with a healthy distrust of the excesses of majoritarianism unrestrained by law and reason. He believed that two major instruments in American society could be used to prevent the tyranny of the majority and ensure liberty: the press and the judiciary. Both institutions would need to be independent of the executive and legislative branches of government.

But Tocqueville harbored a fear that majoritarian tyranny was never far away, even in a healthy democracy like America.

Former Associate Justice Sandra Day O'Connor commented that the Bill of Rights is "a decidedly antimajoritarian document."[435] Originally intended by the anti-Federalists to be a limitation on federal power, the rights of individuals guaranteed by the Bill of Rights provide limitations on the actions of the political branches of government (with the exception of the Tenth Amendment, which is expressly aimed at preserving states' rights). As James Madison expressed to Congress, the Bill of Rights is directed "sometimes against the abuse of the executive power, sometimes against the legislative, and in some cases against the community itself, or, in other words, against the majority in favor of the minority."[436] As Edmund Burke warned, "in a democracy, the majority of the citizens is capable of exercising the most cruel oppression upon the minority."[437] The Supreme Court and the judiciary are uniquely situated as the guardians of constitutional rights of minorities, be they political, religious, ethnic, or otherwise.

But it is precisely this countermajoritarianism that brings the Supreme Court under attack from critics across the political spectrum and accusations that it is an "antidemocratic" institution. For those on the conservative side of the spectrum, there is much irony since historically, the Court's countermajoritarianism has more often than not been a conservative bastion within government. A majoritarian Court would have succumbed to Jefferson's Republicans after John Adams left the presidency, been dominated by Lincoln's Unionists during the Civil War, and accepted unquestioningly Franklin Roosevelt's New Deal legislation. It is no coincidence that the argument for a majoritarian Court comes at a rare time when the Republicans dominate the executive branch and both houses of Congress. No Republican argued for majoritarianism during the heyday of judicial activism on the Warren Court in the 1960s when Democratic majorities prevailed in the U.S. Senate and U.S. House of Representatives.

For the liberal side of the spectrum, the Court's countermajoritarianism facilitated major decisions on behalf of racial minorities, criminal defendants, environmentalists, blue collar workers, migrant labor, and other underrepresented groups when political institutions were unable or unwilling to act on their behalf. As the framers of the Constitution were well aware, prior to the ratification of the Constitution, political and religious minorities were at the mercy of majoritarian state governments. The Quakers of Pennsylvania had been disenfranchised because their beliefs did not jibe with the majority that controlled the state legislature. Though John Marshall's defense of treaty rights of the Cherokees and Earl Warren's declaration that segregation of schools was unconstitutional faced resistance in implementation and enforcement, the fact remains that the Court was at times the only major governmental institution protecting the constitutional rights of political, religious, and ethnic minorities.

**Majoritarian Balance: Where Congress "Overrules" the Court.** Judicial power is not without limits. Hamilton noted in "Federalist No. 78" that the Court is not superior to the legislature, except where the latter passes legislation that violates the "fundamental" law (i.e., Constitution). Even where legislation is struck down by the Court, Congress can effectively "overrule" the Court by either changing the offending language of statutory provisions or by amending the Constitution (a process initiated by Congress but requiring ratification of the states). Neither approach is easy since neither are within the plenary powers of Congress. Legislation requires the signature of the president or, in the case of veto, a two-thirds vote of Congress to override. But the task is more daunting where the Constitution must be amended for a statute to stand, since Article V requires a two-thirds vote of both houses of Congress as well as approval by three-quarters (thirty-eight) of the fifty states. Despite the challenge, this approach was successful in several cases. The *Dred Scott* decision was effectively overturned by the Thirteenth Amendment which was ratified in 1865. The Court's 1895 decision to declare the power to collect an income tax unconstitutional was overcome by the Sixteenth Amendment ratified in 1913. The Twenty-sixth Amendment of 1971 overcame a ruling by the Court striking down a statute authorizing eighteen-year-olds to vote. Not surprisingly, constitutional amendments are rare.

**Is It Policy or Legal Interpretation?** As constitutional scholar C. Herman Pritchett stated, "Judges make choices, but they are not the 'free' choices of congressmen."[438] The legislature and the executive may reach decisions with no other justification than that the result constitutes "good policy." On the other hand, judges must apply a legal methodology or at least justify the result by means of legal principles. In an ideal state, judicial methodology would be policy or end-result neutral. But such objectivity is an unrealistic expectation for a process that is inherently subjective. Though it aspires to a higher level of scrutiny, judicial interpretation is neither scientific nor precise. As Holmes put it in *Towne v. Eisner*, "A word is not a crystal, transparent and unchanged; it is the skin of a living thought and may vary greatly in color and content, according to the circumstances and the time in which it is used."[439] Thus, finding the true meaning of words in the Constitution or laws in a manner faithful to the framers is not always easy. But as Holmes and others discovered, attempting to place methodology and principle over political result can bring political opprobrium.

Interpretation will be influenced by the form of questions presented to the Court, which will differ fundamentally from that of policy issues faced by Congress. Roughly half of the cases deal with a question of the constitutionality of laws or acts of government officials. It may be the act of a federal or state official, executive or legislative. In other cases, it may be the rights of private citizens vis-à-vis federal or state law. Even these cases (e.g., *Dred Scott*) may involve significant political issues.

Many decisions of the Court result in substantial political consequences, regardless of which party the interpretation of the law supports, such as illustrated by the cases of *United States v. New York Times, Roe v. Wade, INS v. Chadha, Bowsher v. Synar, United States v. Nixon,* and *Bush v. Gore.* Some argue that the Constitution actually encourages challenges to the legality of government actions.[440] Controversy is inherent and intended in such a system. But where there are losers in cases with high political stakes, there will often be accusations of partisan motivation and activism.

**Avoiding Politics Altogether: The Political Question Doctrine.** As long ago as 1849, Chief Justice Roger Taney applied the "political question" doctrine, whereby the Court would be obligated to exercise self-restraint in political matters. Where issues are political in nature and otherwise lack justiciable standards, the judiciary should defer those issues to the political branches of government. This approach has its critics as well. The Court has frequently used this approach to avoid weighing in on issues of constitutional consequence, such as war powers. But this doctrine has not been easy to apply because many legal issues have political implications, as Tocqueville noted, or more recently Justice Stephen Breyer. Justice Robert Jackson, a judicial conservative, went further, stating that "all constitutional interpretations have political consequences."[441] Furthermore, the political question doctrine, where applied, gave rise to allegations that the Court was avoiding its duty to adjudicate questions of law merely because of political ramifications. For example, the Court avoided legislative apportionment cases as a political question for many years despite well-founded arguments that gross inequities were being perpetrated in violation of the spirit of the Constitution.[442] But bearing in mind Justice Jackson's observation, a more productive debate is engendered by looking at the meanings of activism and restraint rather than deciding whether a case is "political question."

**Judicial Activism versus Judicial Restraint.** The use of these categories has appeal to those in search of simpler meanings and understandings of the holdings of the Court. But such generalizations often risk oversimplification of judicial behavior, especially when these categories and associated terminology become code words for political orientation. Such is the case of categories like *activism, strict constructionism,* and *judicial restraint.* That is not to say that these categories are not important elements in understanding how justices approach the law and cases but that they are fraught with misleading preconceptions that limit their utility when it comes to understanding decision making of the Court. With that caveat, these terms warrant further examination.

Baum defines judicial activism as the Court's willingness to make significant changes in public policy, particularly in policies established by other institutions.[443] It may stem from both the nature of the Constitution and a realization of the Court's power. Some commentators see the Constitution inviting creative interpretation through its vagueness. David Savage makes this point while describing the Constitution as "a dry organization plan for the government—hugely significant but dull."[444] In a very cynical (some would say realistic) view about the power of the Court, Chief Justice Charles Evans Hughes stated, "The Constitution is what the Supreme Court says it is." Yet despite its implication that the Court has unlimited powers of interpretation, Hughes, as a seasoned politician, certainly understood as well as anyone the limitations of the Court's power and the cost of rendering decisions unhinged from a solid basis in the Constitution.

Activism may manifest itself in decisions overturning executive and legislative acts or policies. It may also appear in the form of affirmative actions by the Court operating under a "duty" under the Constitution to protect fundamental values like liberty, especially when other branches fail to act. William O. Douglas is a good example of an activist in the truest sense, championing the use of the judiciary for policy-making. He boasted that "I don't follow precedents; I make 'em."[445] He further stated that it was his intent to "bend the law" in order to reach desired results.

But activism has been used alternatively by conservatives and liberals throughout the history of the Court. That point is made most eloquently by Judge Robert Bork, who pointed out the activism of the Court of the late nineteenth century, incorporating a "liberty of contract" right into "substantive" due process via the Fourteenth Amendment.[446] Despite much historical revisionism, liberalism was not associated with activism on the Court until the 1950s. Older liberals on the Court, such as Felix Frankfurter and Robert Jackson, were noted for conservative judicial principles and resisted the growing libertarian assertiveness of Douglas and Black. Even today, the sometimes popular approaches of equating activism with liberalism and associating restraint with conservatism are inaccurate and misleading. If one adopts a broader definition of the terminology which includes furthering political agendas on the Court, then, as Professor Mark Tushnet opines, "everyone is a judicial activist."[447]

Accusations of activism are a convenient means to attack specific decisions as illegitimate and the product of the Court's nonelected, "undemocratic" nature. Nevertheless, it is clear that the Court risks its own credibility when it goes too far in effecting policy. Justice Byron White warned that "the Court is most vulnerable and comes nearest to illegitimacy when it deals with judge-made constitutional law having little or no cognizable tools in the language or design of the Constitution." Controversial policy-oriented decisions often bring opprobrium, and the credibility of the Court is undermined when the executive and legislative branches fail to support the decision.

By contrast, judicial restraint may be defined as the "avoidance of judicial activism."[448] Commentators such as Mark Levin argue for judicial restraint because of the illegitimacy of the Supreme Court's sitting in "final judgment of essentially all policy issues, disregarding its constitutional limitations."[449] As he states, "judicial decisions should not be based on the personal beliefs and policy preferences of a particular judge."[450] But "restraint" by this definition does not reflect the absence of policy or political content. As judicial scholar Ronald Dworkin points out, even the choice of original understanding "is itself a political decision."[451] Or as Robert Bork put it, "constitutional philosophies always have political results."[452] Recognition of that reality explains in part why various political causes across the spectrum have taken positions alternately in support of activism or restraint depending upon the issue, the wording of the Constitution, and the currently prevailing interpretation thereof.

**Judicial Restraint and Legal Realism.** Beginning with his publication of a series of his lectures in *The Common Law* in 1881, Oliver Wendell Holmes critiqued the formulaic, "logical" approach to the law described and popularized by Harvard dean Christopher Columbus Langdell. He believed that the lofty formulas and tests applied to "discern" the law obscured underlying moral, political, or ideological motivations. Holmes wrote that "the life of the law is not logic; it is experience . . . the prevalent moral and political theories, intuitions of public policy, avowed or unconscious, even the prejudices which judges share with their fellow men, have a good deal more to do with than the syllogism in determining the rules by which men should be governed. The law embodies the story of a nation's development through centuries, and it cannot be dealt with as if it contained only the axioms and corollaries of a book of mathematics."[453]

Describing himself as the "original realist," Holmes tried to minimize the influence of politics and ideologies of individual justices through the exercise of judicial restraint, deference to legislation and legislative bodies, and adherence to procedures that would restrict decisions to the application of strictly judicial standards.[454] This is exemplified by Holmes's spirited dissent in *Lochner* (appendix 4), which inveighed against activism on behalf of business interests and advocates of social Darwinism, such as Herbert Spencer. Holmes's restraint could be seen in his description of the Court's role in reviewing laws passed by Congress: "the gravest and most delicate duty that this Court is called upon to perform."

But later legal realists, such as Brandeis and Cardozo, are accused of pursuing their own activism on behalf of progressive legal reforms.[455] Attacks on the legal realists' promotion of social policy were levied by Justice George Sutherland who in the 1934 case of *Home Bldg. & Loan v. Blaisdell* declared that "whether the legislation under review is wise or unwise is a matter with which we have nothing to do. Whether it is likely to work well or work ill presents a question entirely irrelevant to the issue. The only legitimate inquiry we can make is whether it is constitutional. If it is not, its virtues, if it have any, cannot save it; if it is, its fault cannot be invoked to accomplish its destruction. If the provisions of the Constitution be not upheld when they pinch as well as when they comfort, they may well be abandoned."

Similarly, another anti-New Deal justice, Owen Roberts, opined in 1936 that "the duty of the Court is not to substitute policy, rather to measure it against the Constitution." But it cannot escape comment that the anti-New Deal justices were by their actions failing to defer to legislatures and, in effect, substituting their policy for that of the Congress, albeit based upon their interpretation of the commerce clause of the Constitution. Yet the Court's majority consensus on the meaning of the Constitution on New Deal legislation was neither solid nor static. Notably, Justice Roberts eventually changed his stance and supported New Deal legislation.

The classification of the diverse group of legal realists as activists is overreaching and questionable. The so-called activism of Louis Brandeis and Benjamin Cardozo, the second generation of legal realists, was a far cry from the activism of William O. Douglas. Deference to state legislation regulating working hours and conditions is hardly the equivalent of legislating from the bench or finding new rights in the Constitution. Nor was Brandeis's dissent in *Olmstead* an invention of a new right to privacy, but rather a recognition of the intent of the right covered by the Fourth Amendment as applied to new technology. Even Robert Bork, a leading antiactivist, expressed flexibility about applying the Constitution to similar circumstances unforeseen by the framers.[456]

The most credible charge against the legal realists is about those who believe in the indeterminacy of the law, whereby law can be found in places other than the statutes and precedents and, instead, may be found in balancing competing values and interests. However "realistic" that view may be, it can lead to a cynical view of law and the courts. As Justice John Marshall Harlan II, who distinguished himself as a judicial conservative and regular dissenter on the Warren Court, saw it, "a basic change in the law upon a ground no firmer than a change in our membership invites the popular misconception that this institution is little different from the two political branches of the government. No misconception could do more lasting injury to this Court and the system which it is our abiding mission to serve."[457]

While Harlan remained a philosophical link to judicial conservatives like Frankfurter, Reed, and Jackson, the emergence of justices more assertive on civil rights and liberties like Douglas, Black, Murphy, and Rutledge had less to do with abstract principles of legal realism than to do with changing circumstances within and outside of the Court. Even Harlan found sufficient constitutional basis to support the Warren Court's rulings protecting freedom of speech, recognizing a right to privacy, and ensuring separation of church and state.

**Constitutional Interpretation: Four Approaches.** Activism and restraint can be better understood in light of different approaches to interpreting the Constitution. Professor Michael Glennon posits four modes of constitutional interpretation: *textualism, intentionalism, adaptivism,* and *functionalism.*[458]

The *textualist* approach defers to the plain meaning of the text of the Constitution and laws. Under this view, the job of the justices is to interpret, not to rewrite the Constitution. The textual approach is in theory neutral as to result. Contrary to popular belief, the textual approach in practice may lead to either conservative or liberal results. A case in point concerns one champion of this approach, Associate Justice Hugo Black, frequently wrote opinions that riled conservatives and was often accused of "activism," though the textual approach by definition does not vary far from the clear stated meaning of the Constitution. For example, in the case of the *New York Times* v. *United States* (a.k.a. the *Pentagon Papers* case) the edict of the First Amendment that "Congress shall make no law . . . abridging the freedom . . . of the press" was a compelling argument on behalf of freedom of the newspaper to publish a classified report without fear of punishment. The solicitor general's argument that "no law" did not mean "no law" was explicitly rejected. Similarly, in the *Steel Seizure* case, Black relied upon a narrow textual interpretation of the commander-in-chief clause of the Constitution with regard to presidential powers in wartime. Since the Pennsylvania steel mills seized on Truman's orders were not in the "theater of war," the act was considered beyond the president's war powers.

Though the textualist approach is appealing in its simplicity, the application of constitutional text to unanticipated issues is often anything but simple. As Justice Byron White stated in *Chadha v. INS*, the text of the Constitution is "anything but clear-cut" on many if not most issues as the Court faced in the case of the legislative veto. Many issues before the Court concern what is *not* written in the Constitution, such as when President George Washington asserted a presidential right to declare neutrality in the British-French conflict. Furthermore, the textual approach can be used selectively as a result-oriented choice. That is to say, this approach may be used by some only when conducive to a predetermined outcome. Equally significant is the fact that, despite popular myth, application of the textual approach does not guarantee conservative results.

Textualism should not be confused with "strict constructionism," a term that has grown out of favor with conservatives like Scalia.[459] As he stated, "I am not a strict constructionist, and no one ought to be . . . A text should not be construed strictly, and it should not be construed leniently; it should be construed reasonably, to contain all that it fairly means." For Scalia, the text should be interpreted in accordance with its original meaning, a view closer to intentionalism.

*Intentionalism* eschews complete or exclusive reliance on the text and allows one to look to other expressions of the framers' intent, e.g., *Federalist Papers*, Madison's convention notes, records of states ratifying conventions, etc. This approach does not admit reliance on custom or subsequent practice. Many prefer to refer to this approach as "original intent" or "originalist." Originalists such as Scalia will defer to the "plain meaning" of the Constitution, similar to the textualist, but the text is only one means by which to discern original intent. Advocates of this approach proclaim a search for the "lost Constitution" or the "Constitution in exile" from the days before "liberal activism."

This approach has four major criticisms, as Glennon describes them.[460] First, the framers would likely have been dubious about intentionalism and anyone who deemed himself or herself able to precisely determine the intent of the framers. Often there was no collective intent but rather inclination or even coercion to compromise in pursuit of consensus. Secondly, it is hard to discern intent from the fifty-five men who met in Philadelphia in the summer of 1787 and have long since passed from the earth. There were no verbatim notes, only the writings of a few, such as James Madison. Thirdly, it is doubtful that the framers wanted their intent to be sought to resolve questions in interpreting the meaning of the Constitution. Finally, the framers' intent is not necessarily relevant to our government and issues that exist over two hundred years later. These limitations on the utility of intentionalism have caused justices to look tradition and custom as a guide to interpretation.

*Adaptivism* relies upon custom and subsequent practice to determine the meaning of the Constitution. Holmes believed that the law could embody conventional usages and "the story of a nation's development through centuries."[461] In this view, the original meaning is less important where it would be unrealistic and impractical to assume that the framers could divine all future exigencies. Instead, flexibility and pragmatism should prevail to adapt the Constitution to modern meanings. But many conservatives criticize adaptivism as license to change the meaning of the Constitution. It is certainly true that traditions and customs can be "cherry-picked" to support a particular end result. Perhaps more importantly, adaptivism does not guarantee a liberal result any more than textualism and intentionalism guarantee a conservative result. Even conservatives such as Rehnquist, Scalia, and Thomas have recognized that where the text and original intent is unclear, justices may consider long-standing traditions about constitutional rights as a guide to interpretation.[462] In *Washington v. Glucksberg*, Chief Justice Rehnquist rejected a constitutional right to physician-assisted suicide as contrary to a "consistent and almost universal tradition" against such. And Justice Scalia would give deference to the "legal traditions of the American people."[463] Consequently, it would be inaccurate to classify adaptivism as an exclusively liberal or activist approach to the law.

*Functionalism* goes farther than adaptivism in creative interpretations of the Constitution. This approach seeks to interpret the Constitution in a way to further objectives of efficiency and equity. Regarding the objective of efficiency, critics argue that convenience and efficiency are not the primary objectives of our democratic government as laid out in the Constitution. Chief Justice Burger ruled against legislative "veto" powers in *INS v. Chadha*, acknowledging that the framers of the Constitution in some cases intentionally imposed "clumsy, inefficient, and even unworkable" burdens on governmental processes to act as a check on "arbitrary governmental acts." Regarding equity, critics argue that this objective can easily be subverted by political agendas.

In the most zealous view of functionalism, the so-called living constitution is a document inviting new interpretations and incorporation of principles of policy. There is no question that functionalism in this form can facilitate judicial activism. A functionalist may read new values or policies into the Constitution. But the substance of the values or policies may be liberal or conservative. Functionalism can be seen in Justice Douglas's finding of a general right of privacy in the Bill of Rights in the case of *Griswold* or Justice Peckham's applying a right of liberty of contract to the states under the Fourteenth Amendment in *Lochner*.

But politics aside, functionalism within the limits of the traditional judicial role may have a legitimate place in constitutional interpretation. Even Judge Bork recognized that judges may on occasion need to apply "old values to new circumstances," such as in the case of electronic surveillance, something clearly not contemplated by the drafters of the Fourth Amendment's search and seizure clause.[464] He was willing to accept new interpretations of the Constitution provided that it was an application of the original "central value" rather than the "creation of a new principle" or new right.[465]

**Summation of Political Channelization.** Political issues come to the Supreme Court embodied in legal cases and controversies. Political inputs come from many sources within and outside of the Court, pressuring the justices in favor of specific results. But a measure of judicial independence ensures some separation from the majoritarian politics of the other branches of government. Activism and restraint can be seen in constitutional interpretation as a matter of degree on a continuum from textualism and intentionalism to adaptivism and functionalism. When subjected to these criteria, decisions of the Supreme Court cannot always be pigeonholed into the categories of "activist," "liberal," or "conservative," especially when the decisions have credible foundations based upon the text of the Constitution or intent of the framers.

# CHAPTER 12

## WHEN LABELS FAIL

*Throughout the history of the Supreme Court, justices have defied political categorization and labels. Whether it be justices who strictly adhere to judicial methodology that abhors results-conscious decision making, justices whose beliefs change over time, or justices who defy the political branches of government simply because they can, judicial independence ensures that justices can define their own categories or refuse categorization altogether.*

**The Elusive Quest for Categorization.** When narrowly focused political criteria is used for evaluation of judicial candidates, presidents should not be surprised when nominees "go astray" on the Court. The natural tendency to apply overly broad categories like "conservative" or "liberal" can lead to disappointing results. This is not to say that the judiciary is wholly a "nonpolitical" branch of government, but rather a recognition that whatever "politics" means in the judicial branch, it is far different in content and character than in the executive and legislative branches. Despite what many would be inclined to believe, party politics of Republicans and Democrats don't always translate easily or consistently into particular judicial decisions or holdings. As Professor Ronald Rotunda observed, "it is (a) common and erroneous belief that judges rule as Democrats or as Republicans once they are on the bench."[466]

While it is understood that there will frequently be party-line solutions to various controversial cases and issues, the long-standing practice and tradition of the judiciary is for judges to make decisions based upon accepted principles of judicial procedure and reasoning, despite flaunted examples to the contrary. As seen through the history of the Court, principles of constitutional and statutory interpretation cannot be simplistically associated with particular political results.

Additionally, political parties are not unitary entities but tend to consist of varying ideological constituencies. Particularly when parties strive for wide appeal in the "big tent" mode, party labels are less than useful categorizations. President Eisenhower learned how big the Republican "tent" was when he nominated Earl Warren to replace Fred Vinson as chief justice. Eisenhower thought he was appointing a solid "Republican" to the Court when he selected the former three-term governor of California and one-time Republican vice presidential candidate. As is often the case, simple party identifications may be misleading in the manner by which they fail to account for diverse ideological viewpoints within a party, not to mention individual predilections as a result of experiences. In Warren's case, his party identification harked back to the turn-of-the-century progressive politics of California governor Hiram Johnson. Eisenhower's later selection of William Brennan, with noted sympathies for working-class and egalitarian causes, was perhaps more predictable. If Eisenhower intended to use the nomination to capture Democratic swing voters in the election for his second presidential term, perhaps he was successful in that objective alone.

Observing the simplistic futility of the broad Republican label, some have divided the party into "modern" and "traditional" camps.[467] The so-called modern Republicans (the late Chief Justice Rehnquist and Justices Thomas and Scalia) represent the more conservative "Goldwater-Reagan" wing of the party, largely influenced by Republican growth in the South and West. On the other hand, the traditional Republicans (Justices Stevens, Souter, Kennedy, and O'Connor) represent the more liberal northeastern wing of the party. Aside from the regional anomalies (Scalia is from the East and Kennedy and O'Connor are from the West), these distinctions provide little to predict behavior on the Court. For example, the modern Republicans voted with the traditional Republicans in forty-nine out of seventy nonunanimous cases during the 2004 term.[468] In only six of that term's cases did the two groups vote on opposite sides in 5-4 decisions. On questions of federalism, Justices O'Connor and Kennedy frequently voted with Chief Justice Rehnquist and Justices Scalia and Thomas.

It must also be observed that other frequently used labels like "liberal" and "conservative" are not necessarily helpful, as has been recognized by writers as diverse as columnist George Will and Professor Laurence Tribe.[469] When asked whether he was a liberal or a conservative, Associate Justice Potter Stewart responded, "I am a lawyer . . . I have some difficulty understanding what those terms mean even in the field of political life . . . And I find it impossible to know what they mean when they are carried over to judicial work."[470] As Stewart recognized, the peculiarities of the judicial role do not make for easy placement of conventional political groupings.

Part of the problem of political categorization is that defined categories, even when there is relative agreement that they exist, change over time. Liberalism, in particular, has changed in meaning significantly in the last two hundred years. Classical liberalism, with historical roots in the eighteenth century, often associated with modern libertarianism, championed the cause of the individual against the state. Economic liberties went hand in hand with political liberties, perhaps captured best by John Locke's natural rights of "life, liberty, and property" as expounded on in his *Second Treatise on Civil Government.* These rights found their way into the Declaration of Independence (with Jefferson substituting "pursuit of happiness" for "property") and the Fifth and Fourteenth Amendments to the Constitution. As such, they are more than ideological beliefs but are values embedded in the Constitution.

Economic liberalism, as advocated by Adam Smith and David Ricardo (and more recently by Milton Friedman), is not the same as contemporary American liberalism, which is associated more frequently with social issues and egalitarian causes. Economic liberals today believe strongly in deregulation domestically and free trade internationally. More often than not, this philosophy is championed by Republicans but the trend of deregulation of the airlines and other industries begun under President Carter and the sponsorship of the North American Free Trade Agreement by President Clinton argues against any one party lock on economic liberalism.

For much of history, the term "liberal" was associated with probusiness, free market orientations, as is still the case in continental Europe. Until Franklin Roosevelt's day, the term "liberal" was often associated with the probusiness community in the United States; but Roosevelt frequently used the term in association with his New Deal programs and in his outreach to Wall Street. Consequently, the term is now more often associated with "big government" and regulation, quite the opposite of its origins. Nor was liberalism associated with judicial activism in Roosevelt's day. Many justices who were known to be politically liberal, such as Robert Jackson and Felix Frankfurter, were methodologically conservative on the Court. Even William O. Douglas did not show an activist bent until much later in his tenure on the Court.

The political categories "Left" and "Right" are simplistic and frequently inadequate, especially when applied to a judicial setting.[471] The left-right frame-of-reference terminology originated in the French Legislative Assembly of 1791, where the Feuillants, Monarchiens, and Constitutionals sat on the right side of the chamber and the Montagnards, Jacobins, and Girondins sat on the left. The shortcomings of this manner of political classification could be seen early on as the revolutionary Girondins switched from left to right in 1792 when they disagreed with the left on the execution of King Louis XVI. And though the Montagnards were radical egalitarians, they were liberal on economic issues, as were the Monarchiens. The eighteenth-century seating assignments of French legislators were even more inadequate in characterizing the rise of nineteenth- and twentieth-century nationalism and socialism. The centralization and aggrandizement of governmental authority at the expense of local and individual authority were often grounds for commonality of regimes of the left and right, especially when looking at what Ayn Rand called "statist" regimes, particularly states controlled by Communists, Fascists, and National Socialists (aka Nazis).[472] Those single party-based totalitarian regimes stand in contrast to Western liberal systems favoring pluralism and governments that have only limited authority to encroach on individual rights. Rand's statist-versus-libertarian model is in many ways more useful than the old left-versus-right construct.

Notwithstanding the nonutility of broad political categorizations and ideological orientations, values expressed by *libertarianism* and *egalitarianism* are worthy of further discussion when it comes to discerning judicial performance. Both libertarian and egalitarian values have come to represent civil liberties and civil rights as recognized in case law, though not without much debate in the legal community about what specific rights are constitutionally grounded. The Warren Court was criticized by Yale law professor Alexander Bickel for, in effect, importing egalitarian views into the desegregation decision of *Brown v. Board of Education* and the "one man, one vote" legislative apportionment decision of *Baker v. Carr.*[473] But the terms liberty and equality have significance deeper than vague political values since they can be directly related to liberties and rights encompassed by specific language in the Constitution (especially the first ten amendments and the Thirteenth, Fourteenth, Fifteenth, Nineteenth, Twenty-fourth, and Twenty-sixth Amendments). Indeed both liberty and equality were values touted extensively by Madison and Hamilton in the *Federalist Papers.* The delegates to the constitutional convention in Philadelphia in 1787 held spirited debates about how to preserve liberty and secure political equality. The anti-Federalists left no small mark on the Constitution by their insistence on a bill of rights. The clear intent of the framers of the Constitution regarding the preservation of certain liberties explains why conservative *originalist* justices like Scalia can unabashedly reach "unconservative" results on cases from flag burning to infrared house searches. In such cases, libertarians and egalitarians are not easily linked into traditional political categories of right and left, nor can they be classified as activists where their values are embedded in the Constitution.

In summary, traditional political categories are too simplistic and imprecise to be useful when discussing politics in reference to the legislative and executive branches of government. They become even less precise when filtered through the prism of judicial procedure and principles.

**Beyond "Black and White" Labels: Alternative Categories and Influences.** Popular labels fail precisely because the subjects will often defy the simplification of performance and belief systems. The problem is particularly acute with judges who have crosscutting ideologies, that is, beliefs that lead to either liberal or conservative results depending upon the circumstances of the case at hand. Political scientists often look to "political culture" to describe national core beliefs and values that are widespread and transcend narrow party boundaries. Libertarianism and federalism are examples of two belief systems that tend to cut across party boundaries. The core values of libertarians and federalists are the subject of some dispute about their precise meaning, warranting further examination.

**Libertarianism.** This ideology is often mistakenly associated with conservatism. The reality is more complicated. In general, libertarians support the rights of states to govern themselves with minimal interference by the federal government. Representing long-standing core beliefs of many, they oppose big government and support economic "liberty" through the loosening of government regulation of the economy. They are embedded in American political culture and are in many ways the ideological descendants of Jeffersonian Republicans. They also have inherited Jefferson's support for individual liberties, even at the expense of law enforcement. Libertarians will often be associated with conservative causes like the right to bear arms.

But contemporary libertarians of the ideologically "purist" variety generally support individual liberties across the board. They oppose mandatory military induction (i.e., the draft) and laws outlawing the use of marijuana, whether for medicinal or recreational use. On the subject of the foregoing individual liberties, strict libertarians are at odds with social conservatives, such as former attorney general John Ashcroft. Ashcroft's curtailment of civil rights with regard to access to counsel and detention without hearing for suspected terrorists, as well as expanded federal control over law enforcement, is counter to basic libertarian tenets. It is no surprise that many libertarians strongly oppose aspects of the USA Patriot Act. On the Court, one can even see the libertarian tendencies of justices with solid "conservative" credentials like Scalia and Thomas on occasion when it comes to individual liberties, albeit inconsistently. Libertarianism remains a subtle but persistent presence on the Court in both liberals and conservatives. No lawmaker or officeholder should be surprised or disappointed when these justices and the Court decide that the government has gone too far with regard to certain constitutionally protected rights.

**Federalism (and Anti-Federalism).** Few politicians today identify themselves as "federalists" per se, yet issues concerning the relation between states and the federal government frequently lurk behind other issues coming to the Court. Even the Federalist Society, despite its name, is a group of "conservatives and libertarians" who are interested in promoting a broad-based agenda, not merely "federalism (and) limited constitutional government." Federalism in their usage has little to do with the original Federalist Party's desire to strengthen central power but is, ironically, nomenclature for states' rights. Since the demise of the Federalist Party and John Marshall's departure from the Court in the early nineteenth century, the label "federalist" has not been popular. Yet the influence of Federalist founders like Alexander Hamilton, who believed in a strong executive branch and expansive federal powers, lives on. The reassertion of federal power after the Civil War, the invocation of John Marshall's name (and *McCulloch v. Maryland*) in the cause of Franklin Roosevelt's New Deal programs, and the racial integration of schools all heralded the growth of the federal government. Although the latter two causes have typically been associated with the Democratic Party, it must be remembered that it was Republican president Eisenhower who first used U.S. troops to enforce Republican chief justice Warren's decision in favor of integration of schools. Many Republican presidents have been elected hailing respect for states' rights, such as Richard Nixon and Ronald Reagan, but when in office have actually strengthened federal power. Indeed, the long-term historical trend since the founding of the Republic has been the strengthening of federal power, notwithstanding the intervention of a bloody Civil War, resistance to desegregation, and continuing electoral campaign appeals to states' rights. Republicans, such as Nixon, often forget their states' rights pledges when it comes to law enforcement, strengthening the federal role therein. The George W. Bush administration is no exception to this, as can be seen by the extraordinary federal measures curtailing civil rights of suspected terrorists and detainees, as discussed previously. Law enforcement measures of this severity have not been seen since the First and Second World Wars in this country. A failure to appreciate where the justices stand on federalism will likely lead to surprises when decisions are made by the Court on legal issues arising from these measures. One legacy of "conservative" chief justice Rehnquist is a working majority on the Court that is willing to defer to state legislative authority and invalidate federal laws lacking a solid constitutional basis. Many "unconservative" decisions may result from his influence.

**Roots of Modern Western Conservatism.** No discussion on the subject of conservatism or any ideological bent can be complete without an exploration of historical roots. When one ventures into the origins of conservatism, it is easy to discover contradictions in contemporary criteria. Most notably, what popularly passes for conservatism today in many ways more closely resembles eighteenth-century liberalism.

Of particular note, the development of political philosophy in the seventeenth and eighteenth centuries paralleled the development of legal philosophy. It is no coincidence that Edmund Burke and John Adams were both schooled in the law. Though Burke never practiced law, he drew much knowledge of law and legislation as a member of the British House of Commons. Burke's and Adams's views on morality, individualism, order, property, prescription, and stability all affected their approach to the law as an essential institution in society.

**Traditional or "Classical" Conservatism.** According to Russell Kirk in his foundational treatise, *The Conservative Mind from Burke to Eliot*, there are six canons of conservative thought.[474] They are

1) Morality: "Belief in a transcendent order, or body of natural law, which rules society as well as conscience."
2) Individualism: "Affection for the proliferating variety and mystery of human existence, as opposed to narrowing uniformity, egalitarianism, and utilitarian aims of most radical systems." Especially as opposed to collectivism. But "libertine" individualism that separates the individual from societal order is scorned.
3) Order: "Conviction that civilized society requires orders and classes, as against the notion of a classless or egalitarian society." Stability is itself an important value and end result.
4) Respect for Private Property: "Persuasion that society and property are closely linked."
5) Rules and Prescription: "Faith in prescription and distrust of (those) . . . who would reconstruct society upon abstract designs. Custom, convention, and old prescription are checks both upon man's anarchic impulse and upon the innovator's lust for power."

6) Skepticism about Change: "Recognition that change may not be salutary reform, hasty innovation may be a devouring conflagration, rather than a torch of progress . . . prudent change is the means of social preservation."

In connection with a moral order with prescriptive values, a reliance on tradition and convention, and a resistance to change, we may look to an individual's theistic or religious orientation from which these beliefs may be based. Justice Antonin Scalia, with a solid Roman Catholic background, and Justice Clarence Thomas, a recent returnee to Catholicism, are perhaps the best examples, though they also express libertarian values on occasion. Traditional conservatism shapes not only one's values but one's judicial methodology. In judicial experience, the English system of common law is a legal system of decision making based upon precedent and analogy. In such a system, convention and tradition promoting "prudent" rather than radical change play important roles. At this level, contemporary social conservatives would seem to be very comfortable with the values of traditional conservatives.

But where traditional conservatives value law as a system for prescribing behavior and maintaining order, they do not place sole reliance upon the state for achieving order. Instead, they believe that law must function in a context of greater societal influences, such as the church, community, and family. One of the most eminent founders of modern Western conservatism Edmund Burke believed in legal prescription and common law, but his skepticism of the laws of man kept him from endorsing a theocracy.[475] To Burke, man's imperfectability would always separate him and his laws from the moral order of God.[476] Writing of the excesses of the French Revolution in 1790, he deplored the state's assumption of "moral competence" and the "epidemical fanaticism" against which wisdom and reason are "least able to furnish any kind of resource."[477] Thus, one would expect traditional conservatives to be hesitant about any radical realignment of the relation between church and state, especially where the state could usurp the church's role in upholding the moral order in society.

The antiegalitarianism present in both Burke and his American philosophical counterpart John Adams would likely offend many social conservatives in America today. Despite Adams's belief in natural rights, his firm stance against slavery, and his one-time close friendship with Thomas Jefferson, Adams did not believe that all men were created equal.[478] This elitist form of traditional conservatism, never enjoyed widespread acceptability in America, can be little more than a point of contrast with other forms of conservatism, especially in the judicial context. Instead, the presence of two Republican-appointed Italian Americans and an African American, among others, on the present Supreme Court (Scalia, Alito, and Thomas) speaks loudly about American acceptance of egalitarianism, despite presidential denials of selection based upon ethnic criteria. The fact that all three appointments were made by Republican presidents is an indication of how contemporary "conservatism" differs from traditional conservatism.

Related to the antiegalitarianism of traditional conservatism is skepticism about populism, popular causes, and majoritarianism in general. Edmund Burke warned that "in a democracy, the majority of the citizens is capable of exercising the most cruel oppressions upon the minority, whenever strong divisions prevail in that kind of polity, as they often must and that oppression of the minority will extend to far greater numbers, and will be carried on with much greater fury, than can ever be apprehended from the dominion of a single scepter."[479]

Though Burke was not antidemocratic, he feared the excesses of majoritarianism, which he believed must be restrained through the protection of natural rights. He believed in the concept of ordered liberty secured through "a constitution of things in which the liberty of no man and no body of men and no numbers of men can trespass on the liberty of any other person, or any description of persons, in the society."[480] Burke's acceptance of egalitarianism was limited to equality of rights under law as opposed to equality of results or equality of classes.

Thus, traditional conservatism by its very nature is curmudgeonly and antipopulist, more appealing to individualistic intellectuals than to the masses. Though traditional conservatism never really gained widespread acceptance in America, other forms of conservatism with broader appeal emerged. When John Adams appointed John Marshall to the Court, he had in mind the preservation of principles of early-American Federalism.

**Federalist Conservatism.** Historians will rightly debate whether Federalism was truly a conservative movement at the time it emerged. The founding fathers had examples of confederations, such as the Swiss model, where cantons shared power, upon which to design a system of government. But the American abandonment of the Articles of Confederation and the adoption of a federal system in 1788 was a move into new governmental territory. Nevertheless, the emerging opposition to the concentration of power in a central federal government at the expense of the states gave rise to Jefferson's Republicans as the new party for change. In another sense, the "High Federalists" like Alexander Hamilton, who advocated a strong executive branch during the constitutional convention of 1787, harked back to a monarchy and could thus be considered "conservative." On the Court, John Marshall emerged as the leading example of a judicial Federalist, with the legacy of *McCulloch v. Maryland*. But federalism would not be eternally viewed as a conservative force. Marshall's name would later be used to support expanded federal powers for Franklin Roosevelt's New Deal programs. Hence, many contemporary conservatives identify themselves with the anti-Federalist tradition.

Nevertheless, federalism in the traditional sense is subtle and wields influence even on politicians who proclaim themselves in favor of states' rights. The expansion of federal powers has continued to increase without exception under every Republican as well as Democratic administration since Franklin Roosevelt. From Nixon's federal wage and price controls to the federal takeover of airport security under George W. Bush, traditional conservatives' affinity for rules, law, and order will frequently find federal answers to issues. The tendency to find federal solutions comes into conflict with the anti-federalist trend on the Court, as described previously.

**Libertarian Conservatism.** As discussed previously, libertarianism in its purist ideological form may lead to liberal or conservative results depending upon the issue or "liberty" in question. Recognizing this dichotomy, some have resorted to using terminology such as "libertarians of the right" or "libertarians of the left." But per earlier commentary, the two-dimensional "left-right" model is problematic and misleading. The subject category of "libertarian conservative" is a libertarian who places priority on selective libertarian causes, such as states' rights, economic liberties, and particular individual rights. A conservative libertarian would generally place a higher emphasis on the Second Amendment's "right to bear arms" than with the rights of an indigent defendant to be represented by an appointed counsel. But libertarian conservatives have on occasion been zealous defenders of a wide variety of the Bill of Rights causes.

Libertarians will differ from traditional conservatives on the latter's insistence on society's need for rules, law, and order. They will oppose government regulation and taxes. Causes championed by the Cato Institute are a useful barometer for libertarian views, albeit of a more purist variety. Libertarians will frequently diverge from the hard morality of social conservatives, preferring the preservation of individual liberty and freedom of action to morality imposed by religious groups or government. Libertarian conservatives tend to be concerned about individual freedoms to the detriment of egalitarian principles, with some exceptions to be discussed later. American libertarians believe in a natural order of economic and social classes, as do traditional conservatives, but more in the nature of Jefferson's "aristocracy of talent" than an aristocracy based upon bloodlines. This characteristic is clearly descended from Jeffersonian Republicanism, once considered radical antiroyalist sedition. But in America, the "conservative" revolution of 1776 did more to preserve a status quo where the seeds of the English stratified class system or landed gentocracy never fully took root.

Creeping libertarianism and concern about protecting individual rights will often sway conservative justices like Antonin Scalia, who voted twice that flag burning was protected as free speech under the First Amendment and voted to ban warrantless searches of homes via infrared detectors as violative of the Fourth Amendment. Where social conservatives of an earlier era were more concerned about law and order, this libertarian tendency seems to escape the notice of contemporary social conservatives who are more fixated on "morality" issues like abortion and separation of church and state. Four decades earlier, the social conservatives were outraged at the libertarianism of Chief Justice Earl Warren, a Republican who believed in both economic and individual liberties.

Campaign finance reform is another area where contemporary "law-and-order" conservatives depart from libertarian conservatives.[481] Whereas Scalia and Thomas placed priority on campaign spending as an extension of First Amendment freedom of expression rights, Chief Justice Rehnquist had no problem with the regulation of corporate and union political spending. He supported such reforms with decisions in 1976, 1986, and 1990. His departure from his usual allies undermines the notion that there are clear boundaries about what is the "conservative" view du jour.

Libertarianism of the conservative persuasion has a particular appeal to the working class, a legacy of the decidedly "unconservative" Jeffersonian Republicans and Jacksonian Democrats. A strong egalitarian, anti-elitist influence distinguishes this group from Hamiltonian and Adamsonian Federalists. Notably, the egalitarianism of this group (composed largely of white males) has historically extended predominantly to members of their own race and gender. But the boundaries between this group and the neoconservatives are not always clear.

**Neoconservatism.** Sometimes referred to as neocons, the neoconservatives claim ideological roots in the 1964 presidential campaign of Senator Barry Goldwater. With a combination of conservative populism and libertarianism ("extremism in defense of liberty is no vice, moderation in defense of liberty no virtue"), Senator Barry Goldwater inspired a generation of conservatives, including William Rehnquist who served in his election campaign. Yet the current crop bearing the title "neoconservative" is different in many significant ways from its ideological forebears, including Goldwater himself. Where they display libertarian views on many issues, such as gun control and states' rights, there is a strong influence of social conservatism, especially with religious overtones, that militates against all but economic-oriented strains of libertarianism. The strident advocacy of traditional Judeo-Christian values can be seen with regard to gay rights and abortion issues and the role of the courts concerning those matters, such as causes taken up by Christian activists, like Gary Bauer and Ralph Reed. Where social conservative values conflict with libertarian values, the social conservative priorities seem to prevail. Thus, the name and legacy of Goldwater has been lent to a fundamentalist movement that bears little resemblance to the mostly secular conservative following of forty years earlier. Goldwater strongly believed in separation of church and state and disdained the rise of the religious right.[482]

The neocons have a measure of populist appeal, unlike the elitist traditional conservatives who had no love of egalitarianism nor majoritarianism. Their activism has successfully attracted many disenchanted former liberals and Democrats. Irving Kristol, considered by some as the "neocon godfather," defined a neoconservative as "a liberal mugged by reality."[483] But in the courts, social and religious conservatives may be pitted against libertarians in cases such as involved the comatose Terri Schiavo. In 2005, House Majority Leader Tom DeLay drew much criticism from his own party for his verbal attack on federal judges in the wake of their refusal to reverse rulings supporting the termination of life-support systems for Ms. Schiavo.

Additionally, traditional conservatives should be leery of neoconservative zealotry for change, the mixing of religion and politics, and the value-laden intervention into the private affairs of citizens. In their advocacy of radical change to the judiciary, such as ending lifetime tenure of judges, the neoconservatives of today represent revolution not conservation.[484] More significantly, traditional conservatives with values based in faith, such as T. S. Eliot, have long feared state involvement in the areas of religion and culture.[485] Though most traditional conservatives would not have supported entirely Jefferson's vision of secularism in the First Amendment, they would have no problem agreeing with the prohibition of the establishment of a "national religion." The framers of the Constitution and the First Amendment free exercise and establishment clauses indeed preferred instead a measure of separation of church and state. They need not have looked far into the past to remind themselves of the devastation of religious warfare during Oliver Cromwell's Protestant revolution in England and the bloody fight against papal political power during the Thirty Years War in continental Europe. For Catholics, the First Amendment ensured that a Cromwell-like zealot would not exercise power over them in America. For Protestants, the First Amendment ensured that they would not be governed by papal decree. For both, the First Amendment ensured the government would stay out of the church's business.

Indeed, the most forceful original proponents for a Constitution that prohibits the establishment of a national religion were not atheists or agnostics. Instead, they had strongly pro-religious motivations. For a nation of great religious diversity, the First Amendment establishment clause would prevent treatment experienced by the revisionist Puritan Roger Williams, who was banished from the Massachusetts Bay Colony. He later founded Rhode Island to reinforce a wall of separation between church and state and to ensure freedom of worship.[486] Even during the time of the Articles of Confederation, many state constitutions restricted the right to vote and the ability to hold political office based upon one's religious beliefs.[487] But Article VI of the Constitution expressly rejected the use of any "religious test" as a qualification for holding public office. Furthermore, the ratifiers of the Constitution in at least two states rejected suggestions to add language endorsing Christianity.[488] Nor did widely divergent Protestant groups want a national religion or any other order resembling the Church of England. Ignoring much of the history of the First Amendment, the neoconservatives appear to be reacting more to "radical secularism" than attempting to restore original interpretations to the First Amendment, which was designed to ensure religious freedom. It has even become fashionable to recast George Washington as something other than one of the leading American opponents of a state religion.[489]

Certain other neoconservative ideas run directly counter to well-established principles of originalism, as adhered to by the Court's justices. For example, "unitary executive" theory, whereby presidential declarations of interpretation while signing legislation are accorded significant weight, is a contravention of the originalist approach that would defer to the intent of the legislators. Judge Alito's adherence to this belief during Senate confirmation hearings, which became a cause for many senators to oppose the nomination, may emerge as a point of contention on the Court when executive authority is challenged in the future.

For the reasons mentioned above, no one currently on the Supreme Court fits squarely within the neocon category. Justice Scalia's conservatism shares many values with social conservatives but in practice is more in the nature of the traditional conservative with the occasional libertarian result. Justice Thomas as well shares some values with the neoconservatives but harbors a strong libertarian streak. Chief Justice Roberts represented gays at one point in his legal career. Though many of these justices lean to the textualist-intentionalist, anti-activist side of judicial interpretation, none appear to subscribe to the radical changes to the judiciary proposed by some neoconservatives.

In sum, neoconservatives, with an unusual combination of social conservatism, selective libertarianism, working-class populism, religious fervor, and political activism, represent a new political force that is attempting to change the course of the Supreme Court. Inherent contradictions of interests within the group may lead to an eventual split between libertarians, social conservatives, various religious factions, and different economic classes.

**Roots of Modern Western Liberalism.** As in the case of the roots of conservative thought, exploration of historical roots of liberalism result in the revelation of many contradictions with contemporary criteria for liberalism. The term "liberal" is often used today in pejorative derision, belying common roots of modern conservatism and liberalism, especially when it comes to approaches to the law as an essential instrument for society.

**Traditional or "Classical" Liberalism.** The renowned scholar Friedrich A. Hayek traced the origins of liberalism to French and English Enlightenment philosophers, including René Descartes, Thomas Hobbes, Jean-Jacques Rousseau, and Voltaire.[490] With the backdrop of an evolving constitutional monarchy in England, a growing mercantile class, the advancement of physical and social sciences, and a newfound respect for learning, liberalism advocated the promotion of reason and rationalism. The emerging liberal concept enshrined both economic and individual liberties. John Locke wrote of "life, liberty, and property" as "natural rights" in his 1689 publication, *Second Treatise on Civil Government.* In the wake of the "Glorious Revolution" of 1688, where Parliament secured constitutional powers over the monarchy, Locke promoted the concept of the rule of law to secure these natural rights. From these many sources, one may extract the following tenets of classical liberalism:

1) Rationalism. The belief that through reason man can triumph over the state of nature and primitivism. In the area of law, a written constitution and a bill of rights represent rationalism applied to government.
2) Optimistic View of Human Nature. A belief in a progression of human development and betterment through enlightenment and learning.

3) Convention and Tradition. Old prejudices and superstitions are viewed as an impediment to progress rather than as the embodiment of the collective wisdom of generations and society.
4) Egalitarianism. A distinct enmity toward class distinctions, though many if not most liberals of the eighteenth century did not believe in racial equality. But this egalitarianism had other limits. For example, most liberals of this era disagreed with the radical egalitarianism of the French Revolution and did not support massive redistribution of wealth.
5) Liberty. Belief in a natural right to liberty. This is valued even at the expense of order.
6) Social Compact. The notion that individuals band together to form government and bequeath certain powers in that government. From the compact flows rights of individuals in relation to the state.

In what may appear to be a contradiction, some conservatives can claim historical foundations in natural rights and natural law theory as well as liberals.[491] The conservative Edmund Burke believed in natural rights, a product of his earlier philosophical support for the Glorious Revolution and political support for the American Revolution. But the elder Burke used his belief in natural rights as a basis for criticism of radical egalitarianism and other excesses of the French Revolution. Thus, Burke's fight was less with liberalism (since he was a liberal by most criteria up until 1789) than it was with radicalism. Burke was, in fact, successful in convincing most English liberals, expatriate Thomas Paine aside, about the dangers of the unrestrained ideological zealotry in Paris.

Natural law theory remains historically relevant to the study of law, though overshadowed by later legal movements such as positivism and realism. It still surfaces periodically. During his confirmation hearings, Clarence Thomas was ridiculed for his professed adherence to natural law theory. But Thomas's rare but periodic votes in favor of individual liberties may reflect latent belief in natural rights.

As regards to eighteenth-century liberalism, support for natural rights linked economic and individual liberties. The protection of economic liberties was championed in Adam Smith's publication, *The Wealth of Nations,* which appeared in 1776, the same year the American Continental Congress declared political independence from Britain. Indeed, the liberal English Whig Party of the era distinguished itself from the Tories by supporting independence of the American colonies. Smith praised "the liberal plan of equality, liberty, and justice."[492] Both Smith and fellow Scot David Hume believed in a system of the rule or supremacy of law.

John Locke was a great influence on the founding fathers, including James Madison and Thomas Jefferson. His influence can be seen in Constitution and the due process clauses of the Fifth and Fourteenth Amendments. After the American Revolution and after the Constitution supplanted the Articles of Confederation, antiroyalism was replaced with anti-Federalism in the form of resistance to the growth of central governmental power at the expense of states' rights. Jefferson's Republicans, in protest of John Adams's administration's Alien and Sedition Acts and federal institutions like the Bank of the United States, took up the mantle of the cause and ending the reign of the Federalists in all but the judicial branches of government. Jefferson's interpretation of the establishment clause of the First Amendment, drawing a clear line between church and state, would in time prevail over a narrow reading of that text.

The cause of traditional liberalism was continued by President Andrew Jackson and his nominee to be chief justice, Roger Taney. Andrew Jackson's brand of liberalism promoted the concept of egalitarianism, albeit for mostly white males, not insignificant since the right to vote had been restricted to white landowners until the presidential election of 1824. English liberals of the mid-nineteenth century fought against the infamous "Corn Laws" and other forms of protectionism and mercantilism, which were abhorrent to liberal economic theory.

But the concept of American liberalism changed in the twentieth century. In a great departure from traditional liberalism, the Franklin Roosevelt's administration used the term "liberal" in association with New Deal programs, which involved expanded federal government. Up to that time, "liberalism" had positive implications for the business community and was considered a means by which Roosevelt could promote his programs to business leaders. The New Deal's federal powers owed much more to the judicial record of John Marshall than to Roger Taney. Clearly, Roosevelt's liberalism, and that of successive Democratic administrations, is not traditional liberalism. Though long forgotten in American politics, the traditional meaning of the term "liberal" persists today in continental Europe, where the label "liberal" will often identify you with probusiness interests and "moderate" politics.

The legacy of seventeenth- and eighteenth-century liberalism lives on, but not with the original name. Contemporary libertarianism incorporates many of liberalism's original values but without the stigma of the label "liberal" is now subjected to.

**New Deal Liberalism.** As mentioned above, Franklin Roosevelt's use of the term "liberal" in association with New Deal programs in order to garner the support of the business community forever changed the meaning of liberalism in America. What places this group in the liberal camp (by contemporary standards) is its progovernment, egalitarian, populist, and proregulation view toward business. Like John Marshall, they favored expanded federal powers but without the "Federalist" label. In his early tenure on the Court, William O. Douglas, an outspoken advocate for the New Deal and former Roosevelt appointee as chairman of the Securities and Exchange Commission, was a good example of this category. In reaction to conservative opponents of Roosevelt, the New Deal liberals of the 1930s despised judicial activism and argued for judicial restraint.[493] They rallied against judicial activism that had promoted liberty of contract as a hallowed right and blocked progressive legislation to regulate wages, hours, and child labor for political rather than judicial reasons. Roosevelt appointed Justices Felix Frankfurter and Robert Jackson to the Court because, among other things, of their views on judicial restraint.[494] But by the 1950s, Roosevelt appointees William O. Douglas and Hugo Black found the Court to be fertile ground to protect and promote civil rights and civil liberties, to the dismay of Frankfurter and Jackson. From this point on, Douglas and Black resembled the libertarian liberal more than the New Deal liberal.

**Libertarian Liberalism.** Like those libertarians associated with conservative causes, libertarian liberals place a high priority on individual liberties, but with more sympathy to egalitarian objectives, recognizing the importance of civil rights. The American Civil Liberties Union is most often associated with such causes, though they have often taken on cases, such as litigation supporting the right of Nazis to march in Skokie, Illinois, in 1977, that have alienated many liberal supporters.[495] William O. Douglas and Hugo Black transitioned from the staunch supporters of New Deal governmental powers to strong advocates of civil liberties and civil rights. Unlike the original New Deal supporters, Douglas and other libertarian liberals believed in an activist judiciary. Together with William Brennan, Arthur Goldberg, and Thurgood Marshall, the libertarian liberals would forever change the Court by landmark rulings on freedom of speech, desegregation, and criminal procedure.

**Contemporary Liberalism or Liberalism in Transition.** The liberalism of the 1960s and 1970s that had promoted hard affirmative action quotas, trade protectionism as opposed to free trade, a woman's right to abortion, and federal management of the business sector as opposed to deregulation has been under siege in recent years by popular "conservatism," even within the Democratic Party itself. The Supreme Court nominees of President William Clinton reflect many of the contradictions experienced by contemporary liberals. Justice Stephen Breyer is liberal by some standards but is often tough on crime. Justice Ruth Bader Ginsburg questions the foundation of a woman's right to abortion based upon a nebulous "right of privacy" as opposed to the equal protection clause. But the liberals of the Supreme Court will have a chance to redefine themselves with upcoming decisions on federal power concerning eavesdropping, redistricting, election finance, and environmental regulation, among other things.

## Sui Generis—Those Who Defy Ideological Categorization

**Methodology over Politics.** Certain justices are noted for attempting to assert judicial methodology over political identification. Legal realists, such as Justices Holmes and Brandeis, sought to carve out a realm of principles over politics for the Court. Holmes stated that the job of the Supreme Court is not to "do justice" but to "apply the law." Such an approach is often not without cost. Holmes alienated President Theodore Roosevelt by giving priority to methodology over political result in the *Northern Securities* antitrust case, ending a cordial relationship with the president who named him to the Court. Justices Black and Frankfurter applied rigid tests in their pursuit of "strict constitutionalism." Hugo Black described the role of the Supreme Court as to "explain and expound" on the Constitution. Strict interpretation of the Constitution does not necessarily mean a conservative result. In the Pentagon Papers case, Black's majority opinion was based upon the clear text of the First Amendment, "Congress shall make no law . . . abridging the freedom of speech, or of the press." To what extent new justices on the Court will approach the law like Holmes, Brandeis, Black, and Frankfurter remains to be seem, especially with pressure from pundits and talk show hosts who seem to place more emphasis on results of decisions than methodology.

**Conflicting Ideological Themes.** Sometimes various "liberal" themes are in conflict with each other, as is often the case for "conservative" themes. For example, liberty and equality are frequently in conflict in affirmative action cases. Likewise, law-and-order (social) conservative values may challenge traditional states' rights views, particularly when it comes to federal powers. And libertarian conservatives may chafe at intrusive government surveillance of private homes. Justice Scalia is an ideological conservative whose adherence to conservative themes often results in decisions that disappoint law enforcement advocates, big business, and others usually associated with conservative causes. For example, in *Kyllo v. United States,* he wrote that thermal imaging devices, which would allow police to view objects thought walls, violated Fourth Amendment protections against unreasonable searches. He found that modern technology enabled law enforcement officials to violate the original intent of the Fourth Amendment, for citizens to be secure in their homes. In *Kelo v. City of New London,* his support for traditional views of the "taking" clause caused him to dissent in an opinion that favored developers.[496] In *Whitman v. American Trucking,* he wrote for the majority supporting the Environmental Protection Agency's powers, as delegated by the Clean Air Act, to set air quality standards.[497]

**Justices Who Change Over Time.** With justices appointed to life terms, they are free to change their position over time, as Hamilton would have predicted. There has been much literature on the "institutionalist" factors on the Court, i.e., forces within and around the Court and the justices that may impel change of heart, reconsideration of the issues, or reevaluation based upon new information. As John Yoo, a former George W. Bush administration Justice Department official, stated, "the president cannot control the people he puts on the Supreme Court. You can't control them even when you're trying to pick them for a specific issue."[498] There is a certain futility about selection of justices that is inherent in the system by design. Neither Alexander Hamilton nor James Madison would necessarily be surprised nor disappointed. Two prime examples of justices who changed over time are Anthony Kennedy and William O. Douglas.

Anthony Kennedy initially sided with conservatives on many issues, to such an extent that some referred to him as "Bork without the beard."[499] He had served for twelve years on the U.S. Court of Appeals for the Ninth Circuit with a "solidly conservative" record.[500] Early in his tenure he sided with Justice Scalia when he supported school prayer. But by 1992, in the case of *Lee v. Weisman*, Kennedy switched sides, quite literally. Initially supporting the right to school prayer in that case, he decided "my draft looked quite wrong" and threw his vote to the other side, reversing the majority and the result.[501] In the same year, he abandoned the conservatives on the Court with regard to abortion in *Casey v. Planned Parenthood*.[502] In 2003, he found that homosexual sodomy was protected by the Constitution in *Lawrence v. Texas*.

William O. Douglas, in his early decisions, opined that the Court should not read "notions of public policy" into the Constitution.[503] Yet Douglas later championed the incorporation of new rights into the Constitution, such as his expansive interpretation of the right of privacy in *Griswold v. Connecticut*. The contrast is truly great between the young Douglas as the New Deal Democrat who consistently supported the government's power, including the internment of Japanese Americans, and the older Douglas, who was a staunch advocate for individual liberty. Douglas also became a strong personal advocate of environmental causes, on and off the Court. He published widely and led a protest for preservation of the historic Baltimore and Ohio Canal.

But Kennedy and Douglas are not the only justices who have changed over time. Some justices may have changed as a result of political pressure. Owen Roberts, a Hoover appointee who initially opposed New Deal laws, switched sides to support the legislation about the time of Roosevelt's Court-Packing Plan. Other justices found that principles of stability and stare decisis required deference to decisions that have become accepted law over time. William Rehnquist in *Dickerson v. United States* came to support the *Miranda* decision after many previous opinions that attempted to whittle down those rights. He also voted against unlimited executive detention power over suspected unlawful combatants in *Hamdi v. Rumsfeld*.

From the earliest days of the Supreme Court, justices have carved paths of their own. John Marshall, who argued and lost a case before the Supreme Court on behalf of state power, became the federal government's strongest advocate for thirty-five years on the Court. Joseph Story, as Madison's 1812 appointee, became philosophically close to Marshall and the Federalists, supporting broad federal powers at the expense of states' rights. Even Roger Taney, the preeminent states' rights advocate on the Court, for a long time held political office in the state of Maryland as a Federalist.

In many cases, justices have appeared to act in defiance of their past activities and political associations. Felix Frankfurter, a founder of the ACLU, supported the government's abridgement of civil liberties and civil rights during World War II and the Red Scare of the 1950s. Hugo Black, the former Ku Klux Klan member and Alabama senator, supported the Court's unanimous decision for school desegregation in *Brown v. Board of Education*. He supported free speech in, among other cases, the *New York Times Co. v. United States* (1971) a.k.a. the *Pentagon Papers* case. Earl Warren as Republican governor of California supported internment of Japanese Americans during World War II but became a strong advocate of civil liberties and civil rights on the Court.

More than a few justices showed little allegiance to the politics of the president who appointed them or the stances of his party. Harlan Stone, the appointee of conservative Republican president Coolidge, voted to support much of Franklin Roosevelt's New Deal legislation. Roosevelt later "rewarded" him by elevation to the position of chief justice. James C. McReynolds was a Woodrow Wilson appointee who disappointed Wilson by failing to support progressive legislation and rankled Franklin Roosevelt by ruling against New Deal programs. Harry Blackmun was a Nixon law-and-order appointee who later frequently sided with Court liberals such as William Brennan and Thurgood Marshall. To the chagrin of social conservatives, Blackmun changed his view on the death penalty in 1994. Byron White was the Kennedy appointee considered a solid New Deal Democrat who became very conservative on criminal issues over time.

But not all presidents are disappointed with independent-minded justices. John Paul Stevens was appointed by moderate Republican president Gerald Ford, but he frequently sides with Ginsburg and Breyer, the only justices appointed to the Court by a Democratic president. President Ford remarked that he was proud of his appointment.[504]

Justices may learn and grow on the job as a result of the social and intellectual exchanges while on the Court. As Michael Greve from the American Enterprise Institute stated in the wake of the revelation of Blackmun's papers and the Kennedy-Blackmun rapprochement, "the social dynamics among the justices matter a whole lot."[505] Chief Justice Rehnquist observed that a justice's loyalty to the president that appoints him or her may not withstand "institutional pressures" within the Court itself.[506] These pressures, he said, tend to "weaken and diffuse" the outside loyalties of any new appointee. Professor Richard Freeman of the University of Michigan observed that "the dynamic of the Court can be very important, the nine justices speaking to each other and, very importantly, to their clerks."[507]

In conclusion, the independence of the judiciary gives justices the freedom to learn, grow, and change their opinions over time, exactly as the framers of the Constitution would have intended. Or put another way, justices will continue to defy categorization simply because they can.

# CONCLUSION

*The Constitution, which ensures the independence of justices of the Supreme Court through terms of "good behavior," by direct implication enables the justices to act in accordance with prerogatives and motivations very different than those of the legislative and executive branches. By all indications, the framers of the Constitution would be neither disappointed nor surprised that justices of the Court defied control by the political branches and eschewed easy political categorization. There is one certainty: we can expect more "surprises" from the justices and the Court.*

As the Supreme Court's prescribed role in governance is inherently different from the executive and legislative branches, justices will continue to defy political categorization. Charged as the final arbiter in interpreting the Constitution, the Court will inevitably find itself at odds with the other branches of government, as the framers would have expected. Between 1803 and 1993, the Court overturned 127 federal laws and 1,212 state and local laws. That may represent only a fraction of the over sixty thousand laws passed by Congress, but that is a power that cannot be ignored. No less significant is the Court's power to invalidate actions of the chief executive, as in the *Steel Seizure* case and *United States v. Nixon.*

Yet for all the power granted it under the Constitution, the Supreme Court is not simply another policy-making institution of government. The choices of judges "are not the 'free' choices of congressmen."[508] The Court is intended to function as a "forum of principle" rather than a mere political body.[509] In the absence of the guidance of principle, the Court risks political subversion as a "naked power organ."[510] Despite ample historical warning about the consequences of politicization, the Court now finds itself under immense pressure to turn against such sound juridical principles. And the president was recently under intense pressure from special interest groups to appoint justices with specific agendas and results in mind.

Selecting justices on the basis of simplistic political categorization is not only unhelpful from a perspective of maintaining independence of the judiciary, it is unwise from the perspective of maintaining a healthy constitutional democracy. Instead, as Professor Rotunda advises, it is important to select justices based upon factors more relevant to judicial temperament, intellectual ability, and personal integrity.[511] Many of the recent attacks on the Supreme Court can be more accurately described as advocacy for a change in the *political direction* of the Court rather than advocacy for adoption of *nonpolitical methodology*. These attacks represent the greatest challenge to the independence of the Court since Franklin Roosevelt's Court-Packing Plan.

Yet the Constitution endures, with wisdom transcending the ages. The founding fathers equipped the Supreme Court with the power to safeguard individual liberty against the tyranny of the majority. It is well to remember the words of Alexander Hamilton in "Federalist No. 78," paraphrasing Montesquieu:

> There is no liberty if the power of judging be not separated from the legislative and executive powers.

# Appendix 1

## FEDERALIST PAPER NO. 78: ALEXANDER HAMILTON

We proceed now to an examination of the judiciary department of the proposed government.

In unfolding the defects of the existing Confederation, the utility and necessity of a federal judicature have been clearly pointed out. It is the less necessary to recapitulate the considerations there urged as the propriety of the institution in the abstract is not disputed; the only questions which have been raised being relative to the manner of constituting it, and to its extent. To these points, therefore, our observations shall be confined.

The manner of constituting it seems to embrace these several objects: 1st. The mode of appointing the judges. 2nd. The tenure by-which they are to hold their places. 3rd. The partition of the judiciary authority between different courts and their relations to each other.

*First.* As to the mode of appointing the judges: this is the same with that of appointing the officers of the Union in general and has been so fully discussed in the two last numbers that nothing can be said here which would not be useless repetition.

*Second.* As to the tenure by which the judges are to hold their places: this chiefly concerns their duration in office, the provisions for their support, the precautions for their responsibility.

According to the plan of the convention, all judges who may be appointed by the United States are to hold their offices *during good behavior;* which is conformable to the most approved of the State constitutions, and among the rest, to that of this State. Its propriety having been drawn into question by the adversaries of that plan is no light symptom of the rage for objection which disorders their imaginations and judgments. The standard of good behavior for the continuance in office of the judicial magistracy is certainly one of the most valuable of the modern improvements in the practice of government. In a monarchy it is an excellent barrier to the despotism of the prince; in a republic it is a no less excellent barrier to the encroachments and oppressions of the representative body. And it is the best expedient which can be devised in any government to secure a steady, upright, and impartial administration of the laws.

Whoever attentively considers the different departments of power must perceive that, in a government in which they are separated from each other, the judiciary, from the nature of its functions, will always be the least dangerous to the political rights of the Constitution; because it will be least in a capacity to annoy or injure them. The executive not only dispenses the honors but holds the sword of the community. The legislature not only commands the purse but prescribes the rules by which the duties and rights of every citizen are to be regulated. The judiciary, on the contrary, has no influence over either the sword or the purse; no direction either of the strength or of the wealth of the society, and can take active resolution whatever. It may truly be said to have neither FORCE nor WILL but merely judgment; and must ultimately depend upon the aid of the executive arm even for the efficacy of its judgments.

This simple view of the matter suggests several important consequences. It proves incontestably that the judiciary is beyond comparison the weakest of the three departments of power; that it can never attack with success either of the other two; and that all possible care is requisite to enable it to defend itself against their attacks. It equally proves that though individual oppression may now and then proceed from the courts of justice, the general liberty of the people can never be endangered from that quarter; I mean so long as the judiciary remains truly distinct from both the legislature and the executive. For I agree that "there is no liberty if the power of judging be not separated from the legislative and executive powers." And it proves, in the last place, that as liberty can have nothing to fear from the judiciary alone, but would have nothing to fear from its union with either of the other departments; that as all the effects of such a union must ensue from a dependence of the former on the latter, notwithstanding a nominal and apparent separation; that as, from the natural feebleness of the judiciary, it is in continual jeopardy of being overpowered, awed, or influenced by its coordinate branches; and that as nothing can contribute so much to its firmness and independence as permanency in office, this quality may therefore be justly regarded as an indispensable ingredient in its constitution, and, in a great measure, as the citadel of the public justice and the public security.

The complete independence of the courts or justice is peculiarly essential in a limited Constitution. By a limited Constitution, I understand one which contains certain specified exceptions to the legislative authority, such, for instance, as that it shall pass no bills of attainder, no ex post facto laws, and the like. Limitations of this kind can be preserved in practice no other way than through the medium of courts of justice, whose duty it must be to declare all acts contrary to the manifest tenor of the Constitution void. Without this, all the reservations of particular rights or privileges would amount to nothing.

Some perplexity respecting the rights of the courts to pronounce legislative acts void, because contrary to the Constitution, has arisen from an imagination that the doctrine would imply a superiority of the judiciary to the legislative power. It is urged that the authority which can declare the acts of another void must necessarily be superior to the one whose acts may be declared void. As this doctrine is of great importance in all the American constitutions, a brief discussion of the grounds on which it rests cannot be unacceptable.

There is no position which depends on clearer principles than that every act of a delegated authority, contrary to the tenor of the commission under which it is exercised, is void. No legislative act, therefore, contrary to the Constitution, can be valid. To deny this would be to affirm that the deputy is greater than his principal; that the servant is above his master, that the representatives of the people are superior to the people themselves; that men acting by virtue of powers may do not only what their powers do not authorize, but what they forbid.

If it be said that the legislative body are themselves the constitutional judges of their own powers and that the construction they put upon them is conclusive upon the other departments it may be answered that this cannot be the natural presumption where it is not to be collected from any particular provisions in the Constitution. It is not otherwise to be supposed that the Constitution could intend to enable the representatives of the people to substitute their *will* to that of their constituents. It is far more rational to suppose that the courts were designed to be an intermediate body between the people and the legislature in order, among other things, to keep the latter within the limits assigned to their authority.

The interpretation of the laws is the proper and peculiar province of the courts. A constitution is, in fact, and must be regarded by the judges as, a fundamental law. It therefore belongs to them to ascertain its meaning as well as the meaning of any particular act proceeding from the legislative body If there should happen to be an irreconcilable variance between the two, that which has the superior obligation and validity ought, of course, to be preferred; or, in other words, the Constitution ought to be preferred to the statute, the intention of the people to the intention of their agents.

Nor does this conclusion by any means suppose a superiority of the judicial to the legislative power. It only supposes that the power of the people is superior to both, and that where the will of the legislature, declared in its statutes, stands in opposition to that of the people, declared in the Constitution, the judges ought to be governed by the latter rather than the former. They ought to regulate their decisions by the fundamental laws rather than by those which are not fundamental.

This exercise of judicial discretion in determining between two contradictory laws is exemplified in a familiar instance. It not uncommonly happens that there are two statutes existing at one time, clashing in whole or in part with each other and neither of them containing any repealing clause or expression. In such a case, it is the province of the courts to liquidate and fix their meaning and operation. So far as they can, by any fair construction, be reconciled to each other, reason and law conspire to dictate that this should be done; where this is impracticable, it becomes a matter of necessity to give effect to one in exclusion of the other. The rule which has obtained in the courts for determining their relative validity is that the last in order of time shall be preferred to the first. But this is a mere rule of construction, not derived from any positive law but from the nature and reason of the thing. It is a rule not enjoined upon the courts by legislative provision but adopted by themselves, as consonant to truth and propriety, for the direction of their conduct as interpreters of the law. They thought it reasonable that between the interfering acts of an *equal* authority that which was the last indication of its will should have the preference.

But in regard to the interfering acts of a superior and subordinate authority of an original and derivative power, the nature and reason of the thing indicate the converse of that rule as proper to be followed. They teach us that the prior act of a superior ought to be preferred to the subsequent act of an inferior and subordinate authority; and that accordingly, whenever a particular statute contravenes the Constitution, it will be the duty of the judicial tribunals to adhere to the latter and disregard the former.

It can be of no weight to say that the courts, on the pretense of a repugnance, may substitute their own pleasure to the constitutional intentions of the legislature. This might as well happen in the case of two contradictory statutes; or it might as well happen in every adjudication upon any single statute. The courts must declare the sense of the law; and if they should be disposed to exercise WILL instead of JUDGMENT, the consequence would equally be the substitution of their pleasure to that of the legislative body. The observation, if it proved anything, would prove that there ought to be no judges distinct from that body.

If, then, the courts of justice are to be considered as the bulwarks of a limited Constitution against legislative encroachments, this consideration will afford a strong argument for the permanent tenure of judicial offices, since nothing will contribute so much as this to that independent spirit in the judges which must be essential to the faithful performance of so arduous a duty.

This independence of the judges is equally requisite to guard the Constitution and the rights of individuals from the effects of those ill humors which the arts of designing men, or the innuence of particular conjunctures, sometimes disseminate among the people themselves, and which, though they speedily give place to better information, and more deliberate reflection, have a tendency, in the meantime, to occasion dangerous innovations in the government, and serious oppressions of the minor party in the community. Though I trust the friends of the proposed Constitution will never concur with its enemies in questioning that fundamental principle of republican government which admits the right of the people to alter or abolish the established Constitution whenever they find it inconsistent with their happiness; yet it is not to be inferred from this principle that the representatives of the people, whenever a momentary inclination happens to lay hold of a majority of their constituents incompatible with the provisions in the existing Constitution would, on that account, be justifiable in s violation of those provisions; on that the courts would be under a greater obligation to connive at infractions in this shape than when they had proceeded wholly from the cabals of the representative body. Until the people have, by some solemn and authoritative act, annulled or changed the established form, it is binding upon themselves collectively, as well as individually; and no presumption, or even knowledge of their sentiments, can warrant their representatives in a departure from it nor to such an act. But it is easy to see that it would require an uncommon portion of fortitude in the Judges to do their duty as faithful guardians of the Constitution, where legislative invasions of it had been instigated by the major voice of the community.

But it is not with a view to infractions of the Constitution only that the independence of the judges may be an essential safeguard against the effects of occasional ill humors in the society. These sometimes extend no farther than to the injury of the private rights of particular classes of citizens, by unjust and partial laws. Here also the firmness of the judicial magistracy is of vast importance in mitigating the severity and confining the operation of such laws. It not only serves to moderate the immediate mischiefs of those which may have been passed but it operates as a check upon the legislative body in passing them; who, perceiving that obstacles to the success of an iniquitous intention are to be expected from the scruples of the courts, are in a manner compelled, by the very motives of the injustice they meditate, to qualify their attempts. This is a circumstance calculated to have more influence upon the character of our governments than but few may be aware of. the benefits of the integrity and moderation of the judiciary have already been felt in more States than one; and though they may have displeased those whose sinister expectations they may have disappointed, they must have commanded the esteem and applause of all the virtuous and disinterested. Considerate men of every description ought to prize whatever will tend to beget or fortify that temper in the courts; as no man can be sure that he may not be tomorrow the victim of a spirit of injustice, by which he may be a gainer today. And every man must now feel that the inevitable tendency of such a spirit is to sap the foundations of public and private confidence and to introduce in its stead universal distrust and distress.

That inflexible and uniform of the Constitution, and of individuals, which we perceive to be indispensable in the courts of justice, can certainly not be expected from judges who hold their offices by a temporary commission. Periodical appointments, however regulated, or by whomsoever made, would, in some way or other, be fatal to their necessary independence. If the power of making them was committed either to the executive or legislature there would be danger of an improper complaisance to the branch which possessed it; if to both, there would be an unwillingness to hazard the displeasure of either; if to the people, or to persons chosen by them for the special purpose, there would be too great a disposition to consult popularity to justify a reliance that nothing would be consulted but the Constitution and the laws.

There is yet a further and a weighty reason for the permanency of the judicial offices which is deducible from the nature of the qualifications they require. It has been frequently remarked with great propriety that a voluminous code of laws is one of the inconveniences necessarily connected with the advantages of a free government. To avoid an arbitrary discretion in the courts, it is indispensable that they should be bound down by strict rules and precedents which serve to define and point out their duty in every particular case that comes before them; and it will readily be conceived from the variety of controversies which grow out of the folly and wickedness of mankind that the records of those precow dents must unavoidably swell to a very considerable bulk and must demand long and laborious study to acquire a competent knowledge of them. Hence it is that there can be but few men in the society who will have sufficient skill in the laws to qualify them for the stations of judges. And making the proper deductions for the ordinary depravity of human nature, the number must be still smaller of those who unite the requisite integrity with the requisite knowledge. These considerations apprise us that the government can have no great option between fit characters; and that a temporary duration in office which would naturally discourage such characters from quitting a lucrative line of practice to accept a seat on the bench would have a tendency to throw the administration of justice into hands less able and less well qualified to conduct it with utility and dignity. In the present circumstances of this countly and in those in which it is likely to be for a long time to come, the disadvantages on this score would be greater than they may at first sight appear; but it must be confessed that they are far inferior to those which present themselves under the other aspects of the subject.

Upon the whole, there can be no room to doubt that the convention acted wisely in copying from the models of those constitutions which have established good behavior as the tenure of their judicial offices, in point of duration; and that so far from being blamable on the account, their plan would have been inexcusably defective if it had wanted this important feature of good government. The experience of Great Britain affords an illustrious comment on the excellence of the institution.

**PUBLIUS**

# APPENDIX 2

## ANTI-FEDERALIST PAPER NO. 80 THE POWER OF THE JUDICIARY, "BRUTUS," JANUARY 31, 1788

*Note: Published under the pseudonym "Brutus," the likely author is Robert Yates, a New York judge. He was one of three New York delegates to the constitutional convention in Philadelphia in 1787. The other delegates were Alexander Hamilton and John Lansing, mayor of Albany. Yates and Lansing were close allies of New York governor George Clinton, who objected to giving Congress the power to tax. Yates and Lansing left the convention early in protest of the Virginia Plan, among other things. This left Hamilton to represent the state of New York, but only in the capacity of a nonvoting member.*

(From the eleventh essay of "Brutus" as published in the *New York Journal,* January 31, 1788)

The nature and extent of the judicial power of the United States, proposed to be granted by the constitution, claims our particular attention.

Much has been said and written upon the subject of this new system on both sides, but I have not met with any writer who has discussed the judicial powers with any degree of accuracy. And yet it is obvious, that we can gain but very imperfect ideas of the manner in which this government will work, or the effect it will have in changing the internal police and mode of distributing justice at present subsisting in the respective states, without a thorough investigation of the powers of the judiciary and of the manner in which they will operate. This government is a complete system, not only for making, but for executing laws. And the courts of law, which will be constituted by it, are not only to decide upon the constitution and the laws made in pursuance of it, but by officers subordinate to them to execute all their decisions. The real effect of this system of government, will therefore be brought home to the feelings of the people, through the medium of the judicial power. It is, moreover, of great importance, to examine with care the nature and extent of the judicial power, because those who are to be vested with it, are to be placed in a situation altogether unprecedented in a free country. They are to be rendered totally independent, both of the people and the legislature, both with respect to their offices and salaries. No errors they may commit can be corrected by any power above them, if any such power there be, nor can they be removed from office for making ever so many erroneous adjudications.

The only causes for which they can be displaced, is, conviction of treason, bribery, and high crimes and misdemeanors.

This part of the plan is so modelled, as to authorize the courts, not only to carry into execution the powers expressly given, but where these are wanting or ambiguously expressed, to supply what is wanting by their own decisions.

That we may be enabled to form a just opinion on this subject, I shall, in considering it, lst. Examine the nature and extent of the judicial powers, and 2nd. Inquire, whether the courts who are to exercise them, are so constituted as to afford reasonable ground of confidence, that they will exercise them for the general good.

With a regard to the nature and extent of the judicial powers, I have to regret my want of capacity to give that full and minute explanation of them that the subject merits. To be able to do this, a man should be possessed of a degree of law knowledge far beyond what I pretend to. A number of hard words and technical phrases are used in this part of the system, about the meaning of which gentlemen learned in the law differ. Its advocates know how to avail themselves of these phrases. In a number of instances, where objections are made to the powers given to the judicial, they give such an explanation to the technical terms as to avoid them.

Though I am not competent to give a perfect explanation of the powers granted to this department of the government, I shall yet attempt to trace some of the leading features of it, from which I presume it will appear, that they will operate to a total subversion of the state judiciaries, if not to the legislative authority of the states.

In article 3d, sect. 2d, it is said, "The judicial power shall extend to all cases in law and equity arising under this constitution, the laws of the United States, and treaties made, or which shall be made, under their authority, etc." The first article to which this power extends is, all cases in law and equity arising under this constitution.

What latitude of construction this clause should receive, it is not easy to say. At first view, one would suppose, that it meant no more than this, that the courts under the general government should exercise, not only the powers of courts of law, but also that of courts of equity, in the manner in which those powers are usually exercised in the different states. But this cannot be the meaning, because the next clause authorises the courts to take cognizance of all cases in law and equity arising under the laws of the United States; this last article, I conceive, conveys as much power to the general judicial as any of the state courts possess.

The cases arising under the constitution must be different from those arising under the laws, or else the two clauses mean exactly the same thing. The cases arising under the constitution must include such, as bring into question its meaning, and will require an explanation of the nature and extent of the powers of the different departments under it. This article, therefore, vests the judicial with a power to resolve all questions that may arise on any case on the construction of the constitution, either in law or in equity. lst. They are authorised to determine all questions that may arise upon the meaning of the constitution in law. This article vests the courts with authority to give the constitution a legal construction, or to explain it according to the rules laid down for construing a law. These rules give a certain degree of latitude of explanation. According to this mode of construction, the courts are to give such meaning to the constitution as comports best with the common, and generally received acceptation of the words in which it is expressed, regarding their ordinary and popular use, rather than their grammatical propriety. Where words are dubious, they will be explained by the context. The end of the clause will be attended to, and the words will be understood, as having a view to it; and the words will not be so understood as to bear no meaning or a very absurd one.

2nd. The judicial are not only to decide questions arising upon the meaning of the constitution in law, but also in equity. By this they are empowered, to explain the constitution according to the reasoning spirit of it, without being confined to the words or letter. "From this method of interpreting laws (says Blackstone) by the reason of them, arises what we call equity"; which is thus defined by Grotius, "the correction of that, wherein the law, by reason of its universality, is deficient; for since in laws all cases cannot be foreseen, or expressed, it is necessary, that when the decrees of the law cannot be applied to particular cases, there should somewhere be a power vested of defining those circumstances, which had they been foreseen the legislator would have expressed . . . ." The same learned author observes, "That equity, thus depending essentially upon each individual case, there can be no established rules and fixed principles of equity laid down, without destroying its very essence, and reducing it to a positive law."

From these remarks, the authority and business of the courts of law, under this clause, may be understood.

They [the courts] will give the sense of every article of the constitution, that may from time to time come before them. And in their decisions they will not confine themselves to any fixed or established rules, but will determine, according to what appears to them, the reason and spirit of the constitution. The opinions of the supreme court, whatever they may be, will have the force of law; because there is no power provided in the constitution that can correct their errors, or control their adjudications. From this court there is no appeal. And I conceive the legislature themselves, cannot set aside a judgment of this court, because they are authorised by the constitution to decide in the last resort. The legislature must be controlled by the constitution, and not the constitution by them. They have therefore no more right to set aside any judgment pronounced upon the construction of the constitution, than they have to take from the president, the chief command of the army and navy, and commit it to some other person. The reason is plain; the judicial and executive derive their authority from the same source, that the legislature do theirs; and therefore in all cases, where the constitution does not make the one responsible to, or controllable by the other, they are altogether independent of each other.

The judicial power will operate to effect, in the most certain, but yet silent and imperceptible manner, what is evidently the tendency of the constitution: I mean, an entire subversion of the legislative, executive and judicial powers of the individual states. Every adjudication of the supreme court, on any question that may arise upon the nature and extent of the general government, will affect the limits of the state jurisdiction. In proportion as the former enlarge the exercise of their powers, will that of the latter be restricted.

That the judicial power of the United States, will lean strongly in favor of the general government, and will give such an explanation to the constitution, as will favor an extension of its jurisdiction, is very evident from a variety of considerations. lst. The constitution itself strongly countenances such a mode of construction. Most of the articles in this system, which convey powers of any considerable importance, are conceived in general and indefinite terms, which are either equivocal, ambiguous, or which require long definitions to unfold the extent of their meaning. The two most important powers committed to any government, those of raising money, and of raising and keeping up troops, have already been considered, and shown to be unlimited by any thing but the discretion of the legislature. The clause which vests the power to pass all laws which are proper and necessary, to carry the powers given into execution, it has been shown, leaves the legislature at liberty, to do everything, which in their judgment is best. It is said, I know, that this clause confers no power on the legislature, which they would not have had without it-though I believe this is not the fact, Yet, admitting it to be, it implies that the constitution is not to receive an explanation strictly according to its letter; but more power is implied than is expressed. And this clause, if it is to be considered as explanatory of the extent of the powers given, rather than giving a new power, is to be understood as declaring that in construing any of the articles conveying power, the spirit, intent and design of the clause should be attended to, as welt as the words in their common acceptation.

This constitution gives sufficient color for adopting an equitable construction, if we consider the great end and design it professedly has in view. These appear from its preamble to be, "to form a more perfect union, establish justice, insure domestic tranquility, provide for the common defense, promote the general welfare, and secure the blessings of liberty to ourselves and posterity." The design of this system is here expressed, and it is proper to give such a meaning to the various parts, as will best promote the accomplishment of the end; this idea suggests itself naturally upon reading the preamble, and will countenance the court in giving the several articles such a sense, as will the most effectually promote the ends the constitution had in view. How this manner of explaining the constitution will operate in practice, shall be the subject of future inquiry.

2nd. Not only will the constitution justify the courts in inclining to this mode of explaining it, but they will be interested in using this latitude of interpretation. Every body of men invested with office are tenacious of power; they feel interested, and hence it has become a kind of maxim, to hand down their offices, with all its rights and privileges, unimpaired to their successors. The same principle will influence them to extend their power, and increase their rights; this of itself will operate strongly upon the courts to give such a meaning to the constitution in all cases where it can possibly be done, as will enlarge the sphere of their own authority. Every extension of the power of the general legislature, as well as of the judicial powers, will increase the powers of the courts; and the dignity and importance of the judges, will be in proportion to the extent and magnitude of the powers they exercise. I add, it is highly probable the emolument of the judges will be increased, with the increase of the business they will have to transact and its importance. From these considerations the judges will be interested to extend the powers of the courts, and to construe the constitution as much as possible, in such a way as to favor it; and that they will do it, appears probable.

3rd. Because they [the courts] will have precedent to plead, to justify them in it [extending their powers]. It is well known, that the courts in England, have by their authority, extended their jurisdiction far beyond the limits set them in their original institution, and by the laws of the land.

The court of exchequer is a remarkable instance of this. It was originally intended principally to recover the king's debts, and to order the revenues of the crown. It had a common law jurisdiction, which was established merely for the benefit of the king's accountants. We learn from Blackstone, that the proceedings in this court are grounded on a writ called quo minus, in which the plaintiff suggests, that he is the king's farmer or debtor, and that the defendant hath done him the damage complained of, by which he is less able to pay the king. These suits, by the statute of Rutland, are expressly directed to be confined to such matters as specially concern the king, or his ministers in the exchequer. And by the articuli super cartas, it is enacted, that no common pleas be thenceforth held in the exchequer contrary to the form of the great charter. But now any person may sue in the exchequer. The surmise of being debtor to the king being matter of form, and mere words of course, the court is open to all the nation.

When the courts will have a precedent before them of a court which extended its jurisdiction in opposition to an act of the legislature, is it not to be expected that they will extend theirs, especially when there is nothing in the constitution expressly against it? And they are authorised to construe its meaning, and are not under any control.

This power in the judicial, will enable them to mould the government, into any shape they please. The manner in which this may be effected we will hereafter examine.

**BRUTUS**

# APPENDIX 3

## FEDERALIST PAPER NO. 81: ALEXANDER HAMILTON

LET US now return to the partition of the judiciary authority between different courts and their relations to each other.

"The judicial power of the United States is" (by the plan of the convention) "to be vested in one Supreme Court, and in such inferior courts as the Congress may, from time to time, ordain and establish."

That there ought to be one court of supreme and final jurisdiction is a proposition which has not been, and is not likely to be contested. The reasons for it have been assigned in another place and are too obvious to need repetition. The only question that seems to have been raised concerning it is whether it ought to be a distinct body or a branch of the legislature. The same contradiction is observable in regard to this matter which has been remarked in several other cases. The very men who object to the Senate as a court of impeachments, on the ground of an improper intermixture of powers, advocate, by implication at least, the propriety of vesting the ultimate decision of all causes in the whole or in a part of the legislative body.

The arguments or rather suggestions, upon which this charge is founded are to this effect: "The authority of the proposed Supreme Court of the United States, which is to be a separate and independent body, will be superior to that of the legislature. The power of construing the laws according to the spirit of the Constitution will enable that court to mold them into whatever shape it may think proper; especially as its decisions will not be in any manner subject to the revision or correction of the legislative body. This is as unprecedented as it is dangerous. In Britain the judicial power, in the last resort, resides in the House of Lords, which is a branch of the Legislature; and this part of the British government has been imitated in the State constitutions in general. The Parliament of Great Britain, and the legislatures of the several States, can at any aims rectify, by law, the exceptionable decisions of their respective courts. But the errors and usurpations of the Supreme Court of the United States will be uncontrollable and remediless." This, upon examination, will be found to be made up altogether of false reasoning upon misconceived fact.

In the first place, there is not a syllable in the plan under consideration which directly empowers the national courts to construe the laws according to the spirit of the Constitution, or which gives them any greater latitude in this respect than may be claimed by the courts of every State. I admit, however, that the Constitution ought to be the standard of construction of the laws, and that wherever there is an evident opposition, the laws ought to give place to the Constitution. But this doctrine is not deducible from any circumstance peculiar to the plan of convention, but from the general theory of a limited Constitution; and as far as it is true is equally applicable to most if not to all the State governments. There can be no objection, therefore, on this account to the federal judicature which will not lie against the local judicatures in general, and which will not serve to condemn every constitution that attempts to set bounds to the legislative discretion.

But perhaps the force of the objection may be thought to consist in the particular organization of the proposed Supreme Court; in its being composed of a distinct body of magistrates, instead of being one of the branches of the legislature, as in the government of Great Britain and in that of this State. To insist upon this point, the authors of the objection must renounce the meaning they have labored to annex to the celebrated maxim requiring a separation of the departments of power. It shall, nevertheless, be conceded to them, agreeably to the interpretation given to that maxim in the course of these papers, that it is not violated by vesting the ultimate power of judging in a part of the legislative body. But though this be not an absolute violation of that excellent rule, yet it verges so nearly upon it as on this account alone to be less eligible than the mode preferred by the convention. From a body which had had even a partial agency in passing bad laws we could rarely expect a disposition to temper and moderate them in the application. The same spirit which had operated in making them would be too apt to operate in interpreting them; still less could it be expected that men who had infringed the Constitution in the character of legislators would be disposed to repair the breach in the character of judges. Nor is this all. Every reason which recommends the tenure of good behavior for judicial offices militates against placing the judiciary power, in the last resort, in a body composed of men chosen for a limited period. There is an absurdity in referring the determination of causes, in the first instance, to judges of permanent standing; and in the last, to those of a temporary and mutable constitution. And there is a still greater absurdity in subjecting the decisions of men, selected for their knowledge of the laws, acquired by long and laborious study, to the revision and control of men who, for want of the same advantage, cannot but be deficient in that knowledge. The members of the legislature will rarely be chosen with a view to those qualifications which fit men for the stations of judges; and as, on this account, there will be great reason to apprehend all the ill consequences of defective information, so, on account of the natural propensity of such bodies to party divisions, there will be no less reason to fear that the pestilential breath of faction may poison the fountains of justice. The habit of being continually marshaled on opposite sides will be too apt to stifle the voice both of law and of equity.

These considerations teach us to applaud the wisdom of those States who have committed the judicial power, in the last resort, not to a part of the legislature, but to distinct and independent bodies of men. Contrary to the supposition of those who have represented the plan of the convention, in this respect, as novel and unprecedented, it is but a copy of the constitutions of New Hampshire, Massachusetts, Pennsylvania, Delaware, Maryland, Virginia, North Carolina, South Carolina, and Georgia; and the preference which has been given to these models is highly to be commended.

It is not true, in the second place, that the parliament of Great Britain, or the legislatures of the particular States, can rectify the exceptionable decisions of their respective courts, many other sense than might be done by a future legislature of the United States. The theory, neither of the British, nor the State constitutions, authorizes the revisal of a judicial sentence by a legislative act. Nor is there anything in the proposed Constitution, more than in either of them, by which it is forbidden. In the former, as well as in the latter, the impropriety of the thing, on the general principles of law and reason, is the sole obstacle. A legislature, without exceeding its province, cannot reverse a determination once made in a particular case; though it may prescribe a new rule for future cases. This is the principle and it applies in all its consequences, exactly in the same manner and extent, to the State governments, as to the national government now under consideration. Not the least difference can be pointed out in any view of the subject.

It may in the last place be obsessed that the supposed danger of judiciary encroachments on the legislative authority which has been upon many occasions reiterated is in reality a phantom. Particular misconstructions and contravention's of the will of the legislature may now and then happen; but they can never be so extensive as to amount to an inconvenience, or in any sensible degree to affect the order of the political system. This may be inferred with certainty from the general nature of the judicial power, from the objects to which it relates, from the manner in which it is exercised, from its comparative weakness, and from its total incapacity to support its aspirations by force. And the inference is greatly fortified by the consideration of the important constitutional check which the power of instituting impeachments in one part of the legislative body, and of determining upon them in the other, would give to that body upon the members of the judicial department. This is alone a complete security. There never can be danger that the judges, by a series of deliberate usurpations on the authority of the legislature, would hazard the united resentment of the body intrusted with it, while this body was possessed of the means of punishing their presumption by degrading them from their stations. While this ought to remove all apprehensions on the subject it affords, at the same time, a cogent argument for constituting the Senate a court for the trial of impeachments.

Having now examined, and, I trust, removed the objections to the distinct and independent organization of the Supreme Court, I proceed to consider the propriety of the power of constituting inferior courts, and the relations which will subsist between these and the former.

The power of constituting inferior courts is evidently calculated to obviate the necessity of having recourse to the Supreme Court in every case of federal cognizance. It is intended to enable the national government to institute or authorize, in each State or district of the United States, a tribunal competent to the determination of matters of national jurisdiction within its limits.

But why, it is asked, might not the same purpose have been accomplished by the instrumentality of the State courts? This admits of different answers. Though the fitness and competency of those courts should be allowed in the utmost latitude, yet the substance of thc power in question may still be regarded as a necessary part of the plan, if it were only to empower the national legislature to commit to them the cognizance of causes arising out of the national Constitution. To confer the power of determining such causes upon the existing courts of the several States would perhaps be as much "to constitute tribunals," as to create new courts with the like power. But ought not a more direct and explicit provision to have been made in favor of the State courts? There are, in my opinion, substantial reasons against such a provision: the most discerning cannot foresee how far the prevalency of a local spirit may be found to disqualify the local tribunals for the jurisdiction of national causes; whilst every man may discover that courts constituted like those of some of the States would be improper channels of the judicial authority of the Union. State judges, holding their offices during pleasure, or from year to year, will be too little independent to be relied upon for an inflexible execution of the national laws. And if there was a necessity for confiding the original cognizance of causes arising under those laws to them, there would be a correspondent necessity for leaving the door of appeal as wide as possible. In proportion to the grounds of confidence in or distrust of the subordinate tribunals ought to be the facility or difficulty of appeals. And well satisfied as I am of the propriety of the appellate jurisdiction in the several classes of causes to which it is extended, by the plan of the convention I should consider everything calculated to give, in practice, and unrestrained course to appeals, as a source of public and private inconvenience.

I am not sure but that it will be found highly expedient and useful to divide the United States into four or five or half a dozen districts, and to institute a federal court in each district in lieu of one in every State. The judges of these courts, with the aid of the State judges, may hold circuits for the trial of causes in the several parts of the respective districts. Justice through them may be administered with ease and dispatch and appeals may be safely circumscribed within a narrow compass. This plan appears to me at present the most eligible of any that could be adopted; and in order to it, it is necessary that the power of constituting inferior courts should exist in the full extent in which it is to be found in the proposed Constitution.

These reasons seem sufficient to satisfy a candid mind, that the want of such a power would have been a great defect in the plan. Let us now examine in what manner the judicial authority is to be distributed between the supreme and the inferior courts of the Union.

The Supreme Court is to be invested with original jurisdiction only "in cases affecting ambassadors, other public ministers, and consuls, and those in which A STATE shall be a party." Public ministers of every class are the immediate representatives of their sovereigns. All questions in which they are concerned are so directly connected with the public peace, that, as well for the preservation of this as out of respect to the sovreignties they represent, it is both expedient and proper that such questions should be submitted in the first instance to the highest judicatory of the nation. Though consuls have not in strictness a diplomatic character, yet, as they are the public agents of the nations to which they belong, the same observation is in a great measure applicable to them. In cases in which a State might happen to be a party, it would ill suit its dignity to be turned over to an inferior tribunal.

Though it may rather be a digression from the immediate subject of this paper, I shall take occasion to mention here a supposition which has excited some alarm upon very mistaken grounds. It has been suggested that an assignment of the public securities of one State to the citizens of another would enable them to prosecute that State in the federal courts for the amount of those securities; a suggestion which the following considerations prove to be without foundation.

It is inherent in the nature of sovereignty not to be amenable to the suit of an individual without its consent. This is the general sense and the general practice of mankind; and the exemption, as one of the attributes of sovereignty, is now enjoyed by the government of every State in the Union. Unless, therefore, there is a surrender of this immunity in the plan of the convention. it will remain with the States and the danger intimated must be merely ideal. The circumstances which are necessary to produce an alienation of State sovereignty were discussed in considering the article of taxation and need not be repeated here. A recurrence to the principles there established will satisfy us that there is no color to pretend that the State governments would, by the adoption of that plan, be divested of the privilege of paying their own debts in their own way, free from every constraint but that which flows from the obligations of good faith. The contracts between a nation and individuals are only binding on the conscience of the sovereign, and have no pretensions to a compulsive force. They confer no right of action independent of the sovereign will. To what purpose would it be to authorize suits against States for the debts they owe? How could recoveries be enforced? It is evident that it could not be done without waging war against the contracting State; and to ascribe to the federal courts, by mere implication, and in destruction of a preexisting right of the State governments, a power which would involve such a consequence, would be altogether forced and unwarrantable.

Let us resume the train of our observations. We have seen that the original jurisdiction of the Supreme Court would be confined to two classes of cases, and those of a nature rarely to occur. In all other cases of federal cognizance the original jurisdiction would appertain to the inferior tribunals; and the Supreme Court would have nothing more than an appellate jurisdiction "with such exceptions and under such regulations as the Congress shall make."

The propriety of this appellate jurisdiction has been scarcely called in question in regard to matters of law; but the clamors have been loud against it as applied to matters of fact. Some well intentioned men in this State, deriving their notions from the language and forms which obtain in our courts, have been induced to consider it as an implied supersedure of the trial by jury, in favor of the civil-law mode of trial, which prevails in our court of admiralty, probate, and chancery. A technical sense has been affixed to the term "appellate" which, in our law parlance, is commonly used in reference to appeals in the course of the civil law. But if I am not misinformed, the same meaning would not be given to it in any part of New England. There, an appeal from one jury to another is familiar both in language and practice, and is even a matter of course until there have been two verdicts on one side. The word "appellate" therefore will not be understood in the same sense in New England as in New York, which shows the impropriety of a technical interpretation derived from the jurisprudence of any particular State. The expression, taken in the abstract, denotes nothing more than the power of one tribunal to review the proceedings of another, either as to the law or fact, or both The mode of doing it may depend on ancient custom or legislative provision (in a new government it must depend on the latter), and may be with or without the aid of a jury, as may be judged advisable. If, therefore, the re-examination of a fact once determined by a jury should in any case be admitted under the proposed Constitution, it may be so regulated as to be done by a second jury, either by remanding the cause to the court below for a second trial of the fact, or by directing an issue immediately out of the Supreme Court.

But it does not follow that the re-examination of a fact once ascertained by a jury will be permitted in the Supreme Court. Why may not it be said, with the strictest propriety, when a writ of error is brought from an inferior to a superior court of law in this State, that the latter has jurisdiction of the fact as well as the law? It is true it cannot institute a new inquiry concerning the fact but it takes cognizance of it as it appears upon the record and pronounces the law arising upon it. This is jurisdiction of both fact and law; nor is it even possible to separate them. Though the common-law courts of this State ascertain disputed facts by a jury, yet they unquestionably have jurisdiction of both fact and law; and accordingly when the former is agreed in the pleadings they have no recourse to a jury but proceed at once to judgment. I contend therefore, on this ground, that the expressions, "appellate jurisdiction. both as to law and fact," do not necessarily imply a re-examination in the Supreme Court of facts decided by juries in the inferior courts.

The following train of ideas may well be imagined to have influenced the convention in relation to this particular provision. The appellate jurisdiction of the Supreme Court (it may have been argued) will extend to causes determinable in different modes, some in the course of the COMMON LAW, others in the course of the CIVIL LAW. In the former, the revision of the law only will be, generally speaking, the proper province of the Supreme Court, in the latter, the re-examination of the fact is agreeable to usage, and in some cases, of which prize causes are an example, might be essential to the preservation of the public peace. It is therefore necessary that the appellate jurisdiction should, in certain cases, extend in the broadest sense to matters of fact. It will not answer to make an express exception of cases which shall have been originally tried by a jury because in the courts of some of the States all causes are tried in this mode; and such an exception would preclude the revision of matters of fact, as well where it might be proper as where it might be improper. To avoid an inconveniences, it will be safest to declare generally that the Supreme Court shall possess appellate jurisdiction both as to law and fact, and that this jurisdiction shall be subject to such exceptions and regulations as the national legislature may presonbe. This will enable the government to modify it in such a manner as will best answer the ends of public justice and security.

This view of the matter, at any rate, puts it out of all doubt that the supposed abolition of the trial by jury, by the operation of this provision, is fallacious and untrue. The legislature of the United States would certainly have full power to provide that in appeals to the Supreme Court there should be no re-examination of facts where they had been tried in the original causes by juries. This would certainly be an authorized exception; but if, for the reason already intimated, it should be thought too extensive, it might be qualified with a limitation to such causes only as are determinable at common law in that mode of trial.

The amount of the observations hither to made on the authority of the judicial department is this: that it has been carefully restricted to those causes which are manifestly proper for the cognizance of the national judicature; that in the partition of this authority a very small portion of original jurisdiction has been reserved to the Supreme Court and the rest consigned to the subordinate tribunals; that the Supreme Court will possess an appellate jurisdiction, both as to law and fact, in all the cases referred to them, but subject to any exceptions and regulations which may be thought advisable; that this appellate jurisdiction does, in no case, abolish the trial by jury; and that an ordinary degree of prudence and integrity in the national councils will insure us solid advantages from the establishment of the proposed judiciary without exposing us to any of the inconveniences which have been predicted from that source.

**PUBLIUS**

# APPENDIX 4

## OLIVER WENDELL HOLMES: DISSENTING OPINION IN LOCHNER V. NEW YORK

The opinion is reprinted here from 198 US 74 (1904).

> I REGRET sincerely that I am unable to agree with the judgment in this case, and that I think it my duty to express my dissent.

This case is decided upon an economic theory which a large part of the country does not entertain. If it were a question whether I agreed with that theory, I should desire to study it further and long before making up my mind. But I do not conceive that to be my duty, because I strongly believe that my agreement or disagreement has nothing to do with the right of a majority to embody their opinions in law. It is settled by various decisions of this court that state constitutions and state laws may regulate life in many ways which we as legislators might think as injudicious or if you like as tyrannical as this, and which equally with this interfere with the liberty to contract. Sunday laws and usury laws are ancient examples. A more modern one is the prohibition of lotteries. The liberty of the citizen to do as he likes so long as he does not interfere with the liberty of others to do the same, which has been a shibboleth for some well-known writers, is interfered with by school laws, by the Post Office, by every state or municipal institution which takes his money for purposes thought desirable, whether he likes it or not. The Fourteenth Amendment does not enact Mr. Herbert Spencer's Social Statics. The other day we sustained the Massachusetts vaccination law. *Jacobson v. Massachusetts,* 197 U.S. 11. United States and state statutes and decisions cutting down the liberty to contract by way of combination are familiar to this court. *Northern Securities Co. v. United States,* 193 U.S. 197. Two years ago we upheld tho prohibition of sales of stock on margins or for future delivery in the constitution of California. *Otis v. Parker,* 187 U.S. 606. The decision sustaining an eight hour law; for miners is still recent. *Holden v. Hardy*, 169 U.S. 366. Some of these laws embody convictions or prejudices which judges are likely to share. Some may not. But a constitution is not intended to embody a particular economic theory, whether of paternalism and the organic relation of the citizen to the State or of laissez faire. It is made for people of fundamentally differing views, and the accident of our finding certain opinions natural and familiar or novel and even shocking ought not to conclude our judgment upon the question whether statutes embodying them conflict with the Constitution of the United States.

General propositions do not decide concrete cases. The decision will depend on a judgment or intuition more subtle than any articulate major premise. But I think that the proposition just stated, if it is accepted, will carry us far toward the end. Every opinion tends to become a law. I think that the word liberty in the Fourteenth Amendment is perverted when it is held to prevent the natural outcome of a dominant opinion unless it can be said that a rational and fair man necessarily would admit that the statute proposed would infringe fundamental principles as they have been understood by the traditions of our people and our law. It does not need research to show that no such sweeping condemnation can be passed upon the statute before us. A reasonable man might think it a proper measure on the score of health. Men whom I certainly could not pronounce unreasonable would uphold it as a first installment of a general regulation of the hours of work. Whether in the latter aspect it would be open to the charge of inequality I think it unnecessary to discuss.

# ENDNOTES

1 Two days after his reelection in 2004, when President George W. Bush was asked what kind of justice he would nominate if the ailing chief justice Rehnquist retired, he stated, "I would pick people who are strict constructionists." See Jeffrey Rosen, "Can Bush Deliver a Conservative Supreme Court?" *New York Times*, November 14, 2004.

2 See Ronald Rotunda, Statement to the Senate Judiciary Subcommittee on Administrative Oversight and the Courts, "The Senate's Role in the Nomination and Confirmation Process: Whose Burden?" September 4, 2001. "In spite of all the efforts to predict how nominees will rule and in spite of the modern tools now used to try to divine how the nominee will act once confirmed, the batting averages of presidents and senators and the general public have been remarkably poor."

3 George F. Will, "Judging This Court," *Washington Post*, June 8, 2005, A21.

4 "Federalist No. 51," "Ambition must be made to counteract ambition . . . It may be a reflection on human nature that such devices should be necessary to control the abuses of government."

5 From Chief Justice John Marshall's opinion for the Court in *McCulloch v. Maryland*, 17 US 316 (1819).

6 Michael Glennon, *Constitutional Diplomacy*, 1990, 35-49, as reprinted in Thomas Franck and Michael Glennon, *Foreign Relations and National Security Law* (Saint Paul: West Publishing, 1993), 84-92.

7 This number reflects chief justices from John Jay to John Roberts and counts the recess appointment of John Rutledge in 1795, who served briefly before his nomination was rejected by the Senate.

8 Aristotle, *The Politics* (New York: Penguin Books, 1978), 116-117. See also notes by Thomas Sinclair, 21.

9 Aristotle, *The Politics*, 127-128.

10 James Q. Wilson, *American Government: Institutions and Policies* (Lexington: Heath and Company, 1992), 5th edition, 112.

11 Christopher Collier and James Lincoln Collier, *Decision in Philadelphia: the Constitutional Convention of 1787* (New York: Ballantine Books, 1986), 41.

12 Collier, 41.

13 Collier, 43.

14 James Madison (a.k.a. Publius), "Federalist No. 51," February 6, 1788.

15 Montesquieu, *Spirit of the Laws* (New York: Gryphon Editions, 1984), 185.

16 Collier, 260-1.

17 Collier, 267.

18 Collier, 269.

19 Alexander Hamilton, "Federalist Paper No. 78."

20 Collier, 271.

21 Richard Brookhiser, *Alexander Hamilton: American* (New York: Free Press, 1999), 69.

22 "Federalist No. 78."

23 Ibid.

24 Ibid.

25 Ibid.

26 Montesquieu, *Spirit of the Laws* (New York: Gryphon Editions, 1984), 185.

27 "Federalist No. 78."

28 Ibid.

29 Ibid.

30 "The interpretation of the laws is the proper and peculiar province of the courts," "Federalist No. 78."

31 "Federalist No. 78."

32 Ibid.

33 Sandra Day O'Connor, *The Majesty of the Law: Reflections of a Supreme Court Justice* (New York: Random House, 2003), 49.

34 "Federalist No. 81."

35 Catherine Drinker Bowen, *Miracle at Philadelphia: The Story of the Constitutional Convention May to September 1787* (Boston: Little Brown & Co., 1966), 244.

36 O'Connor, *The Majesty of the Law,* 58.

37 O'Connor, *The Majesty of the Law,* 35.

38 Michael J. Gerhardt, "Here's What Less Experience Gets You," *Washington Post,* March 2, 2003, B1 and B4.

39 David M. O'Brien, *Storm Center: The Supreme Court in American Politics* (New York: Norton, 2000), 105.

40 *Chisholm v. Georgia,* 2 Dall. 49 (1793).

41 *Glass v. Sloop Betsey,* 3 Dall. 6 (1794).

42 *Ware v. Hylton,* 3 US 199 (1796).

43 Washington appointed John Jay (1789), John Rutledge (1789), William Cushing (1789), James Wilson (1789), John Blair (1789), James Iredell (1790), Thomas Johnson (1791), Samuel Chase (1796), and Oliver Ellsworth (1796). Robert Harrison declined in 1790. William Patterson's nomination was withdrawn in 1793, only to be resubmitted and confirmed later that year. William Cushing declined the nomination to be chief justice in 1796. Baum, 281.

44 Four laws were passed in 1798 in response to the concern about foreign threats: the Alien Act, the Sedition Act, the Alien Enemies Act (gave the president the right to arrest and deport citizens from countries at war with the United States), and the Naturalization Act (which increased the number of years of residence required to become a naturalized U.S. citizen from five to fourteen).

45 David McCullough, *John Adams* (New York: Simon & Schuster, 2001), 505.

46 David McCullough, *John Adams*, 607.

47 David McCullough, *John Adams*, 506.

48 *New York Times v. Sullivan*, 376 US 254, 276 (1964). See also O'Connor, *The Majesty of the Law*, 46.

49 David McCullough, *John Adams* (New York: Simon & Schuster, 2001), 521.

50 The first indictment was in 1803 against a Kentucky farmer but never went to trial. Allegations against William O. Douglas arose from a 1963 visit to the Dominican Republic. Bruce Allen Murphy, *Wild Bill: The Legend and Life of William O. Douglas* (New York: Random House, 2003), 433.

51 David McCullough, *John Adams* (New York: Simon & Schuster, 2001), 552.

52 The election of 1800 resulted in an electoral college tie between Jefferson and Burr. The House of Representatives ultimately chose Jefferson to be president.

53 David McCullough, *John Adams* (New York: Simon & Schuster, 2001), 560.

54 Marshall served as President Adams's secretary of state from 1800 to 1801.

55 McCullough, 560.

56 Ibid.

57 William H. Rehnquist, *The Supreme Court: How It Was, How It Is* (New York: William Morrow & Co., 1987), 122. As Adams put it, "My gift of John Marshall to the American people was the proudest act of my life."

58 *Marbury v. Madison*, 5 US 137 (1803).

59 The Judiciary Act of 1801 also created additional circuit court judgeships, which would put an end to circuit-riding duties for justices of the Supreme Court; but the circuit judgeships were abolished in 1802 by a Republican-dominated Congress.

60 David M. O'Brien, *Storm Center: The Supreme Court in American Politics* (New York: Norton, 2000), 364.

61 David M. O'Brien, *Storm Center: The Supreme Court in American Politics*, 101.

62 Rehnquist, *The Supreme Court*, 104-105, and George L. Haskins and Herbert A. Johnson, *Foundations of Power: John Marshall, 1801-1815* (New York: The Macmillan Company, 1981), 91.

63 Ronald Rotunda, Statement to the Senate Judiciary Subcommittee on Administrative Oversight and the Courts, "The Senate's Role in the Nomination and Confirmation Process: Whose Burden?" September 4, 2001.

64 Tribe, 64.

65 *McCulloch v. Maryland*, 17 US 316 (1819).

66 *Gibbons v. Ogden*, 22 US 1 (1824).

67 *Dartmouth College v. Woodward*, 17 US 518 (1819).

68 Bernard Schwartz, *A History of the Supreme Court* (New York: Oxford University Press, 1993), 50-51, 89.

69 Rehnquist, chapter 6.

70 See also *Cherokee Nation v. Georgia*, 5 Peters 1 (1831).

71 David M. O'Brien, *Storm Center: The Supreme Court in American Politics* (New York: Norton, 2000), 372.

[72] Rehnquist, chapter 6. It should be noted that his family owned slaves.

[73] James M. McPherson, *Battle Cry of Freedom: The Civil War Era* (New York: Ballantine Books, 1988), 173.

[74] "There's More Than One Way to Fail the Senate Confirmation Test," *Washington Post*, April 24, 2005, A4. The vote was the first time the Senate rejected a presidential nominee for a cabinet post.

[75] Rehnquist, 127.

[76] *Scott v. Sandford*, 19 Howard 393 (1857).

[77] Bernard Schwartz, 99.

[78] McPherson, 178.

[79] Rehnquist, 144.

[80] McPherson, 221.

[81] McPherson, 126.

[82] McPherson, 246-247.

[83] McPherson, 247.

[84] Sidney M. Milkis and Michael Nelson, *The American Presidency: Origins and Development, 1776-1998* (Washington DC: Congressional Quarterly Press, 1999), 3rd edition, 151.

[85] Milkis, 150.

[86] *Ex Parte Merryman*, 17 Fed. Cas. 144 (1861).

[87] McPherson, 287-8.

[88] McPherson, 289.

[89] McPherson, 352-3.

[90] *Prize Cases*, 67 US 635 (1863).

[91] Milkis, 151.

[92] Bernard Schwartz, *A History of the Supreme Court* (New York: Oxford University Press, 1993), 149.

[93] Schwartz, 150.

[94] Todd S. Purdum, "Presidents, Picking Justices, Can Have Backfires," *New York Times*, July 5, 2005.

[95] William Rehnquist, *All the Laws but One: Civil Liberties in Wartime* (New York: Vintage Books, 2000), 60.

[96] Rehnquist, 123.

[97] Milkis, 152.

[98] Rehnquist, 158.

[99] Rehnquist, chapter 7, 153.

[100] Schwartz, 150.

[101] *Ex Parte Garland*, 71 US 333 (1866).

[102] *Cummings v. Missouri*, 71 US 277 (1866).

[103] McPherson, 786. "The guerilla fighting in Missouri produced a form of terrorism that exceeded anything else in the war . . . the slaughter of unarmed soldiers as well as civilians, whites as well as blacks."

[104] David Savage, *Turning Right: The Making of the Rehnquist Supreme Court* (New York: John Wiley & Sons Inc., 1993), 27-8.

105 For a contrary view, see Mark Levin, *Men in Black: How the Supreme Court Is Destroying America* (Washington DC: Regnery Publishing Inc., 2005), 16. Commenting on "activism" of the Supreme Court in the case of *Plessy v. Ferguson,* "By failing to invoke the plain language of the Fourteenth Amendment, the Court inserted its own segregationist version of what was just."

106 "There's More Than One Way to Fail the Senate Confirmation Test," *Washington Post,* April 24, 2005, A4. Stanton had been removed as secretary of war by President Andrew Johnson, causing the House to initiate impeachment proceedings against the president for violation of the Tenure of Office Act, which prohibited the president from removing Senate-confirmed officials from office without Senate approval. The Senate failed to convict Johnson, and the Supreme Court declared this act an unconstitutional violation of separation of powers in 1926.

107 "There's More Than One Way to Fail the Senate Confirmation Test," *Washington Post,* April 24, 2005, A4.

108 John M. Broder, "Have a Seat, Your Honor (Presidents Wish It Were That Easy)," *New York Times,* July 10, 2005.

109 Ibid.

110 *Hepburn v. Griswold,* 8 Wallace 603 (1870).

111 *Legal Tender* cases, *(Knox v. Lee; Parker v. Davis),* 12 Wallace 457 (1871).

112 Bernard Schwartz, 172.

113 Stephen Murdoch, "Bush v. Gore Revisited," *Washington Lawyer,* April 2003, 21.

114 Charles Lane, "High Court's Credibility, Internal Balance Face Test," *Washington Post,* November 26, 2000, A10.

115 Nicholas E. Hollis, "A Hotel for the History Books," *Washington Post,* March 18, 2001, B8.

116 Bernard Schwartz, 172.

117 Bernard Schwartz, 173.

118 Hollis, B8.

119 Stephen H. Wirls, *The Presidency: A History of the Office of the President of the United States from 1789 to the Present,* Ed. Michael Nelson (New York: Salamander Books, 1996), 110.

120 *Gelpcke v. Dubuque,* 68 US 175 (1864).

121 *Munn v. Illinois,* 94 US 113 (1877).

122 *Chicago, Milwaukee, and St. Paul Railway v. Minnesota,* 134 US 418 (1890).

123 *Wabash, St. Louis, and Pacific Railway v. Illinois,* 118 US 557 (1886).

124 Bryan would later go on to argue against Clarence Darrow who represented John Thomas Scopes against charge of teaching biological evolutionary theory in violation of Tennessee law in 1925. Bryan represented a bygone era of American politics as a man who was socially conservative, but politically liberal, what some would call the "Christian Left." Though were he alive today he would be pleased to see those continuing his fight on behalf of the teaching of creationism, Bryan would likely be appalled by the antilabor, antisocial welfare themes of the "Christian Right."

125 *Plessy v. Fergusson,* 163 US 537 (1896).

126 Frederick Jackson Turner, "The Significance of the Frontier in American History," reprinted in *An American Primer,* Ed. Daniel Boorstin (Chicago: University of Chicago Press, 1966), 544.

127 Milkis, 187.

128 *In re Debs*, 158 US 564 (1895).

129 David M. O'Brien, *Storm Center: The Supreme Court in American Politics* (New York: Norton, 2000), 98.

130 G. Edward White, *Justice Oliver Wendell Holmes: Law and the Inner Self*, New York, Oxford University Press, 1993), 49-64.

131 Edmond Morris, *Theodore Rex* (New York: Random House, 2001), 313.

132 Morris, *Theodore Rex* (New York: Random House, 2001), 464.

133 Morris, 270.

134 Bernard Schwartz, *A History of the Supreme Court*, 183.

135 *United States v. Northern Securities*, 193 US 197 (1904).

136 Morris, *Theodore Rex* (New York: Random House, 2001), 314.

137 Morris, 314.

138 Morris, 316.

139 *Lochner v. New York*, 198 US 45 (1905).

140 *Adair v. United States*, 208 US 161 (1908).

141 *Coppage v. Kansas*, 236 US 1(1915).

142 *Muller v. Oregon*, 208 US 412 (1909).

143 Morris, 465.

144 Laurence H. Tribe, *God Save This Honorable Court: How the Choice of Supreme Court Justices Shapes Our History* (New York: Penguin Books, 1986), 64.

145 Bernard Schwartz, *A History of the Supreme Court*, 215.

146 Bernard Schwartz, *A History of the Supreme Court*, 215. Lee Epstein and Jeffrey A. Segal, *Advice and Consent: The Politics of Judicial Appointments* (New York: Oxford University Press, 2005), 93.

147 *Bunting v. Oregon*, 243 US 426 (1917).

148 *Truax v. Corrigan*, 257 US 312 (1921).

149 *Hammer v. Dagenhart*, 247 US 251 (1918).

150 *Adkins v. Children's Hospital*, 261 US 525 (1923).

151 *Weeks v. United States*, 232 US 383 (1914).

152 *Debs v. United States*, 249 US 211 (1919).

153 *Schenck v. United States*, 249 US 47 (1919).

154 See Holmes's opinion in *Patterson v. Colorado*, 205 US 454, 462 (1907).

155 *Abrams v. United States*, 250 US 616 (1919).

156 Jeffrey Rosen, "Liberty Wins, So Far," *Washington Post*, September 15, 2002, B5.

157 Bruce Fein, "Packing the Supreme Court," *Washington Lawyer*, February 2005, 34.

158 Also known as the Judge's Bill or Judiciary Act of 1925, David M. O'Brien, *Storm Center: The Supreme Court in American Politics* (New York: Norton, 2000), 99.

159 *Olmstead v. United States*, 277 US 438 (1928).

160 See *Katz v. United States*, 389 US 347 (1967).

161 *Buck v. Bell*, 274 US 200 (1927).

162 Ibid.

[163] Peter Carlson, "A Chilling Triumph of 'Science' Over Sanity," *Washington Post*, February 15, 2003, C1 and C4.

[164] Carlson, C4.

[165] *Myers v. United States*, 272 US 53 (1926).

[166] Milkis, 248.

[167] The other chief justice who previously served as secretary of state was John Marshall.

[168] David O'Brien, *Storm Center*, 36.

[169] Sarah Booth Conroy, "Court's Edifice Is Indeed Supreme," *Washington Post*, December 4, 2000, C2.

[170] The lawmakers represented are Menes, Hammurabi, Moses, Solomon, Lycurgus, Solon, Draco, Confucius, Octavian, Napoleon Bonaparte, John Marshall, William Blackstone, Hugo Grotius, Louis IX, King John, Charlemagne, Mohammed, and Justinian.

[171] Geoffrey C. Ward, *A First-Class Temperament: The Emergence of Franklin Delano Roosevelt* (New York: Harper & Row, 1989), xi-xiii.

[172] Germany's chancellor Otto von Bismarck enacted one of the first social welfare plans in order to counter growing political support for the socialists.

[173] *Louisville Joint Stock Land Bank v. Radford*, 295 US 555 (1935), *Humphrey's Executor v. United States*, 295 US 602 (1935); *Schechter Poultry Corp. v. United States*, 295 US 495 (1935).

[174] *Nebbia v. New York*, 291 US 502 (1934).

[175] John E. Nowak, Ronald D. Rotunda, and J. Nelson Young, *Constitutional Law* (Saint Paul: West Publishing, 1978), 146-147.

[176] *United States v. Butler*, 297 US 1 (1936).

[177] Rehnquist, *Supreme Court*, 228.

[178] Robert Bork, *The Tempting of America* (New York: Simon & Schuster, 1990), 55.

[179] John E. Nowak, Ronald D. Rotunda, and J. Nelson Young, *Constitutional Law* (Saint Paul: West Publishing, 1978), 39. The Judiciary Act of 1937, 50 Stat. 24, was passed on March 1, 1937. Justice Van Devanter resigned in May 1937.

[180] *West Coast Hotel v. Parrish*, 300 US 379 (1937).

[181] *National Labor Relations Board v. Jones & Laughlin Steel Corp.*, 300 US 1 (1937).

[182] Ronald Rotunda, Statement to the Senate Judiciary Subcommittee on Administrative Oversight and the Courts, "The Senate's Role in the Nomination and Confirmation Process: Whose Burden?" September 4, 2001.

[183] Bernard Schwartz, *A History of the Supreme Court*, 241.

[184] Tribe, 82.

[185] Jeffrey Rosen, "Courting Trouble," Review of *Wild Bill: The Legend and Life of William O. Douglas* by Bruce Allen Murphy, *Washington Post*, Book World, March 9, 2003, 5.

[186] *United States v. Carolene Products Co.*, 304 US 144 (1938), footnote 4, at 152-3.

[187] *Palko v. Connecticut*, 302 US 319 (1937).

[188] *United States v. Curtiss-Wright Export Corporation*, 299 US 304 (1936).

[189] *United States v. Belmont*, 301 US 324 (1937).

[190] Edwin Corwin, *The Constitution and What It Means Today* (New Haven: Princeton University Press, 1978).

[191] Rehnquist, 68.

[192] Ibid.

[193] Lincoln Caplan, "Forget the Tone. It's Dissent That Matters," *Washington Post*, July 6, 2003, B1-B4.

[194] O'Brien, 47-48.

[195] *Hirabayashi v. United States*, 320 US 81 (1943) and *Korematsu v. United States*, 323 US 214 (1944)

[196] Michael Dobbs, "A Familiar, Thorny Record of Wartime Justice," *Washington Post*, February 8, 2004, B4.

[197] Ibid.

[198] The executions were carried out in August of 1942. See John Lehman's commentary on the subject, "In Too Deep," *Washington Post*, Book World, February 22, 2004, 4.

[199] *In re Yamashita*, 327 US 1 (1946).

[200] Charles Lane, "Supreme Court Revisits Enemy Combatants," *Washington Post*, November 23, 2003, A3.

[201] *Skinner v. Oklahoma*, 316 US 535 (1942).

[202] Bork, 62.

[203] *Jewell Ridge Coal Corporation v. Local 6167, UMW*, 325 US 161 (1945).

[204] Rehnquist, 66.

[205] Ibid.

[206] Jeffrey Rosen, 5.

[207] Todd S. Purdum, "Presidents, Picking Justices, Can Have Backfires," *New York Times*, July 5, 2005. Truman's comments to oral historian Merle Miller.

[208] *Dennis v. United States*, 341 US 494 (1951).

[209] *Yates v. United States*, 354 US 298 (1957).

[210] *Dennis v. United States*, 341 US 494 (1951) at 510.

[211] *Scales v. United States*, 367 US 203 (1961).

[212] David M. O'Brien, *Storm Center: The Supreme Court in American Politics* (New York: Norton, 2000), 101.

[213] Tribe, 62-3.

[214] *Morgan v. Commonwealth of Virginia*, 328 US 373 (1946). Marshall applied an "intent-based" approach using cases going back to 1878 to demonstrate federal control over interstate commerce.

[215] *Sweatt v. Painter*, 339 US 629 (1950).

[216] David M. O'Brien, *Storm Center: The Supreme Court in American Politics* (New York: Norton, 2000), 319.

[217] Juan Williams, *Thurgood Marshall: American Revolutionary* (New York: Random House, 1998), 226.

[218] *Missouri ex rel. Gaines v. Canada*, 305 US 337 (1938) and *Sweatt v. Painter*, 339 US 629 (1950).

[219] Juan Williams, *Thurgood Marshall: American Revolutionary* (New York: Random House, 1998), 263.

[220] Juan Williams, *Thurgood Marshall: American Revolutionary*, 263-8.

[221] Baum, 232.

[222] David Halberstam, *The Best and the Brightest* (New York: Ballantine Books, 1992), 12.

[223] Juan Williams, *Thurgood Marshall,* 291.

[224] Juan Williams, *Thurgood Marshall,* 308.

[225] Juan Williams, *Thurgood Marshall,* 292.

[226] Juan Williams, *Thurgood Marshall,* 294.

[227] Peter Collier and David Horowitz, *The Kennedys: An American Drama* (New York: Warner Books, 1984), 380-1.

[228] Juan Williams, *Thurgood Marshall,* 309.

[229] Juan Williams, *Thurgood Marshall,* 309. "I think Jack was terrific."

[230] *Gideon v. Wainwright,* 372 US 335 (1963).

[231] *Mapp v. Ohio,* 367 US 643 (1961).

[232] *Miranda v. Arizona,* 384 US 436 (1966).

[233] *Baker v. Carr,* 369 US 186 (1962).

[234] Bork, 89.

[235] *Mapp v. Ohio,* 367 US 643 (1961).

[236] Willard Sterne Randall, *Thomas Jefferson: A Life* (New York: HarperCollins, 1993), 135-136.

[237] Franklin Foer, "'Divided by God': One Nation, Under Whomever," *New York Times,* July 24, 2005. Review of Noah Feldman's book *Divided by God: America's Church-State Problem—and What We Should Do About It.*

[238] *Engel v. Vitale,* 370 US 421 (1962).

[239] *Abington School District v. Schempp,* 374 US 203 (1963).

[240] *Murray v. Curlett,* 374 US 203 (1963).

[241] Juan Williams, *Thurgood Marshall,* 328-9.

[242] Juan Williams, *Thurgood Marshall,* 106.

[243] Juan Williams, *Thurgood Marshall,* 317.

[244] Juan Williams, *Thurgood Marshall,* 6.

[245] Juan Williams, *Thurgood Marshall,* 14 and 332.

[246] Juan Williams, *Thurgood Marshall,* 337.

[247] *Harper v. Virginia State Board of Elections,* 383 US 663 (1966).

[248] *Katzenbach v. Morgan,* 384 US 641 (1966).

[249] Ronald D. Rotunda and J. Nelson Young, *Constitutional Law* (Saint Paul: West Publishing, 1978, 691.

[250] *Griswold v. Connecticut,* 381 US 479 (1965).

[251] *Eisenstadt v. Baird,* 405 US 438 (1972).

[252] *Loving v. Virginia,* 388 US 1 (1967)

[253] *Tinker v. Des Moines Independent Community School District,* 383 US 503 (1969).

[254] Rehnquist served longer than Warren and Burger as chief justice counting the terms extending beyond 2001 (1986-2005).

[255] Bork, 69.

[256] Mark Tushnet, *A Court Divided: The Rehnquist Court and the Future of Constitutional Law* (New York: W. W. Norton & Co., 2005), 25.

257 Mark Tushnet, *A Court Divided*, 26.

258 Baum, 35.

259 Woodward, 203.

260 David M. O'Brien, *Storm Center: The Supreme Court in American Politics* (New York: Norton, 2000), 102. See also Bruce Allen Murphy, *Wild Bill: The Legend and Life of William O. Douglas* (New York: Random House, 2003), 429-430. The latter version portrays the impeachment as a preemptive strike by Nixon in anticipation of Haynes's rejection.

261 Charles Lane, "Douglas's Military Claim Questioned by Biographer," *Washington Post*, February 3, 2003, A21.

262 Lane, "Douglas's Military Claim," A21.

263 Jeffrey Rosen, 5.

264 Baum, 46.

265 Savage, 15.

266 Tushnet, 23.

267 Ibid.

268 George Lardner, Jr., "Nixon on Appointing Rehnquist: On Tape He Exults Over 'Hard Right' Nominees," *Washington Post*, October 30, 2000, A25. Quoting from tapes released from the National Archives.

269 Baum, 64.

270 Lardner, A25.

271 *New York Times Co. v. United States*, 403 US 713 (1971).

272 *New York Times Co. v. United States*, 403 US 713 (1971) at 730.

273 *United States v. Nixon*, 418 US 683 (1974).

274 *Furman v. Georgia*, 408 US 238 (1972).

275 *Gregg v. Georgia*, 428 US 153 (1976).

276 David von Drehle, "Death Penalty Divide Frustrated Blackmun," *Washington Post*, March 15, 2004, A4.

277 Ibid.

278 *Eisenstadt v. Baird*, 405 US 438 (1972).

279 *Roe v. Wade*, 410 US 113 (1973).

280 Robert Woodward, *The Brethren: Inside the Supreme Court*, 279-280.

281 *Swann v. Charlotte-Mecklenburg Board of Education*, 402 US 1 (1971).

282 *Oregon v. Mitchell*, 400 US 112 (1970).

283 *Griggs v. Duke Power Co.*, 401 US 424 (1973).

284 *Fry v. United States*, 421 US 542 (1975).

285 Baum, 30.

286 *Buckley v. Valeo*, 424 US 1 (1976).

287 *Richmond Newspapers v. Virginia*, 448 US 555 (1980).

288 *Gannett Co. v. DePasquale*, 443 US 368 (1979).

289 Baum, 154.

290 *Regents of the University of California v. Bakke*, 438 US 265 (1978).

291 Theodore M. Shaw, "Race Still Matters," *Washington Post*, March 1, 2003, A19.

[292] Michael J. Gerhardt, "Here's What Less Experience Gets You," *Washington Post*, March 2, 2003, B1 and B4.

[293] Charles Lane, "In the Center, Hers Was the Vote That Counted," *Washington Post*, July 2, 2005, A8.

[294] Robert D. Novak, "For Conservatives, a Gloomy Scenario," *Washington Post*, June 30, 2003, A15.

[295] *Wallace v. Jaffree*, 466 US 924 (1984). (decided in 1985)

[296] *Lynch v. Donnelly*, 465 US 668 (1984).

[297] Milkis, 356.

[298] Savage, 15.

[299] *Bowsher v. Synar*, 478 US 714 (1986).

[300] *Bowers v. Hardwick*, 478 US 186 (1986).

[301] *Palko v. Connecticut*, 302 US 319 (1937).

[302] *Johnson v. Transportation Agency*, 480 US 616 (1987).

[303] Baum, 34.

[304] Milkis, 354.

[305] Ibid.

[306] Milkis, 355.

[307] Ibid.

[308] Michael J. Gerhardt, "Here's What Less Experience Gets You," *Washington Post*, March 2, 2003, B1 and B4.

[309] *Texas v. Johnson*, 491 US 397 (1989).

[310] *United States v. Eichman*, 496 US 310 (1990).

[311] Michael Kinsley, "Flagging Interest," *Washington Post*, July 22, 2001, B7.

[312] Ibid.

[313] *Patterson v. McLean Credit Union*, 491 US 164 (1989).

[314] *Runyon v. McCrary, 427 US 160* (1988).

[315] Edward Lazarus, *Closed Chambers: The First Eyewitness Account of the Epic Struggles Inside the Supreme Court* (New York: Times Books, 1998), 315 and 322.

[316] Lazarus, 459.

[317] Lazarus, 463.

[318] Fred Barbash, "Blackmun's Papers Shine Light into Court," *Washington Post*, A1.

[319] *Thompson v. Oklahoma*, 487 US 815 (1988).

[320] *Stanford v. Kentucky*, 492 US 361 (1989).

[321] *Penry v. Lynaugh*, 492 US 302 (1989).

[322] *Powell v. Texas*, 492 US 680 (1989).

[323] *Cruzan v. Missouri Health Department*, 497 US 261 (1990).

[324] George F. Will, "Coup against the Constitution," *Washington Post*, February 28, 2003, A23.

[325] "Supreme Discomfort," *Washington Post Magazine*, August 4, 2002, 13.

[326] George L. Watson and John A. Stookey, *Shaping America: The Politics of Supreme Court Appointments* (New York: HarperCollins, 1995), 109-111.

[327] A remark attributed to Flo Kennedy, an official of the National Organization of Women (NOW), a member of the Alliance for Justice. Phelps and Winternitz, *Capitol Games*, 21.

[328] John M. Broder, "Have a Seat, Your Honor (Presidents Wish It Were That Easy)," *New York Times*, July 10, 2005.

[329] "Supreme Discomfort," *Washington Post Magazine*, August 4, 2002, 12.

[330] David M. O'Brien, *Storm Center: The Supreme Court in American Politics* (New York: Norton, 2000), 352.

[331] *County of Allegheny v. ACLU*, 492 US 573 (1989).

[332] Charles Lane, "Papers Underline Issue of Controlling Court," *Washington Post*, March 7, 2004, A11.

[333] The nominees were Zoe Baird and Kimba Wood. In addition, President Clinton's nominee for assistant attorney general for civil rights, Lani Guinier, was withdrawn after opposition arose regarding her controversial views on civil rights.

[334] John M. Broder, "Have a Seat, Your Honor (Presidents Wish It Were That Easy)," *New York Times*, July 10, 2005.

[335] Helen Dewar, "Polarized Politics, Confirmation Chaos," *Washington Post*, May 11, 2003, A5.

[336] *United States v. Lopez*, 514 US 549 (1995).

[337] *Fry v. United States, 421 US 542 (1975).*

[338] *Reno v. ACLU/ALA*, 521 US 844 (1997).

[339] See notes by Bruce Ennis at the ABA's Forum on Communications Law (undated) at http://www.abanet.org/forums/communication/comlawyer/fall99/courtside.html.

[340] *City of Erie v. Pap's A. M. tdba "Kandyland,"* 529 US 277 (2000).

[341] Bruce J. Ennis, ABA's Forum on Communications Law (undated), http://www.abanet.org/forums/communication/comlawyer/fall99/courtside.html.

[342] *Vacco v. Quill*, 117 S. Ct. 2293 (1997) and *Washington v. Glucksberg*, 117 S. Ct. 2258 (1997).

[343] *Miller v. Johnson*, 115 S. Ct. 2475 (1995).

[344] See Justice O'Connor's similar majority opinion in *Shaw v. Reno*, 113 S. Ct. 2816 (1993).

[345] Milkis, 393.

[346] Milkis, 395.

[347] Ibid.

[348] Charles Lane and Amy Goldstein, "At High Court, A Retirement Watch," *Washington Post*, June 17, 2001, A4-A5.

[349] Sanford Levinson, "I Dissent! The Constitution Got Us into This Mess," *Washington Post*, December 17, 2000, B2.

[350] Lane and Goldstein, June 17, 2001, A5.

[351] Ibid.

[352] Charles Lane, "Laying Down the Law, Justices Ruled with Confidence," *Washington Post*, A6.

[353] March 2001 poll by Princeton Survey Research Associates; Charles Lane, "Laying Down the Law," A6.

[354] Ibid.

[355] Ibid.

[356] *Stenberg v. Carhart*, 530 US 914 (2000).

[357] "Is the Law for the Birds," (editorial) *Washington Post*, October 30, 2000, A26.

[358] *United States v. Morrison*, 120 S. Ct. 1740 (2000).

359 *Dickerson v. United States*, 530 US 4285 (2000).

360 Joan Biskupic, "Court Urged to Repeal Miranda," *Washington Post*, April 9, 2000, A1, A8-A9.

361 This is an anomaly of the electoral college system because although Gore carried a narrow majority of the votes of many large states and cities, Bush carried large majorities in most small states and won a sufficient number of larger states to garner an electoral-vote majority. It was not the first time when a candidate defeated an opponent who carries more of the popular vote. It happened in 1876 between Hayes and Tilden and in 1888 between Benjamin Harrison and Grover Cleveland.

362 Charles Lane, "Justices Return Case to Florida," *Washington Post*, December 5, 2000, A1 and A27.

363 Stephen Murdoch, "Bush v. Gore Revisited," *Washington Lawyer*, April 2003, 25.

364 Stephen Murdoch, "Bush v. Gore Revisited," *Washington Lawyer*, April 2003, 25-6.

365 *Bush v. Palm Beach County Canvassing Board*, 531 US 70 (2000).

366 *Bush v. Gore*, 531 US 98 (2000).

367 Dan Balz and Charles Lane, "Divided U.S. Supreme Court Overrules Gore Recount Plea," *Washington Post*, December 13, 2000, A1.

368 Charles Lane, "Civil Liberties Were Term's Big Winner," *Washington Post*, June 29, 2003, A1-A18.

369 Lane, A18.

370 *Federal Election Commission v. Colorado Republican Federal Campaign Committee, 533 US 431 (2001).*

371 *Whitman v. American Trucking Associations*, 531 US 457 (2001).

372 Bruce Fein, "Packing the Supreme Court," *Washington Lawyer*, February 2005, 36.

373 *Illinois v. McArthur*, 531 US 326 (2001).

374 *Kyllo v. United States*, 533 US 27 (2001).

375 George F. Will, "Not Too Strict to Apply Justice," *Washington Post*, June 17, 2001, B7.

376 *Indianapolis v. Edmond*, 531 US 32 (2000). See also Peter Slevin, "Drug Roadblocks Struck Down: Justices Rule Indianapolis Tactic Is Unreasonable Seizure," *Washington Post*, November 29, 2000, A4.

377 *Ferguson v. City of Charleston*, 532 US 67 (2001).

378 *Rogers v. Tennessee*, 532 US 451 (2001).

379 Gallup poll of February 2000. William Claiborne and Paul Duggan, "Spotlight on Death Penalty: Illinois Ban Ignites a National Debate," *Washington Post*, June 18, 2000, A1 and A4.

380 Rhonda McMillion, "Pulling the Plug on Executions," *ABA Journal*, November 2000, 99.

381 Statistics from the Death Penalty Information Center as quoted by William Claiborne and Paul Duggan, "Spotlight on Death Penalty: Illinois Ban Ignites a National Debate," *Washington Post*, June 18, 2000, A1 and A4.

382 Ibid.

383 McMillion, 99.

384 *Penry v. Johnson*, 532 US 82 (2001).

385 Charles Lane, "Death Sentence for Retarded Man Is Overturned," *Washington Post*, June 5, 2001, A3.

386 Charles Lane, "High Court to Review Executing Retarded," *Washington Post*, March 27, 2001, A1, A8.

387 Robert Pierre and Kari Lydersen, "Illinois Death Row Emptied; Citing 'Demon of Error,' Governor Commutes Sentences," *Washington Post*, January 12, 2003, A1 and A11.

388 Speech of Justice O'Connor before a meeting of Minnesota Women Lawyers. Charles Lane, "O'Connor Expresses Death Penalty Doubt," *Washington Post*, July 4, 2001, A1.

389 Ibid.

390 *McCarver v. North Carolina*, 533 US 975 (2001).

391 *Atkins v. Virginia*, 536 US 304 (2002).

392 *Wiggins v. Smith*, 539 US 510 (2003).

393 *The Paquette Habana*, 175 US 677 (1900).

394 Sandra Day O'Connor, *The Majesty of the Law*, 35.

395 *United States v. Oakland Cannabis Buyers' Cooperative*, 532 US 483 (2001).

396 *Circuit City Stores Inc. v. Adams*, 532 US 105 (2001).

397 *Gilmer v. Interstate/Johnson Lane Corp.*, 500 US 20 (1991).

398 David G. Savage, "Opening Closed Doors," *ABA Journal*, November 2000, 32.

399 *Boy Scouts of America v. Dale*, 530 US 640 (2000).

400 *Board of Trustees of the University of Alabama v. Garrett*, 531 US 356 (2001).

401 *Gratz v. Bollinger*, 539 US 244 (2003).

402 *Grutter v. Bollinger*, 539 US 306 (2003).

403 Terrence J. Pell, "Camouflage for Quotas," *Washington Post*, June 30, 2003, A15.

404 Charles Lane, "Papers Underline Issue of Controlling Court," *Washington Post*, March 7, 2004, A11.

405 "Frist Backs Putting Gay Marriage Ban in Constitution," *Washington Post*, June 30, 2003, A2.

406 *Hamdi v. Rumsfeld*, 542 US 507 (2004).

407 Rhonda McMillion, "ABA Successes in Congress," *ABA Journal*, January 2005, 63.

408 Charles Lane, "Justices Order Review of 400-Plus Sentences," *Washington Post*, January 25, 2005, A7.

409 Justice O'Connor wrote, "The beneficiaries are likely to be those citizens with disproportionate influence and power in the political process, including large corporations and development firms."

410 See Michael Kinsley, "Activism, Ripe for the Takings," *Washington Post*, June 26, 2005, B7. He points out the ideological contradictions of the decision, "When the local government showers a big development with money and favors, it's usually not about sovereignty but about lack of sovereignty. Private developers play jurisdictions off against one another, extracting concessions from all that none would actually make a sovereign decision to make. A Supreme Court decision that concessions of this sort were unconstitutional would have taken them off the table and actually increased the effective sovereignty of elected officials."

411 Dahlia Lithwick, "A Revolution That Wasn't," *Washington Post*, Book World, February 20, 2005, 3. Lithwick was referring to conservative frustration with the Court's failing to reverse rulings on affirmative action and abortion in her review of Mark Tushnet's book *A Court Divided: The Rehnquist Court of the Future of Constitutional Law.*

412 Lithwick, "A Revolution That Wasn't," *Washington Post*, Book World, February 20, 2005, 3. Lithwick is critical of Mark Tushnet's thesis of a culture clash between old and new Republicans on the Court.

413 Richard Brust, "Reviewing Rehnquist," *ABA Journal*, May 2003, 43.

414 Brust, 44. Based upon a study by Northwestern law professor Thomas Merrill, from 1987 to 1994, seventeen cases dealt with social issues and thirteen with Federalism. From 1995 to 2002, nine cases dealt with social issues and twenty-five with Federalism.

415 Brust, 44.

416 Brust, 47. This is the interpretation of Professor Jed Rubenfeld of Yale Law School.

417 Edward Lazarus, "The Supreme Court: Why the Scales Won't Tip," *Washington Post*, November 7, 2004, B3.

418 Brust, 44.

419 Brust, 45.

420 Tocqueville, *Democracy in America* (New York: Adlard & Saunders, [reprint of 1838 edition] 1951), 261. "Influence of legal habits extends beyond the precise limits I have pointed out. Scarcely any political question arises in the United States that is not resolved, sooner or later, into a judicial question. Hence all parties are obliged to borrow, in their daily controversies, the ideas, and even the language, peculiar to judicial proceedings."

421 David O'Brien, *Storm Center*, xiv.

422 Lawrence Baum, *The Supreme Court* (Washington DC: Congressional Quarterly Press, 1995), 5th edition, 2-3.

423 Bernard Schwartz, 65.

424 Lawrence Baum, *The Supreme Court*, (Washington DC: Congressional Quarterly Press, 1995), 5th edition, 2-3.

425 Sandra Day O'Connor, *The Majesty of the Law*, 21.

426 Sean Groom, "Clerking at the Supreme Court," *Washington Lawyer*, March 2003, 22.

427 Sean Groom, "Clerking at the Supreme Court," *Washington Lawyer*, March 2003, 24.

428 Lazarus, *Closed Chambers*, 469. This is the view of the Harvard "legal process" school of constitutional interpretation.

429 Savage, *Turning Right*, 11.

430 Robert Dahl, *Preface to Democratic Theory: How Does Popular Sovereignty Function in America?* (University of Chicago Press, 1956).

431 See also Bork, 57.

432 Charles Babington and Mike Allen, "Surprise Retiree Raises the Stakes of Battle to Come," *Washington Post*, July 2, 2005, A12.

433 See Amy Gutmann's remarks in the preface to Antonin Scalia's *A Matter of Interpretation*, xi, "*Stare decisis* by protecting the power of precedent lends stability to the expectations of citizens."

434 Tocqueville, 235-6. Also, p. 252: "In the United States the majority . . . so frequently displays the tastes and the propensities of a despot." Tocqueville is believed to be the first to use the phrase "tyranny of the majority."

435 Sandra Day O'Connor, *The Majesty of the Law*, 59.

[436] Sandra Day O'Connor, *The Majesty of the Law*, 258, citing I Annals of Congress (1834), 437.

[437] Edmund Burke, "Reflections on the Revolution in France," *Edmund Burke: Selected Writings and Speeches* (Chicago: Regnery Publishing Inc., 1963), 583.

[438] C. Herman Pritchett, "The Development of Judicial Research" in *Frontiers of Judicial Research*, Eds. Joel B. Grossman and Joseph Tanenhaus (New York: John Wiley & Sons, 1969), 42. "Political scientists who have done so much to put the 'political' in 'political jurisprudence' need to emphasize that it is still 'jurisprudence.' It is judging in a political context, but it is still judging; and judging is something different from legislating or administering. Judges make choices, but they are not the 'free' choices of congressmen . . . . Any accurate analysis of judicial behavior must have as a major purpose a full clarification of the unique limiting conditions under which judicial policy making proceeds."

[439] *Towne v. Eisner*, 245 US 418, 425 (1918).

[440] Baum, 5.

[441] Robert Jackson, *The Supreme Court in American History*, 1955, 56; as quoted in Nowak, Rotunda, and Young, *Constitutional Law*, 100.

[442] Bernard Schwartz, 278. By the time the Court considered apportionment in *Baker v. Carr*, the most populous of legislative district in Tennessee outnumbered the least by over 19-1.

[443] Baum, 5.

[444] Savage, 3-47.

[445] Bruce Allen Murphy, *Wild Bill: The Legend and Life of William O. Douglas* (New York: Random House, 2003), 340.

[446] Robert Bork, *The Tempting of America*, 44-45.

[447] See Mark Tushnet, *A Court Divided*, 11, "The civics book view of the Court—that conservative and liberal justices divide over whether it should be restrained or activist and that they use original intent or contemporary values in interpretation—is a fairy tale . . . . *Everyone* is a judicial activist."

[448] Baum, 5.

[449] Levin, 12.

[450] Ibid.

[451] Ronald Dworkin, "The Forum of Principle," 56 *NYU Law Review* 469, 470 (1981),

[452] Bork, 177. He caveats this with "They should never have political intentions."

[453] Oliver Wendell Holmes, Jr., *The Common Law and Other Writings*, 1881, as reprinted by Gryphon Editions, 1982, 1.

[454] G. Edward White, *Justice Oliver Wendell Holmes: Law and the Inner Self* (New York: Oxford University Press, 1993), 365. See also David O'Brien, *Storm Center*, 298-299.

[455] David O'Brien, *Storm Center*, 298-299.

[456] Robert Bork, *The Tempting of America*, 168.

[457] Justice Harlan's dissent in *Mapp v. Ohio*, 367 US 643, 677 (1961).

[458] Michael Glennon, *Constitutional Diplomacy*, 1990, 35-49, as reprinted in Thomas Franck and Michael Glennon, *Foreign Relations and National Security Law* (Saint Paul: West Publishing, 1993), 84-92.

[459] Associate Justice Scalia, *A Matter of Interpretation* (Princeton, New Jersey: Princeton University Press, 1998), 23.

[460] Michael Glennon, *Constitutional Diplomacy*, 1990, 35-49, as reprinted in Thomas Franck and Michael Glennon, *Foreign Relations and National Security Law* (Saint Paul: West Publishing, 1993), 88-89.

[461] Oliver Wendell Holmes, Jr., *The Common Law and Other Writings*, 1881, as reprinted by Gryphon Editions, 1982, 1.

[462] Cass R. Sunstein, *Radicals in Robes: Why Extreme Right-Wing Courts Are Wrong for America* (Cambridge: Basic Books, 2005), 92.

[463] See Scalia's dissent in *Stenberg v. Carhart*, 530 US 914 (2000).

[464] Bork, 168.

[465] Bork, 169.

[466] Ronald Rotunda, Statement to the Senate Judiciary Subcommittee on Administrative Oversight and the Courts, "The Senate's Role in the Nomination and Confirmation Process: Whose Burden?" September 4, 2001.

[467] Tushnet, *A Court Divided*, 49-70.

[468] Donald Kommers, Review of Mark Tushnet's *A Court Divided*, vol. 16, no. 1, January 2006, 11-16.

[469] See Tribe, 133, "In discussing judicial appointments in the context of the future direction of the Supreme Court, the short-hand labels "left" and "right," "liberal" and "conservative," are too blunt to be of much value." See George F. Will, "Judging This Court," *Washington Post*, June 8, 2005, A21.

[470] Bernard Schwartz, 272.

[471] See Tribe, 133.

[472] Ayn Rand, "The New Fascism: Rule by Consensus," *Capitalism: The Unknown Ideal* (New York: Signet, 1967), 202.

[473] Alexander Bickel, *The Supreme Court and the Idea of Progress* (New York: Harper & Row, 1970).

[474] Russell Kirk, *The Conservative Mind from Burke to Eliot* (Washington DC: Regnery Publishing, 1994), 7$^{th}$ revised edition, 8-9.

[475] Russell Kirk, *The Conservative Mind*, 35.

[476] Russell Kirk, *The Conservative Mind*, 48-49.

[477] Edmund Burke, "Reflections on the Revolution in France," *Edmund Burke: Selected Writings and Speeches* (Chicago: Regnery Publishing Inc., 1963), 521 and 599.

[478] David McCullough, *John Adams* (New York: Simon & Schuster, 2001), 224. Adams abhorred egalitarianism, though he also objected to England's class system and distinctions based solely upon birth, "The idea of a man being born a magistrate, lawgiver, or judge is absurd and unnatural." p. 222. John Adams enjoyed a close friendship with Jefferson from the time of the writing of the declaration of independence through their service as diplomats together in France, though it later soured with the Republican challenge to the Adams's Federalist administration.

[479] Edmund Burke, "Reflections on the Revolution in France," *Edmund Burke: Selected Writings and Speeches* (Chicago: Regnery Publishing Inc., 1963), 583.

[480] Edmond Burke, "Letter to M. Depont," *Edmund Burke: Selected Writings and Speeches* (Chicago: Regnery Publishing Inc., 1963), 505.

481 Charles Lane, "Rehnquist May Be Key for Campaign Finance," *Washington Post*, August 31, 2003, A6. Quoting Notre Dame Law School professor Richard W. Garnett (and former clerk to Rehnquist), "Rehnquist is more of a law-and-order conservative than a Libertarian-type conservative . . . he may not think the First Amendment sky is falling if the political system is regulated."

482 Barry Goldwater wrote in a 1994 *Washington Post* essay, "I am a conservative Republican, but I believe in democracy and the separation of church and state. The conservative movement is founded on the simple tenet that people have the right to live life as they please as long as they don't hurt anyone else in the process."

483 Michael Kinsley, "The Neocons' Unabashed Reversal," *Washington Post*, April 17, 2005, B7.

484 For example, Mark Levin advocates an end-to-life tenure for judges and a legislative veto over judicial decisions, among other things. See his book, *Men in Black: How the Supreme Court Is Destroying America* (Washington DC: Regnery Publishing Inc., 2005), 201.

485 Thomas Stearns Eliot, *Notes Toward the Definition of Culture* (London: Faber and Faber Ltd., 1948), 75. T. S. Eliot, the Unitarian turned Catholic wrote, "The confusion of culture and politics may lead in two different directions. It may make a nation intolerant of every culture but its own so that it feels impelled to stamp out or to remold every culture surrounding it. An error of the Germany of Hitler was to assume that every culture than that of Germany was either decadent or barbaric . . . The other direction in which the confusion of culture and politics may lead is toward the ideal of a world state in which there will, in the end, be only one uniform world culture."

486 Issac Kramnick and R. Laurence Moore, *The Godless Constitution: A Moral Defense of the Secular State* (New York: W. W. Norton & Co., 2005), 46-48. Roger Williams believed that politics and political power corrupt the church. In 1636, he was banished from the Commonwealth of Massachusetts when he challenged state-enforced religious restrictions.

487 Issac Kramnick and R. Laurence Moore, *The Godless Constitution: A Moral Defense of the Secular State* (New York: W. W. Norton & Co., 2005), 30.

488 Issac Kramnick and R. Laurence Moore, 36-37.

489 See *National Review Online*, "Divining W," February 20, 2006, interview with Michael Novak and Jana Novak on their new book *Washington's God: Religion, Liberty, and the Father of Our Country* (Basic Books, 2006). But see Willard Sterne Randall, *George Washington: A Life*, 235. Before the revolution, Washington was frustrated that potential German servants would not come to America while the existence of the state Church of England preventing the free exercise of religion. Though Washington was unquestionably deeply religious, he practiced his religion mostly in private, had the attributes of both a deist and a Christian (not mutually exclusive), was an active freemason, was very tolerant if not protective of various religions (Quakers, Mennonites, Presbyterians, Jews, etc.), and believed that national unity was dependent upon separating religious from governmental functions.

490 F. A. Hayek, *New Studies in Philosophy, Politics, Economics, and the History of Ideas* (London and Henley: Routledge & Kegan Paul, 1982), 119.

491 I note that many orthodox conservatives are hostile to the concept of natural rights. Russell Kirk devotes much text to distinguishing between Burke's natural rights and Locke's natural rights while acknowledging that both use much of the same terminology.

[492] F. A. Hayek, *New Studies in Philosophy, Politics, Economics and the History of Ideas* (London and Henley: Routledge & Kegan Paul, 1982), 119.

[493] Cass R. Sunstein, "Role Reversal and the High Court," *Washington Post*, July 10, 2005, B7.

[494] Ibid.

[495] Reportedly, thirty thousand members left the ACLU in protest.

[496] *Kelo v. City of New London*, 545 US ___ (2005).

[497] *Whitman v. American Trucking Associations*, 531 US 457 (2001).

[498] Charles Lane, "Papers Underline Issue of Controlling Court," *Washington Post*, March 7, 2004, A11. Yoo made the statement in commenting on revelation from the Blackmun papers about Justice Anthony Kennedy's switching sides on a number of issues.

[499] Jason DeParle, "In the Battle to Pick Next Justice, Right Says, Avoid a Kennedy," *New York Times*, June 27, 2005.

[500] Ibid.

[501] Ibid.

[502] Charles Lane, "Papers Underline Issue of Controlling Court," *Washington Post*, March 7, 2004, A11.

[503] *Olsen v. Nebraska*, 313 US 236 (1941). Also, see Bork, 61. Bork mocks the early decision of Douglas: "Differences of opinion on the wisdom, need, or appropriateness of legislation should be left were they were left by the Constitution—to the states and to Congress."

[504] Todd S. Purdum, "Presidents, Picking Justices, Can Have Backfires," *New York Times*, July 5, 2005.

[505] Charles Lane, A11.

[506] Todd S. Purdum, "Presidents, Picking Justices, Can Have Backfires," *New York Times*, July 5, 2005. Associate Justice Rehnquist's 1984 speech to a Minnesota law school audience.

[507] Ibid.

[508] C. Herman Pritchett, "The Development of Judicial Research" in *Frontiers of Judicial Research*, Eds. Joel B. Grossman and Joseph Tanenhaus (New York: John Wiley & Sons, 1969), 42.

[509] Edward Lazarus, *Closed Chambers*, 469. This is the view of the Harvard "legal process" school of constitutional interpretation.

[510] Herbert Wechsler of Columbia University warned against the Court's political subversion as a "naked power organ," instead of striving to be an institution guided and controlled by principle.

[511] Ronald Rotunda, Statement to the Senate Judiciary Subcommittee on Administrative Oversight and the Courts, "The Senate's Role in the Nomination and Confirmation Process: Whose Burden?" September 4, 2001, "We want fair courts—not liberal courts, not conservative courts, not moderate courts, but fair courts, and by "fair," I mean we want judges who will call them as they see them, without regard to politics . . . If we treat the Supreme Court as an investment and not as speculation, then the president and the senators and the media as well should worry less about how a nominee might vote on any particular issue than about what they think of the nominee's personal integrity, good faith, and intellectual ability."

www.ingramcontent.com/pod-product-compliance
Lightning Source LLC
Chambersburg PA
CBHW061401280526
45784CB00001B/328
*9781425713515*